AUTHOR	CLASS No.
LOFTHOUSE, J.	4 E 42L
TITLE	BOOK No.
Lancashire Villages	08467283

LANCASHIRE VILLAGES

Lancashire Villages

JESSICA LOFTHOUSE

ROBERT HALE · LONDON

© *Jessica Lofthouse 1973*
First Published in Great Britain 1973

ISBN 0 7091 4165 3

Robert Hale & Company
63 Old Brompton Road
London S.W.7

08467283
L000174165
01143389

PRINTED IN GREAT BRITAIN BY
CLARKE, DOBLE & BRENDON LTD.
PLYMOUTH

Contents

Illustrations

8   ILLUSTRATIONS

Introduction

VILLAGE ORIGINS

If any community under one hundred inhabitants is a hamlet, and one over 1,500 is classed as a small town, this certainly reduces the numbers of true villages in Lancashire. So does the dictionary definition: "A village is a collection of dwellings forming a centre of population in a country district—with the simplest form of local government, a parish council—a distinct unit easily distinguishable from the surrounding rural territory—a separate entity divided from other neighbouring communities by open countryside".

In the last decade scores of places which insist they are villages have doubled, trebled and even increased tenfold where they have taken in the overspills of Manchester or Liverpool. They have parish councils, they are in recognizable rural areas; but the surrounding green belts, and white belts, narrow. Many a pleasant village around Liverpool, a ring around Manchester, on the fringe of industrial towns, have been 'taken in'; and though the house-wives still say, "I'm going shopping in the village," no outsider would recognize them as such.

Two centuries ago Lancashire was a county of small villages and a few boroughs and market towns, old trading centres, all close linked and interdependent. Until the 1750s a village was a place where folk lived, worked, produced most of the things they needed, disposing of their surplus and buying what they lacked at the nearest market town. Ormskirk, Preston, Garstang, Lancaster, with Kirkham and Poulton in the Fylde, prospered because of this in west Lancashire; Clitheroe, Blackburn, Chorley, Bolton and Wigan in the middle belt; and in the eastern parts, long before the textile trade changed the pattern of life, places like Colne and Burnley, Haslingden, Bury and Rochdale too.

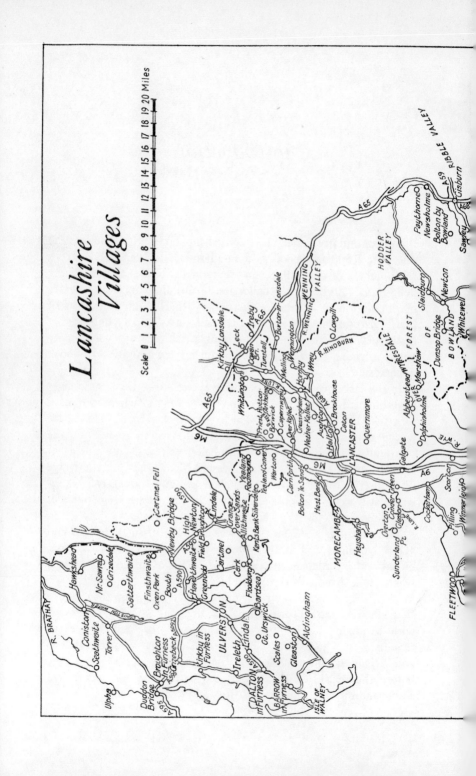

Lancashire Villages

Scale 0 1 2 3 4 5 6 7 8 9 10 11 12 13 14 15 16 17 18 19 20 Miles

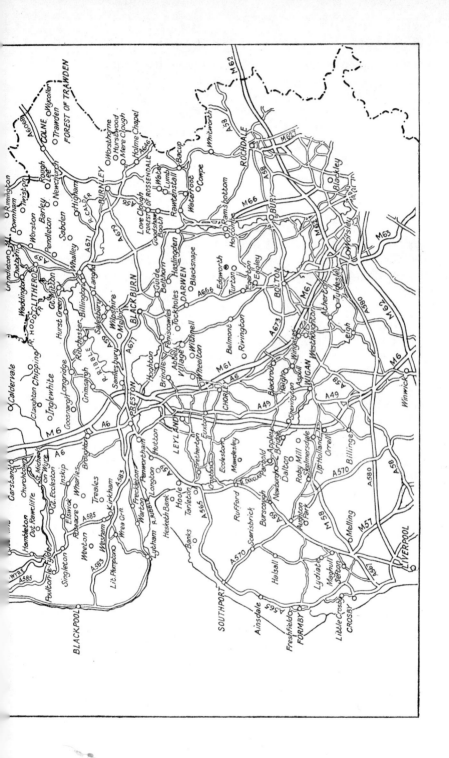

Lancashire was a late developer among the shires—a late starter too, created in the twelfth century. An eleventh-century map would have shown vast areas uninhabited; and what was bog, swamp, moss and mere, uninhabitable. The blanks covered much of the west from the wastes of Chat Moss and Martin Mere and the boglands of the Fylde to the considerable mosses of Cartmel and Furness. None lived in these parts but primitive moss men, wild-fowlers and fishermen.

Tracts as large were devastated after Tostig's rebellion in 1065, and the rest after the harrying of the North by William's men in 1067, when it was left in such a sorry state that William declared it *"deserta"* and designated this and Bowland, Pendle, Trawden and Rossendale *"foresta"*. Reserved for the royal pleasure in the chase, all this remained for centuries undeveloped, trespassing forbidden.

There was nothing to shout about when barons received Lancashire manors from the 'Conqueror', unless they were lucky in the draw. The best land was in the rich valleys of the lower Lune, Wyre, Ribble, Hodder and Calder, lowland enriched by alluvium after receding floodwaters.

The kings reserved vast tracts of poor land for hunting preserves, until in the fourteenth century they allowed clearance for cattle rearing, called vaccaries in Wyresdale, and for scores of small primitive herdsmen or boothsmen in Pendle, Trawden and Rossendale, the beginning of community life in these areas.

Kings and nobles had granted much land to churches and abbeys, which they saw as potentially productive. In Cartmel and Furness, prior and abbot 'opened out' their hinterland, many a wooded clearing becoming a 'thwaite' on the present-day map. Around Pendle and in the Vale of Chipping the many 'leys'—a 'leah' being permanent grassland—resulted from similar clearing of old scrubland. In each, as living space grew so did the population keep pace.

In the fourteenth century our most interesting and historic Lancashire villages were on the map, completely integrated, each with parish church, adjoining hall of the manorial lord, with lord's desmesne and parson's glebe, infields, outfields, meadow and pasture, common and waste, each part essential to their wellbeing then and for centuries to come.

No two are alike, their sites and environs so varied: villages like Wycoller, Hurstwood and Worsthorne in the moors, close against the Pennines; lowland communities once cut off from their neighbours by flooded rivers and vast meres—as Croston and Much Hoole, Halsall and Newburgh, Wrea Green and St Michael's, Stalmine and Pilling. There are 'perfect' villages amongst them: Cartmel and Hawkshead, Bardsea and Aldingham, Hawkshead and the Yealands, Downham, Hornby and Melling; some round greens or along old highways, dipping their feet in babbling brooks or admiring their reflections by still water, beautiful, historic, well-kept, some all of these—and all sitting so pleasantly where they are we can picture them nowhere else. Farming was a major concern of most; craftsmen of varied skills worked in wood, stone and metal, making tools for home, field and farm. Many cottages possessed spinning wheels and a busy loom, producing cloth from wool of their own sheep and local-grown flax.

INDUSTRIAL CHANGES

In their cottages weavers on primitive handlooms, dissatisfied, thought out improvements. The first tentative inventions proved a success. The Kays at Bury devised the fly shuttle. Hargreaves at Stanhill produced his 'jenny' to spin thread more quickly and satisfy the greedy loom. They did not know it but the Industrial Revolution had been sparked off. Crompton, in the rural backwater at Hall i' th' Wood outside Bolton, worked on a machine to do finer spinning than ever before—but not suited to the cottage industry as Hargreaves' 'spinning jenny' had been. Arkwright puzzled out a way of adapting the spinning machine of Thomas Highs of Leigh for water power; as soon as his patent was set aside forward-looking traders set up mills where water was adequate to turn wheels for power. They called themselves manufacturers. The factory system was launched. Many a village was never to be the same again.

> So, come all you cotton weavers, you must rise up very soon
> And you must work in factories from morning until noon.
> You must not work in your garden for a two or three hours a day.
> You've got to stand at the foreman's command and keep the
>   shuttles in play.

After water power, the next phase was steam, and very soon scores of busy wheels silenced, thriving little brookside communi-

ties abandoned. The romantic ruins we come across in lovely
'bottoms' by Brock, Wyre and scores of streams in Lakeland
Lancashire were factories once, left to their fate in the 1820s and
30s. Weekend cottages in enchanting dells were once weavers'
dwellings.

The need was for coal, so industry moved east to the coalfields,
which also yielded stone for building new mills, new towns. As
the moorland climate was suitably damp, here were ideal conditions for the cotton industry. This was the ideal country soon to
be the substructure for Lancashire's prosperity.

The primitive people of the backward moorlands—in Trawden,
Rossendale and south-east Lancashire—felt the impact more than
anyone else. Industry swept into their valleys, forced the old
handloomers and cottage spinsters into the hated mills. Poets
lamented the destruction of the most picturesque places, steam,
smoke and tall chimneys defiling the beauties of Nature, "an
offence to God and Man".

> Ill fares the land to modern ills a prey,
> Where wealth accumulates and men decay.

Some, more forward looking, saw light breaking upon darkest
Lancashire, for "Spirits, boggarts and fairies were now banished
from Rossendale and witches and the devil scared out of Pendle
by the introduction of the steam engine."

Upheaval had also reached south-west Lancashire and the Fylde
where an agrarian revolution was at work. Attempts to drain the
vast mossland and reclaim the land for agriculture, by the 1770s
were succeeding, and at a crucial time. New towns were now mush-
rooming in the east and the west was ready to supply its larders.

Country life was overwhelmed by changes. Few of the old
landed gentry were able to withstand them. They left their ravaged
estates, darkened skies and polluted streams, leaving the new rich
manufacturers to take their places. When an alien population came
north to fill the vacancies in the factories, knowing nothing of
old days, old ways, it was a sad thing.

By the 1870s once-rural hamlets had been caught up in growing
towns, soon to become indistinguishable, mere names on the
outskirts of Bolton, Oldham, Rochdale, Blackburn. One interesting
group admitted one or two mills but never quite lost its village
character or rural interests.

Another most fascinating 'industrial village' was purpose-built, a model village planned by enlightened high-principled manufacturers, many in the Bolton and Irwell area. The survivors, industry having departed during the post-war years, are now highly desirable and residential.

With completely unspoilt villages—far more than one might imagine, our pride and constant delight—I will deal in the predominantly rural western lowland, North Lonsdale and middle-belt Ribble Valley sections of my book.

The headache of present-day planners is the drift from town to country, reversing the processes of the last century. People want a home in the country. They have cars, distance is no very serious problem for them. For the villages it is serious, for a large influx of newcomers with urban ideas and mentality can be sad, and often bad.

The Lancashire new-town planners, in their wisdom, having learned from experience, now envisage a number of villages or neighbourhood units—around them meadows, pastures, farms and play areas, leisure parks and sports fields providing the green belt essential to keep the feeling of separateness and independence. Roads will lead from each to the civic central town; all will have a pride in this, but each will feel he belongs in the smaller unit. This is the new, modern concept, a good one. If this proves pleasant for living then the old countryside, the unspoilt small villages could be saved.

The 1971 census returns reveal that of Lancashire's 5 millions, 4 million live in Greater Liverpool and Manchester, and 800,000 in large towns, leaving the rest, under 200,000, in small market towns and villages. In almost every large town the population has steadily dropped since 1951, and in every rural area there has been a rapid rise.

Here are a few examples, showing the figures from three latest census—1951, 1961, 1971—to the nearest thousand: Blackburn: 111,000, 106,000 and now 101,100, whilst its rural district rose from 13,000 through 15,000 to over 20,000. Preston decreased even more: 121,000, 113,000 to 97,000; its rural district climbing from 38,000 through 49,000 to 52,600. Bolton in the same period lost 13,000, but Turton Urban District, countryside on its northern borders, doubled its population.

The most spectacular rise has been in the onetime farming country of south-west Lancashire, due to Liverpool's overspills, new town development at Skelmersdale and the popularity of Maghull, Aughton and Lydiate; and in similar terrain in the Fylde, around Garstang, Thornton Cleveleys and Poulton-le-Fylde, into which 30,000 newcomers have moved since 1951.

After April 1974 the population of the new County of Lancashire will be 1,341,000. Taken out of old Lancashire will be a total of 4,372,000 into Greater Manchester and Merseyside Metropolitan Counties. At the same time Cartmel and Furness join Westmorland and Cumberland in the new County of Cumbria.

In one area only is the population unchanged. Planning is severely restricted, to preserve the true character of Lakeland, in Cartmel and Furness.

To give an adequate survey of the villages in Lancashire has been a formidable task. Inevitably many are missing. This is not a book about *beautiful* villages for the benefit of visitors, though I hope they will enjoy it too. All types are in: the perfect and the ordinary and the imperfect. As with people, it takes all sorts to make a village and a rural community.

I

West Lancashire Lowlands

On a coloured relief map of Lancashire the western part shows as green, lowland under 200 feet, two big bulges between Mersey and Ribble, Ribble and Lune, roughly west of the M6 motorway or the main-line Liverpool, Preston, Carnforth railway.

This covers rich agricultural land, much of it won from marsh and mere two centuries ago and now virtually the county's larder: north of the Ribble estuary the Fylde of Amounderness; south of it the Leyland Hundred and part of West Derby; the sea on one hand and the holiday coast, the hills enclosing Wyresdale and the steep escarpments of south Lancashire hills—Billinge Beacon, Ashhurst Beacon, Parbold Bottle, High Moor and Harrock Hill—on the other.

From the fells overlooking the Fylde, or from Forton Tower on the M6, a splendid viewpoint, the prospect reaches to the Lakeland mountains of Furness, wherein lies a string of real beauties among our north-west Lancashire villages; on the land between hills and plains are villages often beautiful, always satisfying.

From the escarpments above Parbold and Skelmersdale, though little over 500 feet, one surveys 'no less than sixteen counties'—though the actual total is controversial; down below are many small hamlets and villages among cornfields, potato fields and farmlands stretched like a multi-coloured cloth to the silver rim of the Irish Sea.

There are few towns but many villages in the west, the country-folk converging upon Preston or Garstang or Ormskirk on market days, today as in the past. These villages—none precious or pre-served, honest to goodness like the people who live in them—and the homespun contentment of their surroundings, are the subject of Chapter One of my book.

The most important problem was always traffic on the north-west route to Scotland, and all the road works needed to improve it. How Broughton, Barton, Bilsborough and Brock suffered, and every community on the A6. Now, with the motorway taking heavy and through traffic, they are experiencing a calm not known since the invention of the internal combustion engine. Eventually they may take on the slow pace of villages like Churchtown, Scorton, Forton and Claughton—'next door to full stop'.

The A6 villages look like extensions of Preston: long-drawn-out, leading in towards Lancaster or, so strangers think, very pleasant among trees and blossom, with every front garden displaying massed flowers like a peacock flaunting its tail feathers—colourful, cheerful, suburban.

There is far more, under the surface and back in history. Every highway village had its moments, when Scots came raiding, or Jacobites advanced in the '15 or '45, when Royalist fought Roundhead, when Papists went in fear, and whenever the local gentry—Cliftons, Rigbys, Bartons, Butlers, Singletons or Tylde-sleys—called out their tenants to wars at home or abroad. In the ups and downs of fortune, the landowning families of Amounder-ness took more knocks than most, the reason why so few survived the eighteenth century.

Broughton has a most attractive old core—ancient church, village school, stocks and white-walled cottages—but the tower of the trouble-seeking Singletons has gone. Barton, a few miles north—a contented landscape for fine milch cows, like the cheese and butter adverts—looks so smug who would guess the goings-on in times past? The A6 sweeps across the park, haunt long ago of a ferocious killer boar, the reward for its killing, the heiress's hand in marriage. The peace was shattered by men engaged in Barton-Clifton scraps, affrays and self-explanatory 'blood-wipes', due to a binding promise once made by Bartons to give Cliftons, their overlords, freedom of house and cellars 'for ever'.

No desperate deeds nowadays! Yet one farm, innocent enough to look at, could tell tales of a Jacobite officer who came to buy provisions for the rebel troops. One family knew what happened to him. He was killed, his horse thrown into a pond, saddle bags and sword hidden in the thatch. The 1870s draining of Moses Gill

Field pond uncovered the remains of the horse, the re-roofing of the farm the money and weapons hidden there.

Bilsborough old and new is 'nothing much of a place', but its quiet was ruffled when canal excavators arrived early in the 1800s, and Irish navvies began work on the new railroad in the 1840s. The Roebuck Inn gave the name to its first station—now closed, of course. No stops between Preston and Lancaster!

Myerscough witnessed royal occasions, the last when the Queen opened the College of Agriculture at The Lodge, a large place with a growing use by the farming folk of Fylde and beyond. The Stuart kings were all guests in turn of the Tyldesleys. James I they gave good hunting on his royal progress through the county in 1617. To Charles I they gave undivided loyalty through the Civil War, and with young Charles II Edward Tyldesley rode out and south in 1651—to be killed at the Battle of Wigan Lane. The same lords of Myerscough would have welcomed James II if the fortunes of war had brought him to Lancashire's shores after the Battle of the Boyne.

Many true villages, each distinguishable from its neighbours, belts of comfortable farmland dividing them, continue northwards. None possesses much to interest the tourist, but each has considerable local, parochial pride and goes its own sweet way.

Travellers have long known Galgate, on the old road to Scotland. Scots on their galloway ponies rode along Highland Lane (west of the modern A6) and forded a stream at Scotforth. Some Highlander lost his claymore—later found at the roadside and dubbed a 'Jacobite sword'. Footpads and highwaymen lurked here to waylay travellers slowing down on the long hill. *The Lancaster Gazette* told of many cases, as when in 1821: "John Evatt, hawker, robbed of £50 by three footpads."

This stretch of road, and that near Bailrigg, called Murder Lane after a maid going to the post was foully 'done away with', was frequented by gipsies who chipped away the 'memorial stone' for charms. Galgate has often had to change, adapt to the times. The completion of the motorway was 'the best thing that ever happened'!

Old Galgate developed on Conder banks. Here are located a cotton factory beneath the Six Arches, Thompson and Company's silk spinning mill (founded in 1792 when no silk was coming in from France, and closed down for sale in 1972), a long-abandoned tannery and a defunct ropery. Galgate is no longer a bustling working village—there is no work left. All the bustling activity is by the 'playboys' down at the newly enlarged canal 'marina' by the Plough Inn—very cheerful, with anchorage "for miles of pleasure boats". Recently the terraced houses have gone gay, too, experimenting in paint. Even round the back of the village, my favourite part, colour can hit one in the eye. Sand blasting of grimy old houses reveals the good colour of locally quarried stone.

Being old, and fundamentally old-fashioned, a place where old ideas are not discarded unless the new are found to be much better, Galgate is a storehouse of bygones. I hope the university nearby does not wait too long to collect history from those who have known partakers in it. With industrial archaeology a popular study, Lancaster University is well placed.

In 1952, when writing *Lancashire–Westmorland Highway*, I talked to the oldest natives, many of them octogenarians. Parents and grandparents had worked at the silk mill, which employed most labour, children too, like "John Lee aged about 9 entangled in the machinery and died next day". That was in 1799. They told of schooling—haphazard, 1s. 3d. a week but no go when money ran short; of Dolly Tub Row, where cottagers collected rainwater from the roofs when the pumps did not function; of Ellel Chapel clerk, who in 1804 at last wed the woman he bought twelve years earlier for 4s. 6d; of the old smithy with its anvil stock made from an oak tree stump around which its walls had been built.

Such titbits are only picked up when wandering around. I doubt if passing travellers guess that Galgate is much more than meets the eye. I find the folk friendly, communicative and proud to belong here.

In 1972 Galgate witnessed a civic occasion when the mayor and councillors of Bolton took over a splendid spinning machine long used at the silk mill, to be ceremoniously taken to the town where it was made and now displayed in precincts near the Town Hall.

All these highway villages are remembered as 'places on the A6' and no more. Very different from the impact of villages 'off' the road.

Garstang was for centuries the natural Fylde and Wyresdale trading centre. On market days the narrow street is thronged with countryfolk, natives whose forebears flocked here, plus some of the 5,000 newcomers to Garstang's rural district. The town's prosperity was secured because of the 'never-ceasing passage of travellers, and the industry of the neighbourhood'. Lord Derby built the Wyre bridge. His stepson, Henry Tudor, had given him Greenhalgh where he built a strong castle. Because of the loyalty of the 'Cavalier Earl' in the Civil War, Charles II granted Garstang its Charter of Incorporation. It became chief market for Fylde corn and cattle, fish from the Wyre, and for yarn, linens and cottons produced by cottage industry around.

After the Duke of Hamilton's drainage schemes, his north Fylde estates were now "a rich champagne country growing wheat and other grains", the beginning of its agricultural boom time, its course set fair for the future in farming and marketing. Baines expressed surprise that 'manufacturers did not more extensively prevail'. This did happen in Caterall, Inglewhite, up the Brock to Bleasdale, at Scorton and Dolphinholme whilst local water power was needed for turning wheels. Steam power started an exodus to the carboniferous country, so this countryside escaped the fate of south-east Lancashire!

Exceptions there are, notably Calder Vale still going strong in textiles, delightfully situated, as immaculate as the proud villagers can make it—in the Best Kept Village champion class—visually exciting and a true workaday community!

Nothing of this is on the foreign tourist's itinerary, but Prestonians have enjoyed these vales and villages for generations, needing no Beacon Fell Country Park to introduce them to the pleasures 'on their doorstep'.

BY BROCK, CALDER AND UPPER WYRE

What about Claughton (Cliton)-with-Brock? A local writer, after a happy June day in 1872, described it enthusiastically. "For sweetness of position, shady dells, peaceful glades, woodland scenery, all that makes country life a joy, commend us to Claughton." The miracle is that the picture fits a century later, in spite of motorway upheaval and the envious eyes potential residents cast upon it, so near the M6. Thanks to the continued vigilance of the Fitzherbert-Brockholes, here for centuries, unsuitable intrusions are hardly likely to happen. As an earlier squire fought the 1840 railroad company—and won decorative railings, a cutting to hide the trains etc., so did the present squire insist that M6 construction through his park should leave no permanent scars.

Always a pastoral community, the homesteads are well scattered, and each group a happy surprise, some by the babbling Brock— these sited near early water mills—others thrown high on the slopes or against the park walls. An exceedingly pleasing group including church, presbytery and school are the 'centre' of the village. Because the Brockholes held to Roman Catholic worship, so did many of their tenants. Traditions? That St Kentigern brought Christianity to these parts; that many itinerant priests held secret masses in surrounding farms, and always knew where secret hides offered safety if their whereabouts became known.

I have seen a hide over the front porch of Duckworth Hall; at the presbytery the small portable altar, a simple pewter chalice, and 'host irons' for the making of communion wafers in penal days; and in the baptismal register the signature of George, Prince of Wales and the Hon. Mrs Fitzherbert, godparents of a Brockholes son.

Claughton folk are to be envied. They seem well satisfied with their lot. It looks as if the Fitzherbert-Brockholes will carry on from generation to generation; that the herons will go on nesting in the park heronry; and each spring will be heralded with an exuberance of wild flowers and a perpetual chorale of birds in the nearby Brock woods, all more accessible on a newly-defined nature trail.

For a lonely outlier seek out Bleasdale, gripped between the knees of bald, bare fells. The Brock begins here in a silent bowl where Bronze Age villagers raised a circular stockade of oak logs to defend themselves, though the surrounding bogs were good protection. A century ago this solitude was a centre of industry, with wool spinning and handloom weaving at Hazelhurst, felt workers at Coolam, every cottage—of which there were then many more—a hive buzzing with activity. A hamlet which failed to become a village.

No young folk find work in these parts now. All must be off in the morning early to Garstang or Preston. By day, the villages go to sleep, not a soul stirs, not a discordant sound.

Inglewhite, south of the Brock river, looks the perfect village, playing ring o' roses round a large 'goose green', a market 'cross' on a stepped base as centre. The many lanes signposted to Inglewhite, and signs of old houses which were formerly inns—'Black Bull', 'Queen's Head', 'The Green Man' the only survivor—give a clue to its early importance. The cattle and sheep fairs drew dealers from all parts of the Fylde and beyond, but trade lapsed, the fairs were discontinued, the inns became private houses. No horses are now shod at the smithy, no silk is woven at the old silk mill, and no bone buttons are made in Button Row. All quiet.

The church stands a way off nearer Beacon Fell, at Whitechapel where snowdrops follow January's snows, and children's voices in play and mad-happy larks and frenzied peewits make a joyful medley in early spring. Into its story are woven traditions of a 'convent' at Ashes Farm nearby, of priests' hides, a haunting—always a good cover for mysterious nightly visitations—and the misfortunes of local Jacobite Threlfalls. One was shot 'because he was a Catholic', another slain when militia were carrying him off as suspect in the Lancashire Plot of 1690, and a kinsman accused of sniping at King George's redcoats from a Preston window in the '15.

They say 'nothing ever happens here now'. But where is the familiar 'little man on the cross', why the broken shaft, and where the missing trophies won in Best Kept Village competitions? Vandals! Vandals striking in a quiet backwater like Inglewhite? They can well do without that kind of excitement!

Speak of Goosnargh, two miles south, a century ago 'an old fashioned place, purely rural, its population scattered and with an imperishable passion for cakes'. The only 'old-fashioned' part is now round the fine old church. There is a village school, Oliverson's; a most handsome white-walled Bushell Arms Inn, and what was the seventeenth-century mansion of the Bushells, now a hospital, a splendid building more like a guildhall in a prosperous old borough. Dr Bushell in 1735 stipulated in his will the inmates should be only "decayed gentlemen or gentlewomen or persons of better rank", but no Papist nor any in receipt of poor relief.

The church is one of the most beautiful, with every sign of community pride in it. Goosenarch Chapelry of early times—it was not a parish until Henry VIII's days—took in six titheries (Church Tithery, Beesley, Kidsnape, Longley, Aspenhurst and Threlfall) and was closely linked with Whittingham and Newsham. The church interior with its low, heavy arcades and golden-hued masonry looks old and goes back before the first-known cleric, William de Cortays, priest in 1330. The founder's tomb of the Singletons of Broughton, the fine carved screens of the Chapel of Middletons founded in 1448, floriated crosses and worn effigies, are tangible signs of its antiquity. Modern work is good too: some brilliant stained glass, the royal arms in blue and gold; and a beautiful touch in the west tower, a long blue pendulum moving to and fro against sun-splashed walls.

The population has expanded rapidly, the new outnumbering the old and knowing nothing of Old Goosnargh with its simple pleasures—Whit Tuesday Club Days, Whit Wednesday mayor makings—and better-forgotten customs once rife locally, when the villagers showed scorn of wife beaters by strewing chaff on doorsteps, and any innkeeper found brewing bad ale was forced to walk the church tower battlements, a child in his arms—though what good this did is hard to guess!

When children are on to a good thing they do not let traditions die. House-to-house begging on Shrove Tuesdays—"Please a pancake"—continues, and kindly giving of oranges and Goosnargh cakes to outstretched hands. Provend Day is only remembered by those who as youngsters frequented the inn doors when they knew the great baking of the local 'cakes' was in hand. Fifty thousand batches were made before the expected invasion of Prestonian visitors at Easter and Whitsun. The children waited for handfuls of cake scrapings.

Goosnargh cakes, as we know them now, were a lucky accident made in a hurry one fair day when supplies had run out early. Housewives to help out gathered any left-over ingredients in their kitchens, and there was very little. From butter, flour, loaf sugar and caraway seeds they 'rustled up' a mixture and put it into rapidly cooling ovens. The result was a half-cooked biscuit, but it was such a melt-in-the-mouth confection people clamoured for more of the same softness. So they say.

One of the best things about Goosnargh is an enormous open

space, the vast goose green of early times, wide as Harrogate's Stray and able to accommodate football games, children's play, dog exercisers and strollers, with room to spare; such an enviable public amenity, nothing should ever be allowed to change it.

South of Goosnargh and Whittingham urban influences reach out from Preston, but north beyond the Brock the rural takes over. This was not always so, for Scorton, Dolphinholme and Caldervale were among early industrial villages. Two Fishwick brothers from Burnley arrived at Scorton in 1809 to start a factory with village labour, and after their time Peter Ormrod employed fifty at a doubling mill which supplied his Bolton spinners with yarn. He was a hard master but fair and, looking down on his model village, believed his people were happy and content.

A perfect place everyone thought it: 'many pleasant white-washed cottages with gardens, and trim three-storeyed terraces of workers houses'; but never a public house or beershop so that when folk needed a 'drop of something strong they slipped over to the Old, New or Middle Holly'. They did this in 1872, and still do so in 1972, though the village is made up of people very different from the factory workers. Now business executives from the very modern houses in Scorton Hall grounds, university staff and the like, have joined those putting in the first application for licensed premises.

Industry moved away years ago, the workers' homes are converted, some picturesque thatched cottages have gone, and with one exception all infillings have been discreet. Everyone likes Scorton as it is, pretty as a picture. Only the restless teenagers complain, "It's as dead as ditchwater, nothing ever happens and we have to go to the Hamilton Arms or Garstang if we want fun". Visitors smile, sigh and say they will return. They like it "quiet as a millpond". They enjoy the glorious countryside and the Nickey Nook and Grizedale paths and rambling ways unsurpassed.

Scorton has a neighbour three miles as the crow flies south-wards, also the creation of enlightened industrialists, also a 'model' village impossible to fault, and as much a surprise to those who believed 'mill villages' were synonymous with grime, squalor and immorality. At Caldervale the Jackson brothers in 1835, knowing the horrors of backstreet Manchester, planned in a delectable green hollow by the clear Calder stream firstly a mill and terraces of weavers' cottages, and ten years later a second mill, more rows of houses all with gardens and 'necessaries'—a shop, a temperance hotel, a news room, but never any pub or beershop. Just as at Scorton, where also any policeman depending on catching lawbreakers for a living "would have died of starvation and a broken heart".

The Jackson brothers, of a Quaker family from Wyresdale, were true 'Friends': their garb, broad-brimmed hat, drab clothes, knee breeches and clogs; their attitude benign. They encouraged thrift and good use of leisure, and encouraged gardening, holding annual competitions. After their time Caldervale continued to delight all who strayed into it—"a delightful spot, the prettiest we have seen, you may travel many miles and not meet with another so pleasing".

'How different from the south-east Lancashire cotton towns.' "No girls in shawls hang round doors, no lads play pitch and toss in back alleys, no old women in dirty caps or ragged bare-legged children to be seen." In 1872 the two mills were going strong.

Caldervale always was an exceptional village, and still is, a tight-knit and very proud community bursting with the spirit which makes champions! In 1970 it was best of the Best Kept Villages in its class, following up in 1971 by becoming champion among former winners; and in 1972, instead of resting on its presentation seats during the year of lying fallow, valiant work progressed to make beautiful more waste land going down to the Calder bank, landscaping and shrub planting.

Scores of mills have closed down since the war, but here one of two is doing very well—producing, among other cloths, gaily patterned material much in vogue in the Middle East and African markets. It is good to watch the weavers hurrying to dinner in their own homes at twelve o'clock, and to join the men who, their meal time over, gather on the bridge to meditate on the water and movements of fish.

All ways out of the village are steep, from sheltered vale to windy heights, none more exhilarating than the high platform above the woodlands shared by the parish church and the newly extended village school. The bonniest, merriest children, drawn from the village far below and fell farms all around, let off their energies under a wide sky noisy with bird cries. When they troop indoors and quiet falls I know where many a wandering eye will stray—to the wide new windows, one framing a deep-green forest, a world of magic, mysterious shadows for who-knows-what childhood imaginings.

The county has many such ideal village schools. Small wonder the chance of their children attending them induces many parents to seek homes in the country just for this advantage.

A thousand years ago a Norseman called Dolphin chose a home deep down by the rushing Wyre for his settlement, Old or Lower Dolphinholme. It was to become known for its woolcombers and the abandonment of St Blaise's Day when everyone let down his back hair and men in clogs clumped around doing a three men's morris, a native dance, to the tune of "Wyresdale Greensleeves".

With everything in its favour it could not escape the Industrial Revolution. The Wyre was harnessed by many water wheels, the spinning mill here the largest with a quite enormous warehouse, its blank stone wall soaring above the river bank. Before the bridge was built heavy loads crossed a ford, then struggled up the Wagon Road towards the Trough Road, with supplies of yarn bound for Yorkshire's woollen mills.

The warehouse is now the Memorial Hall, public hall, social club room and badminton court; the Old Mill, now derelict, had a Methodist chapel above and a joiner's shop below; for, after various vicissitudes industry moved out. The two handsome houses by the mill have new occupants, and the 'big house', Wyresdale House owned by the Garnetts, has been divided into flats.

Dolphinholme is a most attractive place, exciting in its way, old and new side by side. By the Wyre men dig in their riverside vegetable plots; plants, they say, do well in the shelter of the warehouse walls. Children race and tumble downhill from school to cottages, three-storeyed, by the bridge. Their father comes out and shows me the 'new' higher road level at his front door, and the old way to the ford at the back. He said he would have been happy living here a century ago, because he "likes working with horses, and all was horse transport then". And Dolphinholme a much livelier place, by all accounts!

We climbed the toiling Wagon Road, then over the pastures towards Wyresdale House where lived that colourful character, John Fenton-Cawthorne, owner of large local estates. When Patchett's new worsted mill was built almost under his nose and workers arrived *en masse*, almost 3,000 by 1800, he threatened to build a rival mill at Corless—though he was not at all interested in industry; he hated it, and the industrial classes.

He did everything with style and panache. Winning his Corless water rights, he fired a victory cannonade from his lawn. To show his dislike for Tom Paine, the 'arch-anarchist', he made an effigy and burnt it on a bonfire. On special occasions he sent an ox to the unfortunates in Lancaster Castle Debtors' Prison. His greatest achievement came when he found Dolphinholme totally unbearable and indulged his desire for peace and privacy by moving to Marshaw, there to reclaim the fells, plant trees by the young Wyre—where so many motorists now park under his pines—and turn barren acres into rich grassland. His greatest folly, a grandiose scheme to erect a Balmoral-type mansion "This Tower shall live in song and Wyresdale be its name. 1806" was his final ruin. He became bankrupt and much of his land was eventually bought by the Earl of Sefton.

Dolphinholme now has a 'normal' village population, and a great many children. The place really comes to life when school is over.

In the eleventh century Theobald Walter gave Furness Abbey land in Lower Wyresdale and a small property for a steading and chapel within the royal forest in Over Wyresdale. After the brethren's short stay, the Prior of Lancaster, then the Duchy, administered Abbeystead, and from their revenues paid a chaplain to care for the spiritual welfare of herdsmen and farmers. Small settlements had then appeared in clearances within the forest— 'vaccaries' or cattle grazings, which brought in more revenue to the royal coffers than hunting. From the vaccaries of Lee, Emmott and Tarnbrook, Marshaw, Swainshead, Haythornthwaite and Catshaw all came to 'Wyda chapel' to worship. They still do.

The church, the Quakers of Lentworth, and then William Cawthorne's grammar school, "free for all children" in his native dale and with a bequest of £15 yearly for the teaching of fifty "pore schollers", were the chief civilizing influences. The Quaker school has gone, converted into a house, but Abbeystead church, beautifully sited in green pastures not far from the dreaming waters of Abbeystead Lake, and Cawthorne's Endowed—now the primary school—still play their part in local life.

The village is pretty as a picture, almost too good to be true, neat, well-cared-for, with hardly a visual flaw in it. A century before the Earls of Sefton bought the village, farms and moorlands, it was in sore need of a new master. Farms were improved, derelict property rebuilt, and the picturesque houses, all tumble-down, were made good as new, like the seventeenth-century post office in a charming garden, pretty enough to put in a frame and hang on the wall.

The occasional bus for Lancaster collects passengers at the Pinfold under the shelter of splendid trees. Across the road rows of youngsters look out through the school playground railings, like a cage full of mischievous monkeys.

Beauty is all around in scattered pieces, in small hamlets, the results of a purely pastoral heritage. Tarnbrook, Marshaw, Lee—higher and lower—and all outlying farms for generations have been cared for by Sefton agents; the grouse moors and pheasantries, by Sefton keepers. In 1972 with the death of the last earl ended the Molyneux line. The future?

LOWER WYRE VILLAGES FROM GARSTANG TO WYRE MOUTH

Three villages following Wyre west of Garstang each perfect in its way, have been protected from centuries-old flood menace by banks of earth, in summer gay with dog daisies and corn marigolds.

High water brought sixth-century Irish missionaries in their coracles to the spot where St Helen's Church was built and they landed also where St Michael's Church now stands, both older than Eccleston—though as a 'church town' it should have pre-eminence.

Blackpool-bound people who stop in Great Eccleston's long 'square' are less interested in churches. Copp church stands aloof, unassuming, on an eighty-five-foot eminence, a 1723 replacement of an older building. Views from here are wide and wonderful, but I find myself counting new tall green silos, 'haylege towers'—whereas folk once named fourteen windmills with thrashing sails—with sun play, cloud galleons, dazzling of sea one way, Wyreside fells the other. The Fylde seems to me a good land; everything about it bucolic, with a rich earthy smell. Even the parsons were part-time farmers, like one William Sharpe, longhorn cattle breeder, his own ploughman, often forking and carting and spreading manure.

The village centre is too involved with Blackpool traffic (though bypassed), so much of old comeliness wiped out by commercialism.

A pity trippery has taken over, except the 'White Bull', with nearby eighteenth-century houses and a few pretty cottages on the approach ways. Yet here once rode proud de Lancasters, de Coucys, Couplands, Rigmadens, local de Ecclestons of the Hall also, and Stanleys, Earls of Derby, who took over their lands and for centuries were the 'great ones'.

The Blackpool highroad cuts through St Michael's, an ugly iron bridge is needed for pedestrians' safety, cottages have been demolished for car space. Yet the heart of the village is heavy with history, proud as St Helen's Church, even more antique. Michael's Church was a Norman foundation, like Poulton's and Kirkham's. Fylde folk, being 'little Englanders', strongly and forcibly prevented foreign tithe and revenue collectors, all French-speaking clerics and agents of Norman abbeys, from completing their business.

St Michael's rich parish King Henry IV gave as endowment for Battlefield Collegiate church after his victory outside Shrewsbury, "all fruits, hay, tithe of lambs, calves, foals, poultry, geese, eggs, milk, flax, hemp, apples, garlick, onions, pigeons, etc. etc". Which shows this countryside, river flooding and moss and mere notwith-standing, was highly productive. Centuries later, after draining and reclamation, the new acres under cultivation made of it a land flowing with milk and honey.

Butlers were manorial lords for centuries. They lie in St Catharine's chantry chapel, divided from the nave by low arcades with sturdy pillars. The covered cup, badge of the family of Theobald Walter, the king's cup bearer, is cut on their 'new steeple' of 1611. A century later Henry Butler was attainted as a Jacobite rebel; his son died in prison after the '15 rebellion. A rush of local buyers pounced to buy their forfeited estates: the Ffrances later as sole landlords become 'squires', claiming the manor house and occupying St Catharine's chantry (which they rebuilt). Most important, Ffrances as moss lords completed ambitious drainage schemes. This brought general prosperity. It has remained rich agricultural land, farming the main industry.

Local clergy were well provided, they entered into local life, as down-to-earth as the rest. Hornbys, father and son, were 'characters'. In 1789 the elder succeeded Anthony Swainson, an Oxford Fellow who kept his own pack of hounds and took leave of each from his deathbed! He had been lax in tithe collecting, so

Ribchester, village on a Roman site

Whalley on Calder banks

Boarsgreave in moorland and meadows

Sabden in a Pendle valley

Worsley, village by coal wharf and canal

Hornby personally supervised the carting of what was his due! His son was a rich landowner: both the 'Brown Cow' and 'Black Bull' were his, he kept good horses, good carriages, and was both scholar and gentleman.

St Helen's Churchtown seems far too big for the small village at its gate, a quiet single street from market 'cross' to 'Punch Bowl'. Originally this inn was 'The Covered Cup', Butlers being important hereabouts too. When St Helen's was Garstang's only church the parish covered 28,000 acres from Over Wyresdale to Pilling, and south to the Brock. In the roll call of local landholders were Kirkland Butlers, Rigmadens of Wedacre, Tyldesleys of Myerscough, Cateralls from over the river, Brockholes—after they arrived from the Ribble Valley—Radcliffes and Banastres. Many were to be papist recusants, Royalists or Jacobites, destined to be knocked by ill fortune, few to survive the eighteenth century. The Fitzherbert-Brockholes of Claughton are notable exceptions.

King Henry IV generously provided four great oaks from his Forest of Myerscough for the north aisle roof. A century later other oak beams were carved with pious or admonitory precepts. In Latin in the Lady Chapel in 1529: "St Mary pray for us. Let people beware of talking together in church. The devil says everything so spoken is spoken to him." Another, in the North aisle, warning, "Always say less than you do!"

The site is of utmost tranquillity, girdled by silver trunks of splendid beeches. Does the circle define a pagan site consecrated by sixth-century Celtic missionaries? Was it always so serene? It is said blood was shed within, and twice it was purified and reconsecrated. Often the river rose, flowed into the nave, all graves were awash and "all the world became a sea."

A pity the curfew was discontinued. It tolled nightly from Old Michaelmas to Shrovetide, finally sounding the 11 a.m. 'start making your pancakes' bell on Shrove Tuesdays. Children were told a huge boulder in Crappen-crop field rolled over "when it heard St Helen's bells". As at Woodplumpton, where the witch's grave stone turned in its socket on "hearing the midnight bell"!

Sound of bell music drifts over the sleeping village. Mr Cookson is playing the carillon in the west tower, he sits on his stool, manipulating levers which pull six ropes—and old hymn tunes sound from the belfry louvres. One is thankful for beauty such

c

as Churchtown's, all the ear hears and all the eye looks on is pleasing.

Rooks caw from the tall trees near the Vicar's Walk. The vicarage garden was Philip's Toft in the thirteenth century. In earlier times, from Robert Persona de Garstang of 1190, Cockersand Abbey brethren served the church.

On 19th/20th August 1972, in celebration of the patronal festival, the market street was thronged by parishioners and friends. A country market was set up—not only for eggs, butter, cheese and poultry such as 1872 farmwives sold, but a multiplicity of wares. Folk walked about in 'heirloom costumes'— almost bringing the past to life!

These churches, and Kirkham's and Poulton's, were for long the chief civilizing influence in the Fylde. Dissent also reared its head in the seventeenth century, nowhere more active than in Elswick near Great Eccleston. In 1672 Charles II granted a licence to preach at Elswick Lees to Cuthbert Harrison, lately ejected from his church at Singleton. Things did not run at all smoothly, for he was at first compelled to hold clandestine meetings in farms and cottages. In 1753 the Independent Chapel, a simple one with bell turret, was built; now it is dwarfed by a 'town style' Congregational Memorial church, still going strong.

Elswick's lanes and straggling houses have changed little since 1872, when it was a "mixed up place among fields, orchards, gardens and trees, its barnlike chapel with more charm than a great cathedral". Average Sunday attendance was 200, farming families "carried lunch in bundles" and after the 'forenoon service' tucked in—the minister and wife ate in the pulpit, some devoured pies in the vestry and children picnicked in the porch. In singing none could excel Elswick's home-grown choir.

South of the Wyre, numerous villages, robbed of old simplicity and rustic charm by intensive farming, battery production, evidence of ultra-modern efficiency, share a long history which they have done their best to forget. Occasionally, good buildings—old, restored, new in good taste—make one feel all is not lost; as at Singleton. This is a smiling village with trees and pleasant houses with charming gardens, where I once talked to the W.I. on local folk-lore, judged the best red rose competition, and went home rejoicing with an armful, in late June when in our hillside gardens laggard roses bore only tight buds.

Thistleton is as pleasant—one farmhouse beautifully thatched by a craftsman brought from Norfolk, rich acres surrounding it, whilst Inskip and Sowerby, once marooned in extensive mosslands, still possess acres of reeds and rushes, left-overs of ancient meres. Long ago Butlers, Cliftons and Molyneux owned this corner of the Fylde, until all came by marriage to the Earls of Derby. 'Derby Arms' is a common inn name, one near Treales and another at Inskip, three lanes end convenient for holding Courts Baron with Stanley's agents 'in the chair'. It is recognizable today by its Museum of Motoring Oddments, a veteran car on its roof, the "biggest tyre in the world", and ale drawn from petrol pumps!

Look for signs of Fylde landowners' beneficence. The Earls of Derby were great providers, gave land for schools, churches and chapels—as did the Dukes of Hamilton in north Fylde.

The Queen, of course, owns much of the Fylde as Duke of Lancaster. The Duchy estates, far larger than in her father's reign—compensation for nationalized coal mines was ploughed into land here—are the most modern and best equipped, the tenants well content with their lot. The new agricultural college at Myerscough, opened by Her Majesty and the oldest farming education college at Winmarleigh—founded in 1891—have a wide influence far beyond the Fylde. The look of well being, evidence that someone cares, is not a matter of chance. It reflects on village and villagers too. No tumbledown cottages, neglected buildings or sign of poor husbandry anywhere to be seen; a rich, contented countryside.

COASTAL COMMUNITIES FROM POULTON TO COCKERSAND

Nether Wyresdale looked to Poulton as chief market for centuries, long before there was a toll bridge at Shard; a ferry in earlier days and the ancient ford, Aldwath, in remote times being vital links with villages north and south of the river. In the market place local folk met travellers going north on the ancient trackway to Pilling, Cockersand Abbey and Lancaster, or making south across the Fylde by the old ridge route to Kirkham and the Ribble fords, so keeping in touch with the outside world.

The high-running tides often make a watery wasteland around 'out on a limb' villages, the Rawcliffes and Hambleton, and especially isolated Stalmine-with-Stainall, Preesall-with-Hackinsall. "Water, water, all around, but none with a liking for imbibing it."

Hambleton, sited high above the river looks exciting, silhouetted against the sunset, boats bobbing near the banks—where the best mussels in English waters were caught on hooks, hence the famous 'Hambleton hookings'.

Butlers had greatest sway hereabouts in early times, and the Sherburnes too—one of whom, Geoffrey the Arblaster, went east to the Ribble in the thirteenth century to become ancestor of the Stonyhurst Sherburnes and Leagram Welds.

Stalmine, the prettiest, neatest village, was not rescued from the encroaching sea until the 1780s, civilization held at bay whilst the tides rolled in, "the dead receiving no rites of church for no priest could reach them, no priest could abide among them". Incredible to imagine now, for Stalmine is bright and bonny, cheerful, prosperous in poultry producing, complete with a church, houses disposed about a green where there used to be annual village sports, bull-baiting and the like on St Oswald's Day. The Seven Stars Inn stands by. The place wears its age lightly. Henry III was king when the church was founded, the Crown was owner of local property and Furness Abbey a tenant.

For bonus, Stalmine had a boggart, the obliging hard-working Hall Knocker, who cheerfully gathered in the marsh sheep, mucked-out farmyards, and made himself general dog's-body, but for his pains was 'laid' after exorcism by the priest and, 'they say', lies quiet under the church threshold stone!

Hackinsall, twinned with Stalmine (as so common in the Hundred of Amounderness), and nearby Preesall, were King John's and he granted estates to a family destined to be here at Parrox Hall to the present time: the Elletsons, who travelled far but returned from the West Indies to this most beautiful home; one of local families to endure longest.

The villagers—as yet careless of the rat race, or knowing little about any Jones's who dictate the pattern of living in more sophisticated villages—have deep affection for these places. Preesall's site, on a low rise, lanes slipping away into sunny hollows, a foreground of the Wyre with fishing boats and pleasure yachts—most attractive! Roads run along banks with cut-away turfbeds on each side, inland dead flat, dead straight, not exciting country, but with a windy-day charm of its own. Once I heard the bus driver chatting up two village girls. Said he, "You should get out of this. It's livelier in a cemetery."

Other coastal villages share Stalmine and Preesall's content, not yet over-run by development though property developers cast envious eyes on the hinterland. The invigorating breezes which give all trees a tipsy list to port and set the countryside into perpetual motion, the satisfied residents declare, "make it fresh, healthy; here you can live to a hundred." At modern Pilling they say this, and at Knott End, which is showing most rapid change.

In recent years Pilling has turned its back on the sea except for cultivating and harvesting the seawashed turf of its salt marshes for lawns, bowling greens and much new landscaping in old towns. All around are low-profiled farms, some with local-grown winter fuel, peat stacked in round robins at back doors. Two centuries ago Pilling Moss, with peat inexhaustible, natives believed, separated the village from its hinterland. Yet Cockersand had granges hereabouts, there was corn growing and a tall windmill to grind it—now, without its sails, a modern round house.

The village has a newer church, bright and cared-for, and an older, lovingly restored, a stone's throw away, a cool place on a sunny afternoon, blue shade in the white-walled nave and beauty in its uncluttered unadorned simplicity. It probably appeared very different to the congregation of Georgian days, when half the inhabitants were willing to share in the profits of wrecking and used their thatches and peat stacks as excellent hides for smuggled contraband. The parson, the long-remembered Parson Potter, 'best preacher and best fighter as ever came into Pilling', was remembered with affection. Best runner too, who, when the call came during matins that a ship had broken its back and spilled its cargo on the nearby shore, shouted to the escaping congregation, "Now then lads, let's start fair! Let me get this surplice off and. . . ." Keen sportsman and gambler too. When he appeared at a cockpit, was he about to report the meeting to the constables? Not he. "Half-a-crown on the red cock!" cries he, and slaps down his wager.

Cockerham church had newsworthy parsons too, and a grammar-school master wily enough to outwit the devil. He possessed a book of magic with hints how to—and using the 'make rope out of sand' trick sent the Old Lad packing.

The Vicars of Cockerham, who acquired former Cockersand Priors' 'perks', claimed—until recent years—all salmon trapped within the monastic fish baulks during 'Vicar's Tide' one night each month.

Cockerham church stands aloof from the village and seems safe from change, whereas the village is growing and space is filling, which means modern houses are invading the spacious vicarage gardens and new bungalows stealing the show from the old traditional cottages. Formerly the Manor Inn was venue for cock-fighting, greyhound coursing, horse racing and gentlemen bowling on the green. The village smithy not only mended farm imple-ments, hammered tools and shod horses, but supplied horse pattens like outsize wooden snow-shoes, needed for ploughing and field work on boggy ground.

Life in the days of Cockersand Priory, St Mary-in-the-Marsh, was geared to the needs of the brethren; all roads led there, cordways over the mosses and paths to priory farms and chapels, to Fluke Hall and Pilling Hay. Caravanners use the same paths to the shore, through stands of bulrushes—take note of tide times!—and many a jaded motorist would do well to follow the same old routes to taste the salt air with cheeks whipped by the fresh sea breezes. On Cockerham Skeers—broken water, rocky ledges—inshore fishermen are bent and busy, and where the tide flows in deeper channels men fish with long drift nets as salmon lures. They make dramatic silhouettes against the bright water; so do the meagre priory ruins, the loneliness accentuated by oyster catchers' cries and curlews in winter.

Here in the priory's heyday ships took sail from Monks Quay for Ireland. Now we see modern shipping on the horizon moving away from Heysham Docks. Between, Lune deeps and tiny dots on the far shores towards Sunderland Point and Overton where the counterparts of Cockerham's fishermen move about their wonted business, with 'eave', or 'haaf', nets as used by their common forebears the Norsemen.

LUNE MOUTH VILLAGES, GLASSON, OVERTON AND
SUNDERLAND POINT

How the wind blows from the priory to the Land Lighthouse, and to Glasson, where it always chases one around. To find shelter look where ancient mariners stand in knots; they know and remain rooted there. They watch with critical eye the 'fair weather fishermen', owners of pleasure craft—Glasson has a gay marina life at the weekends—then with little persuasion talk of a different Glasson, thronged with Baltic shipping, wood-pulp cargoes from Finland, Welsh colliers, Cornish china-clay boats and timber brought in from Canada.

Now, Glasson has walled-in enclosures, a newly found prosperity, in iron foundry, oil refinery, dry docks, cement dumps and warehouses; this is modern 'working' Glasson ticking over. Look beyond the gimmicky cafes and gift shops to the dockside pubs, solid old houses, the inner basin and the long 'cut' linking the port with the canal system; this belongs to Glasson Dock which from 1787 poached Sunderland's shipping, and in turn lost it to Fleetwood, later to be outstripped by Liverpool.

Glasson boomed, and Sunderland became 'Cape Famine'. Wide channels divide them now, and little shipping uses any Lune port. Today Sunderland depends entirely on fishing. For farming there is little enough room, a few small enclosed acres divided by narrow lanes only wide enough for a pony or fisherman's cart, and hedged in by boulder walls, turf sodded, with gorse and quickthorn windbreak defences on top.

"Look o'er yon wall and you'll git your head blown off!" We were there in November, crossing the causeway from Overton as the tide ebbed to clear it. The school mini-bus was behind us. Out tumbled a merry crew and like wild ponies all leapt away to their various homes. Two little girls went ahead of us, dancing on wall tops, balancing on logs, scampering off to the shore.

Changes have reached 'sundered' Sunderland Point, but none drastic. None will come without protest, for none seems anxious for better links with the mainland. They even sigh with relief when the tides flow and the barrier is more than a mental one. "It's nice to be left alone. It's so quiet when everyone's gone."

Apart from new coats of gay paint and new notices of village activities—lectures, evening classes and the like, timed according to the tides—nothing changes. Robert Lawson, the architect of Sunderland's attractive waterfront in 1728, would recognize the same tall houses of First and Second Terrace, his quays—though no tall ships lie there—the sailors' inn, with farm and barn adjacent, and maybe the romantic Caribbean-type last villa with ornamental canopy and balconies which must have been built for some West Indian merchant dreaming of warmer climes, bluer skies. 'They say' the tree by the inn, 50 feet high, its top flattened by sea winds, "grew from a cotton seed" from a bale unloaded here! Natives insist it is a cotton tree: experts pooh-pooh it!

Black Sambo's grave always has flowers upon it, placed by little girls; in November gold chrysanthemums in a jam jar. In 1736 the negro slave who willed himself to die believing his beloved master who had sailed up to Lancaster had abandoned him, was buried here in a sheltered hollow of a sea-edge rabbit warren. Never has it been forgotten, or without fresh flowers. Now a very thick piece of ship's cable surrounds it, as a kerb. The path to it is well trodden.

Near the shore, in Butler's packing shed, we watched the fishermen and quick-fingered children packing in polythene bags "slivers of pure silver, slips of moonlight", whitebait, newcomers to Lune waters after unaccountable migration. These were to be sent to Fleetwood and thence to London buyers, a rare delicacy.

Butlers—like Burrows and Bensons, Viking stock—are all inshore fishermen, all round Morecambe Bay. Here at Sunderland they fish in the old ways, using the haaf nets one notices against the 'Cotton Tree' barn wall, and the cobles and nobbies drawn on the shingle.

Sunderland and Overton are good at sharing church and vicar, school, all activities. Old Overton has come to terms with its new houses, a 'blood transfusion' when it might have died on its feet— and the first feet were set here thirteen centuries ago. Its wind-battered old church was raised three centuries before Heysham's, which celebrated its thousandth year in 1967. Survivors from its past? An inn, the 'Ship', with its redoubtable landlady, 'Ma' Lily McCluskie; white-walled fishermen's cottages—against which men in dark-blue ganseys, arms folded, expressions quite inscrutable, make extremely attractive still-life pictures—and old buildings tucked into sheltering slopes. Overton can be called a typical waterside village, self-contained, going its own way.

Pilling and Cockerham, Glasson and Sunderland, like Overton, are pleasantly relaxed; the villagers live with forces they cannot control, have accepted them and enjoy what they have—clear air, invigorating breezes and, for contemplation, the daily wonder of the tides.

Middleton has been visually less fortunate; mixed blessings, holiday camp and vast chemical works! Heysham has its worries for the future, all depends on the 'Barrage', this is a subject as many-sided as joining the E.E.C., opinions are as divided.

NEAR PRESTON AND ALONG THE RIBBLE ESTUARY

Preston began where tracks made by Ribble fishermen of Walton and Penwortham met on Fishergate Hill, a place of subsequent barter, then trade. Preston became proud because it was a priest's town in St Wilfred's days, and even more proud when with royal charters and a medieval merchant and craftsmen's guild it could exert tight monopolies. But without the estuary folk who came to its markets its prosperity would have had a slower growth. Norsemen of Hesketh and Becconsall and, along the Ribble south banks to Meols and Hawes, descendants of tenth-century sea rovers who forgot their pirating impulses to become lawfully employed inshore fishermen, came to town with 'English' neighbours from Hutton and Tarleton, Warton and Freckleton.

In the seventeenth century the main goods offered on the stalls were "leather, butter, cheese and fruit and garden things, as well as pedlery, and in separate markets pigs, cattle, flesh and fish, corn and coles". But after the eighteenth-century reclamation of the marshes with plentiful crops from new ground the buying power of the villages increased and Preston's prosperity with it.

They will still be coming when the Lancashire new town centred on Preston sends its hundreds of thousands to town for shopping on market days and Saturdays, a pattern time cannot change. I enjoy a day in Preston. Since it is on important highways, there is a feeling of identity with the outside world, which I never experience at Bolton or Blackburn farther inland.

The rich and productive countryside north and south of the estuary—miles of cornfields, potato fields and market gardens— would never have been had not landowners like the Ecclestons and Fermor-Heskeths and Fleetwoods in the south, and Cliftons and Hoghtons in the north, by their draining and reclamation won so much from the former bog and mere and were early starters in the agrarian revolution. It was about the best land in the country, "very fertile, won from the sea it needed for some time no tilling being rich in marine deposits". The mosslords reaped a rich harvest financially so that the meagre population thinly spread over 'barbaric, sterile heathland, their rude hovels licked by the flood tides, could be rehoused till there was hardly a primitive reed-thatched cot left standing'.

Bright ideas were put forward to develop the Fylde coast, with a new Ribble–Kirkham canal, a Poulton branch to the Kendal–Preston canal, and there was even a plan to link Lytham and Kirkham with the Wyre villages by a navigable cut. All forward-looking men had ideas. Some cried out for improved roads so that a mail coach could carry letters, replacing the one post boy! And if communications were improved the very backward villages would reap the benefit. Unfortunately the landlords were dilatory, with little business acumen. No-one could imagine that where Marton Mere's brackish water entering the sea made a 'black pool' there would be a Golden Mile to make millions, or that men like Mr Whiteside, whose inn provided rooms for visitors in 1755, would go down in history as the first of many to cater for the seaside holiday maker. The seaside was unfamiliar to most Lancastrians in 1755, and taking holidays away from home unknown.

The years which saw Blackpool, Lytham and St Anne's firmly set on their course as 'resorts' also decided the fate of villages *en route* for the sea. Not only were they sharing the prosperity of improved farming but also they were all set to be providers for the new holiday coast. Blackpool is extremely fortunate nowadays in its hinterland, constant supplies of local produce, fresh vege-tables and home-grown tomatoes a speciality. It is still living up to its name 'Gefeld', the Fylde, the Field, full of pleasant villages— and inevitably thousands of town workers choose to live there.

The journey to the coast at fifty miles per hour has no great attraction, the villages all much of a muchness. Ashton is leafy, and Lea is long-drawn-out. Who would guess Will Shakeshaft was named among Thomas Hoghton's singing boys at Lea Hall in the years of the young poet's 'disappearance'; or that the way from hall to shore had dark secrets as when a Hoghton in 1568 fled to Flanders with his family, taking a boat from Lea by night and never returning; or that men landed at Lea unmarked, to be passed inland by secret ways to safe retreats, in penal times when a papist priest was forbidden in performing his office.

The coastal villages look much more like villages from the estuary, as I have seen them when sailing down the tide on an Irish car ferry.

The coast road was improved in the early nineteenth century, made a gated way with tolls to pay, 3d. or 4d. It was slow, but in the 1870s no one was in a hurry to cross Freckleton marshes, 5,000 acres of it reclaimed, ploughboys whistling and seagulls screaming behind, "inquisitive calves, and frisky stirks, and cattle refusing to budge from the roadway". Enough of the primeval was left for today's wild fowlers, and hazards too when sea mists come crawling low over the marsh, and the tide creeps in unnoticed.

The Angles sited Freckleton on a rise where the Romans had an outpost 'terminal' and where the Ribble at low tide was fordable. Travellers came to Naze Point and Warton Brows *en route* from the Douglas to Kirkham. The coast here developed into a small port where cargoes from seagoing vessels were unloaded to small boats for Preston. There was some shipbuilding, a factory weaving sailcloth and sacking, later cotton weaving; and young men hankered for the sea. Warton also shared this trade, welcoming travellers and sending its sons away to become seamen and, many, master mariners.

Who recognizes this? "Small, old and quiet as a mountain tarn until the school doors open. Its church is antiquated, its gallery like a water tank, the belfry patronized by jackdaws, starlings and sparrows. The parson has a four-wheeled carriage, enjoys yachting, duck shooting, and keeps cats, monkeys and toads in a menagerie." This was Warton in 1872.

How many passing through Freckleton know of its Aberfan, when stark tragedy came with lightning out of a stormy sky on 23rd August 1944. Down crashed a US plane, wrecking the village school; and one complete age group of infants, twenty-three of them, were killed. Others died too, villagers and airmen. Time has pushed the memories into the background; few ever talk about it, but children play on the Memorial Recreation Ground, gift of the American airmen, and discussion is still going on about how best to spend accumulated funds for the Memorial Hall—after nearly thirty years.

Higher level Clifton is more shapely, its beginning and end quite clear and pretty in between. Wrea Green, described in 1872 as "small, ancient, preeminently rustic with aged cottages, a town's common with geese and ducks having a happy time", is like this now.

It has retained its rural character and spruced itself so much
that it has been among the Best Kept Village winners several
times.

Of course, say envious neighbours, "The green makes it; there
are no interesting buildings." But community feeling is strong. In
August 1972 the village won its fight for the said green, over
which the lord of the manor of Kirkham claimed livestock grazing
rights. Because the village had continuously enjoyed the green for
traditional activities "over and beyond the memory of its
inhabitants", the village won.

Fylde villages, Angle and Norse, for a thousand years have been
twinned—Weeton-with-Prees, Warton-with-Bryning, and here
Ribby-with-Wrea. The Rigbys' ancestral hall site is to be used in
future for Lancashire's Royal Show so placing it firmly on the
county map. A century ago the two villages, incredible though it
may seem, provided work for 475 men. Now all must travel to
Blackpool, Salwick, Lea or Preston.

I wonder what Tommy Noblett, a character of the last century,
would say about all this to-ing and fro-ing? Tommy was sexton
for forty years, lived in one house for fifty, and at the age of 80
thought nothing of walking to Preston and back in one day.
Walking, scorning offers of lifts in gigs, ignoring railways, said
he, "Legs were meant to walk with, and too much riding would
make folk lose the use of them."

A string of estates belonging to Cliftons followed the ridge
above the mosses, desolate before and golden with corn after
draining. They endured longer than any other Fylde family; others
were extinguished by the Civil War, exiled during the Commonwealth or finally crippled after Jacobite risings. Little Lund-cum-
Salwick was theirs and the chantry chapel, "used by no others
except during the Commonwealth when Cliftons were banished",
and during periods of religious strife. Lund was "a very dark corner
with a veritable Roman altar set up as a font" in those days; but
from its landmark windmill hill what a view! All the cottagers—
as in Newton-with-Scales its neighbour—were handloomers forced
to leave their villages and swell the numbers of Preston's factory
workers, a century ago.

Westby, another Kirkham township, among fields of grain, had
both watermill and windmill, the later claimed to be the best
mariners' landmark along the coast. Being Clifton land it had

Roman Catholic priests, one the squire's hunting crony and an intrepid follower of hounds. Another was always accompanied by his dogs, one sleeping in the sanctuary during mass. One priest had in his orchard the best pear trees in Westby; he knew it, the village lads knew it. Each autumn both parties used cunning. The priest won. Firing a gun from his window was a partial deterrent, but far better was tying his ferocious dog to the best bearing tree.

Ask Fylde folk and they will say they consider Weeton about the best of the bunch among its villages. It is very pretty, tidy but not the least old fashioned. Not quite as in 1872: "silent, serenely set, quietly, quaintly looking—its thatched houses standing back from the broad road as if to give it a wide berth and let it go by, unmolested". Its most significant buildings, now as then, were the church, the windmill and the inn, the latter the place to meet the local horny-handed sons of the soil with straws in their mouths. According to Hewitson, "they respected ale, had traditional reverence for gin and water, but their respect for the Lord Derby eclipses all else". Times have changed!

WALTON AND LOWER DARWEN VILLAGES

Who invented the story that "from Walton Bridge looking towards Ribchester you overlook the richest treasure in England"? Was this treasure dug up by chance on Ribble banks at Cuerdale in 1840? A spade struck into a hidden chest, the lead split and out spilled streams of silver coins and many silver ingots. Since that hoard, possibly a treasury chest containing a fleeing army's pay after Brunanburgh, was exposed to the startled gaze of the labourers there have been no more finds! To hope for more around Walton must be unrewarding. In the last century the historic earth has been overlaid thickly by industrial growth, Walton village and broad highways. Walton and Bamber Bridge always channelled trade and travellers towards Preston, so sharing the flow of history.

Its most exciting days, loaded with drama, were in the Civil War. The Battle of Preston in 1648 flowed between Preston and Walton Bridge, and when it was won Cromwell took a well-earned rest to write his despatches at the inn on Darwen Bridge, the 'Unicorn'. Charles II went by three years later. In 1715 Stuart supporters in the first Jacobite rebellion were here, and another

Charles, the Young Chevalier, spent a night at Walton Hall in the '45.

In the eighteenth century the 'Unicorn' was a meeting place for numerous Lancashire 'big names' in a so-called mock corporation. Their complete regalia is in the Harris Museum in Preston, and also the minute books which the curator let me peruse at my leisure.

The first meticulous entries were in 1705, the last casually written in 1796. Stuart loyalists predominate among early paid-up members in Queen Anne's reign—Towneleys, Butlers, Blundells, Tyldesleys. Was the hilarious buffoonery and horse play indulged in by certain of the officers—slut kisser, custard eater, house groper—merely a cover for more serious Jacobite discussions in the years when everyone wondered whether the Queen's choice of successor would be James Edward Stuart or her Protestant kinsman George of Hanover? The corporation's major, his deputy, recorder, physician, pastor and poet laureate (one year he was the Rev. Mr Shakespear) had more important roles.

After the '15, when many members were of families penniless or exiled for their part in it, old Roman Catholic names are fewer. After the '45 enthusiasm waned, attendances were desultory until the society wound up, and the book was used for the scribblings of subsequent 'Unicorn' landlords' children.

Villages near Preston and Walton were at once involved in the factory system in the first stage of industrial revolution. The Darwen water was what the bleachers needed; the dairy herds of the valley supplied the dung and urine needed for dye fixing in the new print shops; large cotton weaving mills followed, all in rural settings. Moons Mill and Kittlingbourne were early starters, and Gregson Lane and Bamber Bridge were two villages with many immigrant Irish who stayed over after the canal, turnpike road and later the railway building. Together with the native hand-loomers here was a ready made labour force. And so it remained for a century and more until slump, recessions, short time, 'rationalization' and the shut-down of some mills forced out long-established families. There is a hard core of village stock staying put, but the young must find work in Preston.

Industrial premises dwindled in number but they carried on long after the manufacturers who founded them were forgotten. About 1800 the owners of Darwen Bank, Cooper Hill and, farther

along the Darwen valley, the Feildens of Feniscowles and Witton
Park, the cotton magnates, replaced the ancient 'extinguished'
gentry on their ancestral homes. Each then seemed settled for
centuries ahead. None remain.

At Hoghton things worked out different. On the surface none
would guess this village, the prettiest by the Darwen, ever had any
industry—the green slope towards the Tower, a farseen landmark,
the farmlands all around well cared for, the buildings in good
shape. The satisfying grouping of church, school and Church Farm
on a shared hilltop, trees behind, the sky above makes, in whole
and in part, a perfect picture of happy contented rurality. Turn
down lanes off the highway: ducks on ponds, geese hissing as you
pass, cows ambling to shippons. Or discover Cripplegate, Goose-
foot, Dearbought and Barracks Lanes. Or watch village cricket on
the sports field, join the villagers at a meeting or social gathering
in the village hall. An ideal village? Housing promoters say so:
"most desirable to live here, our homes excel in their situation"!
New houses everywhere, along byways, down near the Bottoms.

Out of sight, where Darwen emerges into sunlight from a deep
dark ravine, a complete mill village: two mills, sociable rows of
stone-built cottages up steps, some 'prettified' with picture
windows and flush doors, all occupied, but not many by the old
breed of weavers. 'Shut down' came in 1969, the factory buildings
offered for sale in lots. In 1972: great clanking wheel broken,
milldam choked, and in the vast weaving sheds all machinery gone,
only wind stirring cobwebs across doorless, windowless holes.
Hoghton Bottoms was a piece of the Old Lancashire.

SOME LOWLAND VILLAGES OF THE SOUTH-WEST

Because of the comparable terrain, climate and native stock of the
Anglo-Norse Fylde, the villages south of the Ribble estuary match
up with those on the north side. Until one reaches Hoole the
increasing build-up of houses blurring the edges of Penwortham,
Longton, Hutton, almost continuous along the A59, is like that
from Ashton and Lea to Freckleton and Warton. The rest is flat,
devoid of interest, agricultural contributor to Lancashire's larder.
Until the end-products come to the shops the public is not wildly
excited by potato fields, glass-house farming and battery hens
or egg production. Here it is the staple industry.

Neither is residential property of particular interest to those who enjoy something else in a village. The local fears, naturally, are of more building enveloping that already here when the new town 'gets moving'.

"Nestling within trees, under wide spreading foliage, wild flowers in profusion, the air redolent of Flora, hares and rabbits . . . in Crow Wood around its old and curious chapel." Such was Penwortham's scene a century ago, wild life in profusion: "pheasant and partridge . . . near Prior's Oak—and immigrant Irish washing themselves in St Mary's Well"!

'Penverdant' was important when brethren from Evesham were at the priory and early Norman barons at the nearby castle on the mound. Especially so were its fisheries which despatched an annual prior's due of sixty salmon to Evesham. Then the Ribble was fordable at low tides and a ferry plied at others. Whisk away the electricity power station and the two bridges to imagine this. The castle motte east of the church is an excellent viewpoint.

From the Dissolution Fleetwoods were most important here-abouts, quick to purchase abbey land and make their way in the world. One son married Cromwell's daughter. In the church the steel helmet and leather jacket painted with the family badge, martlets—though folk say it "was left here by Cromwell"—probably belonged to a Fleetwood.

Hutton is proud of its old grammar school, its up-to-date county institute—helpful to amateur as well as professional gardeners—and famous police training college—which does far more than police-dog handling, though most of us see only demonstration of that. Like Longton it is roadside, pleasant and developing. Not till Hoole do we really feel we are in a village which seems attuned with its past, with farming, boats, barges and sea-going and coastal craft. Here are inns, and at the village end the old church, the handmade brick of its walls glowing with the stored sunshine of 350 summers.

On the Bretherton lane stands Carr House where lived the Stones family, John gave the church its font, his wife the communion plate, whilst other Stones traded from the Douglas shores. Andrew 'of Amsterdam, merchant' shipped goods to England via Hoole, and Richard, who imported Irish panel boards and timber in 1604 supplied the Shuttleworths, then building Gawthorpe Hall, with 1,000 pieces, storing them till needed in Hoole's tithe barn.

Newburgh, village on the plains

Downham in early spring

Broughton-in-Furness, its face cleaned by the L.C.C.

Hornby in the Lune Valley

Chipping's old grammar school and almshouses

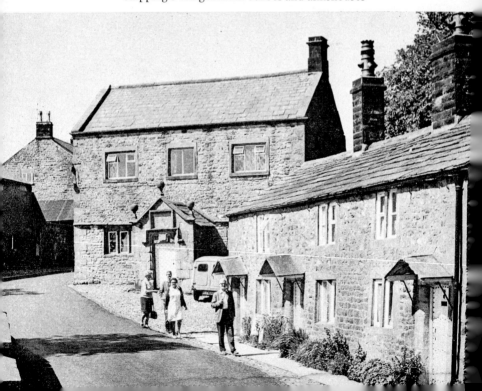

In their house, from the room above the porch in 1639, the young curate and an astronomer friend witnessed and recorded for the first time an astral 'happening', a dark spot on the sun's disc, the Transit of Venus. In the church are many memorials to Jeremiah Horrocks, 'Pride and Boast of British Astronomy'.

Lord Lilford, heir general to many 'discontinued' old Lancashire families, owns Carr House. Here is now displayed the Barry Elder's Dolls Museum—and maybe in the future the Lancaster bomber Lord Lilford bought in May 1972 will find its way to Hoole.

I know a farm not far from the Douglas with its kitchen table concealing a trap door. I have heard tales of smugglers unloading contraband by night at the Douglas edge and footsteps heard beneath the floor, and the lifting of the table and creak of a heavy door.

All this bucolic region came within the 'four quarters' of Croston Parish: Bretherton in the second, Hesketh Bank in the third whilst the fourth was made up of Tarleton "which is so much less than the rest because Much Hoole and Little Hoole are taken out of it by Act of Parliament". So much was bog, mere, watery waste and tidal estuary that outlying villages pleaded for their own churches "because of great inundations of the river Asland by reason of the Douglas, Fumey Pool and Yarrow over-flowing the ways for the most part of winter time". Floods were so bad that none could reach Croston church without a boat. Even by boat the going was impassible after the worst flooding.

The present face of this lowland part of Leyland Hundred is due to successful draining of Martin Mere by cutting a channel to the Ribble. First attempts by Fleetwoods in 1692 were a failure. Eccleston's schemes succeeded because of John Gilbert's ingenuity a century later. Hesketh's nineteenth-century reclamation of their marshes was completely rewarding. The Crossens Drainage Board continues the good work and keeps constant watch over the drains and channels, ensuring that folk around the old mosses sleep easy by night.

Many south-west Lancashire villages today would be unrecognizable to visitors from the past. Where now Tarleton of 1872—"rough, and ready, primitive, with one long bewildering street, and all sizes of houses which looked in need of shaking up and putting in order again"? The villagers have changed too—homely

D

and hospitable, yes, but there is no suspension of all operations on a stranger's approach "as all speculate on why he comes and what he wants". Neither is the current fashion for the youths "beaver hats, fur caps and shaven necks"!

Tarleton, Hesketh and Becconsall, are grown out of recognition with few old features intact—old names, a few surviving marsh-land dwellings. This also goes for most of the south Lancashire villages almost all rapidly expanding and eating up many rural areas.

But some of the old 'bad lands' are to be protected—just in time! Freshfield sand dunes by the sea have been a happy hunting ground for the flower lover and butterfly chaser, Formby shores known for wild life and many rarities in plant life, and Ainsdale's 1,216 acres of foreshore and pine woods for some years a wild life sanctuary. Added to these in 1972 were the unreclaimed areas of Martin Mere—any will-o'-the-wisps, mermen or spectres of the watery wastes remaining?—to be another wild life conservation area.

Around the old mosslands the villages are very civilized. Rufford in 1872 was "indeed a beautiful spot, cottages, and farmhouses looking as if by some happy enchantment they had dropped from some region above, essentially rural, purely rustic, exquisitely pastoral—neither mines, nor quarries, nor manufactures of any kind". Hewitson gave the credit to the chief landowner of Victorian times, Sir T. G. Fermor-Hesketh, who had "replaced miserable small cottages by neat clean dwellings of a selectness seen in few country villages. Here were no lodgers, no wandering vagrants, no dark horses."

THREE PERFECT AND HISTORIC VILLAGES

Rufford is attractive now but has not the instant impact of another rural community renewed by landowners who loved it and ensured its charm should reach into another century. I am thinking of Halsall, islanded for centuries amid vast bogs and meres, its church spire a landmark visible for miles—"Heleshala" in the Domesday Book when Anglo-Norse Chetel held two plowlands here. Chetel was among Halsall's early landholders. Those who followed called themselves Halsalls, named eldest sons from their Church's saint, Cuthbert, and each in his time added beauty to the already venerable foundation. Halsalls were at the hall south of the village from medieval to Tudor times when, in 1593, one founded the grammar school tacked on to the church.

The village has the look of a place well loved and shaped, like Rufford, by those to whom good taste and harmony were all important. Villagers tell me of Lady Lethbridge of the hall, who decided village replanning should preserve its spacious, open character, her friend and neighbour the Marquis of Scarisbrick suggesting the architectural type for new buildings. What they achieved the villagers have always valued. The council houses are as well placed and pleasant—prize-winners in cottage garden competition—and the most modern houses 'New Georgian' and with lawns and trees, fit in happily. So do any conversions.

The near-perfection of Halsall is not by chance. Old residents and newcomers work together to keep it so. Many are enthusiastic members of the Civic Trust.

There the church has always been dominant in local life and affairs. Most activities come under its care—not the W.I., of course. Halsall has everything—sixty Women's Institute members, a Sunshine Club for the older folk, a new youth club for the 12 to 16s, Meals on Wheels and a village luncheon club run by the busy W.V.S. There is cricket and football on a fine sports field, badminton for an indoor winter sport—and during the coldest winters, skating on a flooded field above the sluice gates of a long-abandoned mill pond. Angling is enjoyed in the nearby canal and boating on a very pretty, tranquil stretch which was the first section of the Leeds and Liverpool 'cut'—the sod-cutting ceremony was performed just by the 'Saracen's Head'. Here Liverpool folk stepped out of canal boats and waiting horse-drawn carts carried them off for a day at Southport, then a new resort far ahead of Blackpool. Pigeon-shooting is a necessary sport in a corn-growing region like this. Too many birds are a menace so shoots are organized—but the pigeons, cunning in self preservation, fly for sanctuary to the church tower!

Halsall overflows with wellbeing, harvesting the goodness of the earth. Farmers supply the markets, hauliers are many, transporting sprouts, cabbages and potatoes to Manchester and Liverpool. All and sundry enjoy the harvest suppers and barn dances. They treasure their local heritage too. The rector, Canon Bullough, produced an excellent guide to St Cuthbert's, full of fine photographs of carvings in wood and stone.

St Cuthbert's I would put among the most interesting churches in Lancashire, excelling in interior work of the early fourteenth to sixteenth centuries, surprising to find in a lonely church once marooned in the marshes. Fascinating is the exquisite workmanship of the Chancel's Easter Sepulchre, Rector Halsall's tomb, and the stonework of sedelia and piscina. Unique, I believe, in the array of misericords, is a wrestling match with a monk on the sideline! A changing range of colour, sometimes soft, sometimes glowing, stains the walls of nave and chancel—visual delight, picked up in lovely flower arrangements. Good taste in everything!

Happy the eye in Halsall. Small wonder it has done well in the Best Kept Village competitions. Is there any flaw? It has a bus service—and, in addition, a parish bus doing church runs on Sundays, bringing in scattered parishioners. But—Halsall has no shop, no post office.

The next village, Scarisbrick, has shop and post office by the Morris Dancer's Inn, a useful baby clinic in the same block. All very conveniently contained. Scarisbrick, at the centre of early attempts at reclamation is a very widespread community, growing outwards. Beyond is Churchtown, which, had it remained quite separate from Southport, would be a complete village. The old church, the green and trees, a number of much admired, immaculate white houses, old inns and thatched cottages bowed with age, belong to North Meols, which pre-dated Southport by a thousand years. A pity green belts were not important when the two drew too close together.

As attractive as Halsall in a different way is Newburgh, of the plains but nearer the western escarpment. Like most Newtons, Newbys and Newtowns this is very old, an ancient market where old roads met, yet very much part of the present. As a really go-ahead village it possesses a prominently placed parish notice board. with up-to-date notices and the 'crit' of the last Best Kept Village judges pinned up for all to see, mark and digest to make sure the village earns a place next year!

Like the judges everyone must be 'charmed' by Newburgh—especially by its varied yet harmonious architectural styles, houses of mellow handmade brick and of fine local stone, with the long low lines so well in keeping with the level rural landscape—all good neighbours though no two alike.

Equally at home, handsome 'houses of distinction' like Peter

Lathom's, Ash Tree Cottage, Moorcroft House and Derby House, homes diverse, some proudly dating from the seventeenth and eighteenth centuries, others nameless, undated but equal in charm. Even the new houses, because of trees in their gardens, fit admirably into the village scene. At the centre, near the inn, are a cross on a green and seats for summer idleness and village gossip.

A pity a community with so much—and with a council which cares and people who are proud to belong here—has to endure the pounding of heavy lorries, the fate of every village which became a market because it stood where trading routes met.

Behind the houses are gardens, orchards, play fields, riding school, and arable seemingly to infinity. But not quite to infinity, for south of Newburgh are Lathom and Skelmersdale new town. The one has dwindled and has little left of its days of glory when the Stanleys were in occupation of Lathom House and the neighbourhood shared English history. The other has swallowed up the rather grim little village and its surrounding farmland.

The reason south-west Lancashire is disappointing as far as old villages go, is that so much was bog and watery waste that there never were many. The mere-edge villages, a ring of them surrounding the reclaimed acres of the last two centuries, are nothing more than farms with field workers' cottages—no recorded history, few traditions, little charm apart from what the passing hours bestow, the blush of early morning and the mystery of low-lying mists, the gaudy splendours of sunset which are certainly displays of glorious technicolor in a landscape where nine-tenths is sky.

Villages overlooking the lowlands are rapidly changing character, for Maghull with 21,000, Aughton with 8,000 and Lydiate with over 5,000 since the war have grown up. So have ancient communities on the coast, like Formby, a small place with a harbour before silting put an end to it and the folk turned to agriculture. Crosby (the Great), also a Viking settlement of the tenth century, in the last decade has almost joined up with Waterloo and Seaforth, whilst Little Crosby, of equal age and part of the tenth-century Norse settlement "where a cross was set up", remains small, aloof.

Both Crosbys have common ancestry: they were both granted or acquired by the descendants of the fair-haired Blondell who fought at Hastings. Blundells were at Crosby Hall eight centuries

ago—and are still there, on the same site, which puts the Whit-
lock-Blundells among the oldest families (though in the female
line) in the county.

When writing *Lancashire's Old Families* I found fascinating
material about the family, and incidentally about their tenants
and neighbours around Little Crosby, written down by William
the Cavalier from the Civil War and the Commonwealth to the
Days of William and Mary, and by Nicholas, his grandson, known
as the 'Diarist', who recorded in detail all his doings at home and
supervising the work on his Little and Great Crosby estates.

There is an oft-quoted letter written by William Blundell to
James II in which he says of Little Crosby that there was "not a
beggar, not an alehouse, and not a Protestant in it".

I feel that if one stood long enough in the wandering street old
William Blundell might appear, stopping to talk with the villagers,
jotting down scraps of local wit or wisdom in his notebooks. Or
Nicholas, calling on his cottagers, sharing their good times and
bad, filling the role of squire and father and adviser to all. It was
such a close-knit community that Blundells and their humblest
descendants shared the same ups and downs of fortune, the dark
days crowding out the bright during far too many generations in
the years between the 1590s and 1720s. It shows how loyal they
were for when rich rewards would have been theirs none informed
against the Blundells and their clandestine visitors, papist priests
harboured at the hall. During the Civil War when William Blundell
was in prison or in hiding and the womenfolk were left to carry
on alone, old servants kept the rough Roundhead soldiers in check
when they billeted themselves at the hall.

Here are happenings in a village year in the days of Good Queen
Anne.

Christmas was kept as a religious festival. Merry making was
concentrated on Twelfth Night with the fiddler playing, much
dancing, including Nicholas' own arrangement of the Sword
Dance and the Squire himself trying out conjuring tricks or
playing Cut in the Pantry with a friend from Lady Green. Sometimes the local mummers played at the hall and Crosby lads
performed dramas—'imperfectly', a 'group' touring from house
to house, first giving a boisterous, often ribald play followed by
one with more serious intent, real drama!

Where there was so much standing water a hard winter meant

ice and everyone sporting on the frozen ponds, all the Blundells
sharing the pleasure with the village folk. Frosty mornings meant
hare coursing too.

Plough Monday: out came the ploughs for blessing, then field
work began; oxen used for farm work were six or more years in
the yoke before being sold for meat. Little Crosby had a single
large Town Field cultivated for the growing of rape for winter
fodder. Compare with today's crops, "pottatowes and tornops",
only grown in gardens in Nicholas Blundell's time. When not
turned to crops the Town Field lay fallow. The village stock was
allowed to feed there, so manuring the ground. In the early
eighteenth century little winter fodder was grown so that cattle
and horses grazed the common well into winter. To augment
animal manure as fertilizer folk spread lime, or burnt moss ash
from the bogs, carried seaweed from the shore, or used the most
valued fertilizer, marl.

Shrove Tuesday, the last fling before Lent meant a great con-
sumption of pancakes. Folk ate at friends' houses, then invited
them home to more. The Blundells shared a feast of pancakes with
neighbours then "several came to eat pancakes at the Hall and
all made merry with Tatlock the Fiddler and Anderson the Piper
to play for the dancing". The latter were always on hand for every
merry night and merry making, the piper "having brought up
seven small children, chiefly by his pipes playing".

Marl was a valued fertilizer, but hard labour went into the
getting of it. The various processes needed three months—between
the setting out of the pit in April to the taking away of the last
cartload in July. The villagers had to perform boon work for the
Blundells, six days of their labour during the year as the squire
required—carting marl or lime or coles from Haigh—maybe three
days' reaping, three days' shearing, or, in default, the payment of
a boon hen valued at 6d. But what ever hard labour was asked of
them, everyone knew there would be a grand merrymaking for all
afterwards. When all marl had been removed and before the
water began to fill the great pit, Blundells and all who had shared
the marling used the pit for a bull bait, "squire providing a collar
for the best bulldog of three or more baits". Little children
watched too. None were squeamish about blood sports then.

Best of all was Finishing Day, when "abundance of marlers,
spreaders, water balys and carters" were called to the great feast,

and neighbours, tenants and villagers too sat down to a huge celebration spread. They brought gifts of sugar, chickens and butter. After the appetites and thirsts were satisfied, "we fetched home the maypowl from the pit and had sword dancing", the eight dancers ably trained by Nicholas who also brought tinsel for the garland and shaped the caps the marlers and dancers wore.

In fact the year was one succession of happenings, so life was never stale in old Little Crosby, especially in summer when it was possible to move around with ease. Winter floods confined everyone to the village. From October to March time stood still.

In the Hall gardens grew fruit trees. Nicholas' grandfather recorded that by planting cloves, nutmeg or spices at the roots of apple or pear trees the fruit would take that flavour. Nicholas, a great experimenter, soaked his cherry stones in brandy before planting! He suffered in September from orchard raiders, village lads who were "leathered by their fathers at the Lodge Gates—others looking on—for stealing apples and other peevish tricks". I guess the brandy for the cherry experiment was contraband.

Apple stealing to lively lads, smuggling to 'sporting' men, satisfaction was derived by any who got away with it. Nicholas had the co-operation of Little Crosby men. Diary entries have veiled references: "This night a cargo of 16 large ones brought to White Hall." "W.C. covered the cargo very well with straw." "I furnished C.H. and his brother with two good casks." "A deal of outhousing at the Hous serched for brandy." Read between the lines!

The Sunday nearest St Luke's Day began Crosby Goose Fair, the year's highlight, all the fun of the fair to follow, Blundells dining with their tenants, a great honour, then attending the races on Crosby Marsh, all laying wagers on the runners. Small wonder the Grand National and Aintree Races were established hereabouts, for the country people had long been addicted. The early August horse races on the shore were popular as the Marsh races, and Molyneux and Blundells always there.

Little Crosby tenants living as they did in a state of benign feudalism fast disappearing, the wellbeing of each family from birth to the grave was the concern of the family at the hall. When a village woman was lying-in Mistress Blundell was often present, and the midwife lodged at the hall when cottage room was cramped. The children visited, curious to see the new arrival and bring gifts. When any were ill Nicholas Blundell, with a well-stocked supply of medicines and salves—the doctor advised him what was most efficacious—was there to help. He was not averse to experimenting either, putting his trust in a valued Family Book of Proven Cuars. Some of grandfather William's cures were horrific!

Some remedies tried for outbreaks of spots: "Put Mally into the sellar well." "The children were put in the sea for some outbreaks" "Dr pulled up some of the roots of Mally's head" and Nicholas "Pulled up by the roots his other daughter's hairs". Children were sent out to pick large amounts of eyebright, "very excellent for sore eyes", taken inside, outside "and smoaked".

Sick visiting was undertaken as a matter of course, the squire not refusing a call for help even at midnight. However poor and humble the dead, the Blundells' own coach-carriage was lent for a journey in dignity to the grave.

Little Crosby is rare in having the same family on the spot still. Rarer still, here is a village community which can enjoy rural merrymakings in the same great Hall Barn and granary where their forebears gathered centuries ago. The huge building—massive sandstone walls, ancient timbers—has been made better than new with wooden floor, galleries, balconies and stairs renewed so that now old style, new style, trad and pop, barn dances and discoes can be enjoyed therein. William would be appreciative, and doubtless Nicholas' genial spirit longs for a come-back. Seven young Blundells share the fun today.

THE PARISH OF SEFTON

Across the farmlands southwards the Alt meanders, not as freely as formerly, flooding the surrounding acres and making it necessary for folk to be ferried by boat to church and corn and hay at harvest to be carried on rafts, but confined within safety limits. It makes a border for Sefton parish. Near its banks is the lonely site of the ancestral hall of the Molyneux, followers of the Conqueror and early comers to these parts, like the Blundells. They rose high in rank to become Earls of Sefton, their great house at Croxteth a palace within a vast park. They had been made rich by royal grants and claimed precedence over their neighbours, demanding payment from the Blundells—a 4d. rent and a red rose at Mid-summer as part of feudal service for certain lands—and often riding so roughshod over them they made fierce rivals if not enemies of Blundells and their villagers, and of the Stanleys and their supporters. The country folk and tenants were always involved.

It took centuries—and sharing the same loyalties for King Charles I, the Stuart and Jacobite causes—to end the family feuds. Both Molyneux and Blundells lie quiet beneath the floor of Sefton parish church, where each claimed right of burial during the generations when both were firm papists. The Molyneux family tombs with grave slabs, memorial brasses of earlier Molyneux and cold marble of later viscounts and earls, are a notable collection. Here lie soldiers who fought in the Crusades, at Crécy and Agincourt—and William who "wan the Erle of Huntley's armes at the Battell of Flodden", who fought for and lost so much in the Royalist cause and were later rewarded at the Restoration.

The hall was demolished in 1720, and by the end of the century only the flat site and fragments of a bridge over the moat were left—as I saw it recently, cattle grazing where warriors mustered in court yards and not even a hint in the sea winds of high revelry in the hall, nor even masonry to tell it ever was there. But the Croxteth Molyneux were brought here for burial until the nineteenth century.

Of the dwellings of Sefton tenants, of the old village little is left. The population of Sefton with Lunt today is under 400. Exactly two hundred years ago when Thomas Pennant was here the church looked just as proud in its isolation—there were no other buildings in competition, though the fine corn mill, erected in the 1590s and in use still, was its neighbour by the Alt, and the few dwellings were half hidden in clumps of trees. Trees were rare in this landscape, ditches taking the place of hedges so any were worthy of mention. Local girls threw pins into the wishing well, St Helen's near the church; stray cattle were still impounded in Brickwell Lane pinfold; and there were stocks and a ducking stool, in place but rarely used.

Manor courts were then held with suitable decorum at the 'Punch Bowl'; officials were elected—the constables and bearers of such titles as 'birelagh'—bylaw or barley-men, 'offerers' and 'layers of the mise'. More convivial occasions—at the same old

hostelry—were the gatherings of the Ancient and Loyal Corporation of Sefton, a club of prosperous Liverpool traders and
merchants who from their number chose mayor, bailiffs, recorder,
etc., and butter weigher, controller of gunpowder, as well as the
palaver sitter or Prince of Anamoboe. What was an equivalent of
mayor's Sunday meant morning service at the 'Cathedral'—Sefton
church—dinner at the 'mansion house', the old Church Inn, church
again, and "the rest of the day spent in Conviviality and
Harmony". Politics were banned but feeling must have been
unanimous in 1789 when the corporation passed a resolution to
show how ridiculous they considered "the abolishing of the slave
trade by Fanatic Wilberforce". Obviously they were all involved
in the Africa trade.

In 1773 Sefton township was a place "of fine meadows reaching
almost to the sea, supplying Liverpool with hay". It was watered
"by the Alt, a small trout stream, but under water the whole season
after the first winter floods". And the parish—which included
Aintree, Netherton, Thornton Lunt, Ince Blundell, Great and
Little Crosby, and Halsall and Altcar—suffered. Pennant must
have heard discussions concerning what should be done, but not
till 1777 was an Act passed to regulate the Alt and its tributary
streams, to safeguard 5,000 acres useless half the year. Meetings
were held at Sefton church, on parish level, it being decided that
a tax should be levied on all owners or occupiers of improved
land. So, the Alt was cleared and cleansed, a new channel cut
near outlets at Altcar, Formby and Ravenmeols, and feeders
confined to new courses. All part of the Great South West
Lancashire Reclamation scheme.

All benefited, especially Ince Blundell "land on an 'innis' or
island in the swamps" of medieval times, half enclosed by the
meandering Alt. Early Blundells of Ince gave the monks of Stanlaw,
soon to translate their abbey to Whalley, "the mill, the corn
within it and the fish traps without". One later followed this gift
with common of pasture by the Alt, the Grange, "for sheep, cows,
turbuary and housebote", and gave his villeins, bondsmen or
serfs, to the abbey. There was always trouble about water and
flooding between the abbot and other neighbouring landowners.
When a Blundell of Little Crosby complained that damage to his
property was due to the abbey's neglect, the abbot retorted how
could he help when the Alt flowed and reflowed at *every* tide from

the sea into the Little Crosby ditches? He could not make war with Nature.

Long wide ditches in the Ince Woods, flanking the Liverpool highway, are evidence of the great drainage schemes needed to allow tree planting. The lovely lake within the hall ground also 'tames' the Alt. There is a village of Ince Blundell, nearly 600 people in it, well scattered. And in autumn 1973 £250,000 spent on straightening out the Alt bed—Final taming of the river intended.

In 1974 the Merseyside Metropolitan County will take over many villages between Southport and Liverpool including the Crosbys and Sefton.

2

North-West Lancashire Villages

Heysham is what you want of it: a place to live, outside a town but with its advantages, a good slice of holiday coast with the expected tourist amenities of cafes, gift shops, canned music. There is even a local brew, nettle 'drink'—a pale relation of more potent and now forbidden nettle beer. It has a holiday camp, a zoo and the docks, where one sails in the sunset to Ireland. It is also a journey back into history, best indulged in on quiet evenings in early spring when snowdrops mantle the churchyard, or in winter when crying of wintering seabirds is melancholy on the wind, but NOT in the holiday season.

Upper Heysham is completely modern, but the Lower borrows from the past, and white cottages crowd into the street as it dips to the shore, crammed as Clovelly in summer. Behind Greese Cottage (seventeenth-century and up steps) is the churchyard and St Peter's, which celebrated its millennium in 1967. On the headland amid relics of an abandoned monastery and graves carved out of bedrock, stands St Patrick's Oratory, half a millennium older. Dates—approximate: Patrick washed up on the Skeers about A.D. 460; Norse raiders destroyed the Celtic community, chapel and cells about A.D. 900; after which the Anglian builders sited their new church at lower level, out of sight from the sea.

For the 'touristic', today's visitors come in their tens of thousands. In 1872 the 'select' enjoyed the same pleasures, more simply. Earlier arrivals saw a 'no-village'. "No market, shop, doctor, attorney, no school or manufactory, and no sea-going boat!" Heysham then comprised a few cottages, one or two gentlemen's houses and the Old Hall (now a hotel). The manor was held in turn by Molyneux, Bradleys and lords who claimed "rights of watermill, windmill, dove-cotes, willow groves, salt and fresh marshes, and wreck of the sea".

Residents in modern Heysham are content with its present, pleasant look. The curious stranger has an eye on other things,

and if the sale of church guide-books—like hot cakes, by the
thousands—is any indication the historic is the most popular draw.
Not many villages are so deep-rooted in the past; did any other
keep St Patrick's day as the major festival or keep in touch
down the years with Armagh? "The only English church
evangelized from Armagh."

Rare treasures? St Patrick's oratory on the headland, none
older in the North, its precinct from the fifth century so holy that
men sought burial close against its walls. Many graves lie beneath
the turf but those hollowed from cliff-top bedrock are imperishable. Plenty of atmosphere lingers here, the silence accentuated by
seabirds' mournful crying.

The monastic cells of those who came along after Patrick are
high-level, whilst St Peter's—just over 1,000 years old—was
founded in a sheltered spot. One of the early burials was a
spectacular one. Over the remains of some far-famed great Norse
warrior slain in battle—at Torrisholm?—his followers set a hog-
back tomb cover. Stone carvers skilled in Norse mythology cut
upon it a struggle to the death of evil—serpent, hell hounds, the
devil in a wolf's shape—against the powers of good. All heaven
and earth is caught up in the conflict, but Christ, as a hart, is
shown victorious. This wonderful work of art was dug up in 1800,
placed near the south porch, and has now been brought indoors
for preservation—just in time!

Morecambe was formerly a small fishing village called Poulton-
le-Sands, which became so popular it swallowed such adjoining
villages as Heysham, Torrisholme and Bare, and now threatens to
expand outwards to Hest Bank, Slyne and Bolton. The last named
was formerly most important, astride the great north-west highway. What changes Bolton-le-Sands' main street has seen since
the road improvements of 1754. Postchaises arrived first on the
new turnpike, followed by the carriers' wagons of 1757, great
lumbering carts; and in 1763 there came in at a spanking pace a
flying machine—with six horses, speeding at six miles per hour—
and the diligence—Kendal to London in three days! Mailcoach
days were to follow. When the Kendal canal was completed in 1817
there was general rejoicing and crowds watching the fun from the
bridge by Bolton's new Packet Boat Inn.

In the 1840s came the new railway, and slackening road traffic.
The internal combustion engine brought back trade, but with it

Samlesbury's church on Ribble banks

Sefton church, on the Alt banks

Seventeenth- and eighteenth-century box pews in Samlesbury church

Ribchester parish church

Brindle church

Melling church

such traffic problems that the village had to be by-passed by a new, straight A6, and in due time by the Motorway to the east. The place has almost reverted to its early completely rural past of the eighteenth century.

Formerly the villagers were farmers. Their large flocks were grazed on the tidal salt marshes towards Keer mouth, sheep droppings manuring the land; and seaweed and mussels were gathered in such great quantities they were used as fertilizers too. Men followed the ebb tide, gathering cockles on the Skeers, to be carried by canal-boat to the new Lancashire towns. Year-old hoggs (sheep) were wintered on the marshes. The tall church tower was a guide to mariners and to travellers on the oversands crossing to Hest Bank.

Now, non-productive 'settlers' live in estates covering the green slopes west of the A6, and more are planned. In 1972 the children's seaside holiday home site was sold for £20,000. Everyone, even those who are 'new', fear further urbanization. Gazing at the tranquil, deserted canal, a sort of barrier against the 'tide' of new bungalows; or sauntering on the one long street, a sunny stillness upon it, gossiping people and folk with time to idle, this seems far ahead.

A glance at the public notice board tells of a diversity of happenings—W.I. monthly meetings, whist drives, spring fairs, floral and horticultural society doings and a wide choice of evening classes. The old boys' school (with bell cote and aged tree, the datestone seventeenth century), a library by day, is used for evening meetings. Here there is no excuse for boredom.

The motorway has given a reprieve, one hopes, to old buildings in narrow places threatened by fast traffic. Bolton has several such old corners, and Slyne village too, where travellers turned off to Hest Bank to wait for the ebb tide and the sands guide. Hawks-head Farm was built in the plague year, when a Londoner with a pack of infected second-hand clothes passed by and took the pestilence to Milnthorpe. Other doors opened to cheer Bonnie Prince Charlie as he went by: "James Bibby Built These Houses in 1745."

Tourists always found plenty to interest them. "Beautiful as are the provisions of Nature, Lancashire is more celebrated for its works of art in its wonderfully constructed and beautiful canals." Eighteenth-century notables arrived, admired the canal and

E

continued towards Nether Kellet and Dunold Mill Hole, a stupendous cavern from which a stream issued to turn the mill-wheel. The modern quarrying activity now whitens nearby M6 with lime dust. The descent into the underworld was considered thrilling. "Above our heads are hundreds of yards' thick of rock and minerals." Cave explorers, students from Lancaster, have shown me their scientific charting and naming of the passages, chambers, lakes and cascades—all in a day's work! No throwing about of epithets—"Pleasingly horrible, the fabulous Styx"—not for them!

Nether Kellet is a growing village, its prosperity beginning and ending in lime. The Limeburners Inn was frequented by rowdy workers, who earned the reputation: "Wos and wos, and then comes Kelleters." Here the barrel bottom was reached. A brave woman, Elizabeth Bates, built a Victorian school round her cottage, her aim to take the wild youth and inculcate the three Rs.

Nether Kellet sprawls about large enclosures, with nothing of the pleasant compactness of Over Kellet. Edmund Crouchback gave a Dacre a deerleap in his forest here, before Kelleters of Norse stock became 'Englishmen'. The village, however, is typically English, round a green, with market cross on steps (good for resting), a war memorial and a ring of houses of distinction looking on. Hall Garth stands behind the fine trees, and the Old Vicarage facing—"best house in Kellet". An outer circle tucks away comely houses of lesser degree, some dated—like Hoggarths (1759, and with tales of mad Luke Wilton, a priest's hide and uneven stairs with trip steps) and others of 1673, 1699 and 1744.

Just off the green, the Eagle's Head Inn; beyond, on a windy hill with superlative views, is the old church, very much a centre of modern village life, as for seven centuries past. The village seems to have no problems—apart from lime dust, and the eating away of well-loved limestone hills.

Three delicious hamlets—Capernwray, Priest Hutton and Borwick—are emerging from motorway building into a future envious of their situation. At Borwick, the first canal-side 'five-figure' executive-type houses—about which local opinion differs.

Naturally, highway villages like Bolton-le-Sands suffered changes unknown to communities off the main traffic routes. Warton, the Yealands and Silverdale went their own sweet way, involved as they were in land and sea. Their people were mixed: Celts who kept watch from Warton Crag descended to mix with the new Anglian settlers of the seventh century, and they in turn were infiltrated by Norsemen fleeing from Ireland in the ninth century. Vast areas of salt marsh were flooded by the tides. Although there was great extent of mere and mosses, yet there was enough good land for tillage and limestone heights for pasture.

By the time King John granted Warton its weekly market the villagers and neighbourhood were in one mind about Scots raiders rampaging from the border, approaching from the sands behind Warton, or straying on their local tracks. A century later, when Scots–English enmity was put on a permanent basis by the Edwards, manorial lords built strong-walled peles. Wartonians could share with Yealanders the secure hides within the rocks of Trowbarrow and Cringlebarrow when beacons gave warning from the Crag.

In these villages, North Country history had its stage. Great names came and went: Thane Torfin, the Anglo-Scottish Barons of Kendal, Lancasters, Lindsays (kin to the Bruce), Couplands— and the Thwengs who built the Old Rectory in the fourteenth century—the Middletons of Leighton Hall, Kitsons of Warton Hall and Washingtons of Tewitfield—each has departed. The church tower was gift of a Washington, his family shield carved thereon, the mullets and bars which the new state of America chose and called the Stars and Stripes. For safety, the stone is set on the inside tower wall, George Washington's portrait alongside. Well, the world knows where that family arrived, but on 4th July strangers must wonder why the American flag flutters from the tower, a new flag, a gift from Washington's Capitol.

Another local notable, Matthew Hutton, when Bishop of Durham obtained letters patent "for a Free Grammar School with two chambers for master and Hospital of Jesus in the town of Warton for poor old men". Born at Priest Hutton in this parish, he rose to the eminence of Archbishop of York. His 1594 foundation was replaced by the village school in 1902, and recently a fine modern primary school has been erected in a quiet back lane, one of many new Lancashire village schools on pleasant sites.

The curving street looks good, rising beyond the church and old school, flanked by grey stone cottages, completely at ease with Georgian neighbours, like the one called Washington House.

From Shovel Inn to Old Coach Road all is protected, no old building to be altered without expert consultation.

No Wartonians would say their village is perfect—not like Yealand Conyers, a sedate, exquisitely mannered place; here I have never seen 'intruding' farmyard animals on the road, nor heard screaming children or voices raised. Maybe its Quaker background led to restraint and serenity. The very name of Yealand Conyers is a tranquillizer. Warton is different: people work and children run around; a whirl of activity, the church hall fully booked every day of every month—compared with Yealand Conyers' pool of quiet. Yealand Redmayne, in contrast, contains council houses and families of healthy boisterous children, its average age far lower than its neighbour's and more like Warton's—which has far more in its school now than sixty years ago.

All three have charming houses built of the same native rock—pale-grey stone of lasting beauty—garden walls with menageries of riven limestone beasts as topping, smothering of roses and clematis, honeysuckle and jasmine at different seasons and rare displays of rock plants in spring. Every cottage has settled in for two or three hundred years, growing from the limestone terraces as naturally as the old yews and glorious beeches of Cringle-barrow. Not a niche or cranny but is filled with ferns, saxifrages or cushioned with mosses. Walls, like those in Back Lane, Warton, have enormous footing boulders and its flanking barns huge corner stones.

A village conscious of its perfection can lose it. But where people matter no community is 'unnaturally' perfect. No place like a village for bringing out human foibles and faults. I have never heard of problems at Yealand Conyers, and Redmayne takes life light-heartedly. Warton is different.

Drawing nearer to Lakeland, heart's desire of so many, new-comers are attracted by the natural beauty and rare rural amenities—these they value. Many newcomers are professional people, some of the 'university set', quite well informed about local affairs, and about such things as planning permission, scheduled buildings, definitive footpath maps, the role of parish councils. Architects, lawyers and historians among them are knowledgeable about matters the natives "never worried them-selves about, leaving all to the council". Councils must now sit up and take notice, or someone will give a prod. Women's Institute members play their part, being a good mixture of old, young, native and 'foreign'. When ancient rights are threatened such a village jumps to it, realizing those who destroy their past deserve no future.

Warton was stirred into action when a piece of land, given to the village in the last century so that stock could be watered at the trough thereon, so it was rumoured, was about to be disposed of by the council so that Lancaster U.D.C. could build on it. The amenity-conscious called public meetings, formed a village society and organized the clearing of the land, The Ware, from which young folk removed tons of rubbish. The county during Environmental Improvement year approved when the C.P.R. chose this plot as one of five for landscaping. The council was *not* happy about this offer! Nothing was done!

To rouse interest in their very rich heritage, a very good Warton history was compiled. The natives are not without pride as is soon obvious talking to them, especially to the over-60s who remember 'when it really were a village', and say with conviction they were glad they were lads in Warton sixty, seventy years ago, in spite of the advantages the youngsters have today. How they enjoyed life, adventuring up the quarry walls behind the 'Black Bull'—where Lancaster students practise climbs now with ropes—learning to swim by jumping off an old boat on Carnforth sands, or in the Warm Hole in the Keer by the Iron Works. They roamed the Crag, and gathered samphire for pickling on the sands. At Easter they rolled pace eggs down the slopes by the 'duck pond' and played 'guinea pig' ('piggy' elsewhere), "one hit over barn roof scored fifty." "We all grew up to be battlers. We fought Millheaders, and Carnforth at football, and cricket wi' Yealand on Summer House Hill."

Warton Church has St Oswald, Northumbrian king and martyr, for its patron. Parish boundaries take in Lindeth, where Keer meets the Kent channel; Silverdale with Yealand Redmayne and Conyers, Borwick, Carnforth and Priest Hutton, wide flung and in the past surrounding so much mossland and land inundated at high tides that little was left. But that little was good. "A kind of Canaan, hills, dales pleasant and fruitful—and never a beggar in it."

Except the poor uncomplaining Silverdale curate to whom the vicars of Warton forgot to pay his £5 a year! Poor James

Atkinson, after four years without pay, had "no bread or raiment to put on wife and family", but he stayed to serve his flock who, because of "daily overflowing of seafloods, and ground broken up to the bedrock", found the ancient church way to Warton impassable.

Eighteenth-century Silverdale was a working community of farmers, inshore fishermen, wildfowlers, mossmen, stonegetters and furnacemen at the local iron forges. They trod out the many paths round the mosslands. Flax was grown nearer Yealand Storrs, and linen spun and woven in the villages. Over the limestone knotts are miles of footpaths, trailing down to The Cove, to Jenny Brown Point, into small creeks involved in shipping, and—who knows—once sharing the smuggling of Far Arnside and Jacob's Bay!

Silverdale because of its pastoral beginnings is a place of green fields across which paths reach out to scattered communities like The Cove, The Row, The Green and Lindeth; at the centre, the shops, church, 'tourist amenities' and the Gaskell Institute. Now many new houses and flats appear and population rises, not with young but with retired folk, vintage and veteran, gadabouts who seem never to have a dull moment. "When we come here we can put away our cars, so much going on we don't need them!" Apprehensively some ask, "When will the development stop?" It possibly has. "This is rocky terrain, sewer-laying a costly business.

At Gibraltar we watched men on tractors, with sheepdogs, gathering large flocks from the salt marshes off Jenny Brown Point—all heavy-fleeced, in excellent shape, such grazing being excellent. I was surprised to learn this grazing is rented, these are gisted marshes—marsh, fell heafs and hill pasture in the North often are investments of far-away businessmen. If the owner wishes to slice off this sea-washed turf for sale, none can stop him.

Though this enchanting shoreline is now designated as of natural beauty and to be protected, we have looked over the salt marshes and the channel, trod the flower-sprinkled turf and the secret paths through the yew and holly groves, and wondered— for how long? Where will the Morecambe Bay barrage be, and how will this land and seascape be affected?

In 1860 men raised a mile-long sea wall near Gibraltar, to be continued to Red Bank, Bolton-le-Sands, and to Park Point, to hold back the tides and reclaim Silverdale Sands. George Stephenson planned a railway viaduct across the Kent. Men now envisage a barrage with road on top. The 1860 scheme failed for Nature did not co-operate and the sea wall is under the sand.

The 'ostriches' say the barrage may never happen, that not till 1976–7 will results of investigation be known; and if any one of the four outline schemes goes through it will take anything from eight to fifteen years before construction is completed—if then.

Those 'for' a barrage say only this way can Lakeland lakes, and even lake-less Westmorland dales threatened by 'drowning', be saved. Surely, they say, large expanses of water above the barrage, like estuarine lakes for yachting, boating—and good for eel catching and coarse fishing—would look better than the Kent and Leven sands at ebb tide? And Low Furness would no longer be out on a limb.

Those 'against' say no storage reservoirs covering Kent Sands off Silverdale and Warton—involving Keer Mouth, or Leven Sands 'lost' off Cartmel, could ever compensate for the changing beauty of the channels wrought by the tides; nor for the effect on inshore fishing for flounders and whitebait and shrimps—sure to be adversely affected. Inevitably loss of the intertidal sand banks so valuable in providing food for fish and wading birds—these estuaries are haunts of wintering migrants in great numbers and feeding grounds unexcelled on the western coast—would "set up ecological changes, the ultimate effect impossible to estimate". Also on the seaward side of any barrage the tides would pile up sand and silting would cause ecological and economic change down each estuary—so would Heysham harbour and free passage of shipping be threatened. Do we really want the pipe dream to become reality?

The enthusiastic newcomers find everything they desire at Silverdale: walking for those who walk, sport for those who enjoy it, classes and lectures for those who want them—like Yealand Conyers it is always devoted to worthwhile activities. Some remember Elizabeth Brockbank's Yealand studio, where those who wished were free to come and paint; quite a notable village art society resulted and the pre-war production of Christmas cards. Another Quaker, a Ford, a century ago held woodcarving classes for the women, an attempt to keep the old skills alive. Today the Friends' Room by the Meeting House is busy with lectures and classes, and a village choir meets here, augmented by the good voices and musical enthusiasts of Silverdale.

Yealand Conyers "is where the money is", people have said. One can believe it, seeing fine mansions fronted by immaculate lawns, flower beds and borders fit to be shown in full-colour magazines, and halls equally fine, screened from view by splendid trees. The wealthy Liverpool shipping and Manchester cotton magnates chose these unbeatable sites for their great houses. One was built at Hyning; Lord Ashton later bought the estate, and the late Earl and late Countess Peel lived here, their favourite residence. Fords, Liverpool shipowners, replaced the early Yealand Manor House (a site occupied since a De Jaland heiress married a Conyers in the twelfth century) by a Regency mansion some distance away. They had purpose-designed, made-to-fit Gillow mahogany furniture. The present occupiers are the Provincial Assurance Company.

Over the hill ridge, exquisitely set in a sloping green park, is Leighton Hall. It was given a new façade in Richard Gillow's time, Sir Walter Scott, his friend, suggesting the pseudo-Gothic, which came out very well. The early owners of Leighton had been lords of Yealand until misfortunes of Civil War and Jacobite rebellion overcame the Roman Catholic Middletons. Their tenants survived as farmers, flax growers and handloom weavers. I have seen fine linen sheets from village looms—heirlooms! Cottagers were also makers of straw plait for bonnets. Yealand has neither 'hemplands' nor any home industry now, but farming is good. As for the untouched mossland, this is considered outstanding for its natural beauty and amenity value.

Tourists and countrygoers are served: Leighton Hall is open on certain days as one of the North's historic houses. Leighton Moss, just beyond, is both nature reserve and bird sanctuary with a permanent warden; contrived 'hides' allow the interested wildlife lover and birdwatcher to enjoy it. Silverdale's nature trail in Eaves Wood is for the nature lover, admirable for the young.

During 1972–73 Warton Old Rectory, restored as an ancient building, rare of its kind, delighted antiquarians whose bent is medieval architecture. Experts describe it as a prototype. Here is the halle, with dais end and chapel on one side, arches leading into buttery, pantry and kitchens on the other, and family sleeping chamber above. Little for the uninformed to see, but much for the historian.

There is far more to see and enjoy at the small village of Borwick, just off the A6 and very near the M6. Here in mid-village is the hall of a family of Kendal woollen merchants who prospered and built on to an ancient pele a most handsome Tudor house, with quite enormous stables alongside to accommodate their teams of packhorses. These Bindlosses lived here for generations, growing in importance, staunch Royalists and hosts to young Charles II in 1651 on his way south to fight for his lost crown. His chair is here.

Many changes have come to the hall—but not to the village, which is enchanting, nor more than a ring-o'-roses round a green; delightful houses made of the seventeenth-century stables, and a few very mod. homes on delectable sites overlooking the canal.

Here is a case of the very oldest adapted to the needs of the youngest. I was at a folk concert in the Hall in November, the hosts the Lancashire Federation of Youth Clubs—now the occupiers. The place was floodlit for the event and most dramatic it looked, Tudor gables catching the light and dark shadows cast on walls.

Borwick, like Priest Hutton its neighbour, is a small jewel among our villages.

LUNE VALLEY VILLAGES

They say a health-giving god, called Lon by the Celts, named the Lune; that the Romans under Hadrian named their fort from the river, Lon castrum; and when the Plantagenet kings cut off parts of Cheshire, Yorkshire and Lonsdale, and put the pieces together, they named the new county after their chief seat of government, Lunecaster's shire.

One of the most important highways from the north and Scotland came down the Lune valley and there many villages took over, some the most satisfying in the county. Beautiful valley, smiling farms, every village most pleasant; and, as far as the visitor sees, the people living uncomplicated lives, not a worry line on any brow.

It is so pleasant that any stranger who finds his way here is sure to wonder why there are so few like him, why villages as beautiful as any in Devon or the Cotswolds have not set out to attract tourists. Apart from the few hotels and occasional guest-house, the rare pottery or arts and crafts shop—nothing! No lures, no gimmicks, not a hint of commercialism. Knowing the fate of the Lakeland villages, over-admired beauty queens, one can understand why the inhabitants prefer things as they are.

They have their problems in common with all villages, their distresses concerning Euro-lorries, speeding juggernauts, long loads, for the busy highway from the north-east coast to the west sweeps through some of the oldest and most vulnerable village streets. They are worried that so many cottages have been bought by newcomers, some of whom have no wish to play any part in local affairs, who live elsewhere five days every week and most of the year, leaving the village half dead. If they integrate it is a very different matter. Through their support many a village cricket and football club, annual sports, gala days—and church funds—benefit, it needs majority support to keep all these going.

Few villages provide any employment—in many residents require none, being retired or of adequate means, the young folk going off to Carnforth, Kirkby, Lancaster or Morecambe to work. It is very sad when village schools close—no young families, a scarcity of children. When folk prefer to shop in the town—everyone enjoys Kirkby or Lancaster on market days—the village store cannot pay its way; where the post office is also under the same roof it must close down too when the shop is forced out of business.

These are rural problems, nationwide. Yet Lonsdale folk battle on, with a philosophical approach to life and smiling faces to all comers. My friends from America are quite enchanted, charmed by such 'gentle people' and children with natural good manners.

Their village forebears survived the worst history could do to them. The Angles came to terms with the Norse settlers, they both made the best of their Norman overlords. All combined against the common enemy, the Scots of four centuries. They had divided loyalties though the Wars of the Roses, the Civil War and Jacobite troubles; and when the great landowners went under, the tenants carried on, unperturbed, under new management.

How rich the valley is in complete villages, perfect in the visual sense, rich in architecture spanning Tudor to Victorian, some with ancient churches, and with vicarages and rectories so handsome, within spacious grounds, one might mistake them for the halls of ancestral landowners; and many mansions which were halls of early manorial lords, one to every village.

Some are fortified—like Hornby Castle and Thurland—some Balmoral or mock Gothic like Halton Hall and Gresgarth. There are examples of the best Palladian or Georgian at Burrow Hall, Leck, Quernmore and Whittington. There is comely Tudor or Jacobean like the old halls of Gressingham and others of the same period, now converted to farmhouses; Robert Hall, Claughton and Cragg Hall, these tell how rich was the Lune valley long ago when powerful men chose to live here, found families and identify themselves with the life of this fair countryside.

All this is unchanged since I wrote of it at length in 1952 in *Lancashire's Fair Face*. The country is farmed as before, but vanished are the village craftsmen, gone their workshops. As for the signs of vigorous industry which swept along the Lune and its tributaries—Hindburn, Roeburn, Wenning—in the 1790s; not a wheel remains, hardly a mill wall standing—which is not surprising since the manufacturers of textiles withdrew when steam power was introduced, and makers of bobbins, shuttle and nails fell on lean times by the beginning of this century. Any old mills partly intact are now ripe for conversion, like several disused barns.

Let it not be thought that the villages are about to die. They face the bright future as places in which to live, if not to work. Young marrieds like it here; their children fill the schools of Halton, Caton and Hornby and the atmosphere is charged with optimism.

Take a look at Halton, thrown on a high ridge, its history long and eventful. Norsemen carved a saga on the churchyard cross, Earl Tostig's halle crowned the nearby mound, from which later William's nominees ruled Lonsdale's twenty-two townships.

Halton Hall facing the church is a complex of Balmoral Gothic buildings high above the Lune, where the medieval hall of Garnetts, Dacres and Caruses stood long ago. Along the one street, between 'White Lion' and 'Greyhound', is every kind of village domestic architecture, the ordinary enlivened by a lovely seventeenth-century Manor House and a contemporary farmstead.

Just out of the village at Halton Green, where the rich rolling landscape, good earth and prosperous contented farmland rolls away to the skyline, all is a visual delight. We came in autumn, the dying flame of creepers on aged walls, scents of wood smoke and orchards as we searched in a croft for "stones said to be monastic, and the graves of a farmer and his wife".

Long ago a kind of outlier to Halton was Hoton, now Aughton and pronounced 'Afton', a tiny off-the-highway hamlet, just a handful of cottages and farms and a few folk with big ideas. Come upon it unaware and the quiet and beauty of the valley and far blue hills is enough to smooth any furrowed brow. Only once in a lifetime does it hit the headlines, with its Pudding Festival. The last revival was on 22nd July 1971 when thousands gathered on a field at Oaken Head farm to enjoy "100 acres of attractions". The giant pudding, mixed and boiled by Aughton women and numerous helpers, on calor gas stoves, was borne in triumph on a brewer's dray driven by the huntsman of the Lunesdale Hunt, with escort of mounted police and brass bands blaring. The entire proceedings were graced by Aughton's own Pudding Queen, resplendent in pearl tiara and model gown—no teen-age glamour puss but a bonny woman of Arkholme origin—and from beautiful morning through a dull afternoon to the Festival Dance and the last departing reveller, a glorious day was had by all.

The Lions Club were organizers, half the proceeds going to charity and half to the much-used village hall.

"We only raised £2,700", a village girl told us. 'Only?'

Upriver are three villages of more importance. Gressingham (Ghersintune in the Domesday Book) was given to King John's keepers of the royal aeries of hawks, the Gernetts, whose tombs are in the old church—very old if the round-headed Anglo-Norman door is any indication. No place is more full of nooks and crannies; all the houses seem tempted to run downhill to the bouncing beck, which is in a great hurry to join the Lune. A happy surprise, but not visible from the Halton–Kirkby highway. It was winner of the Best Kept under 300-Population Village award of 1972.

Unseen is the best of Arkholme, which turns its back to the main road. It was Aaram in old records, the 'airdh' or 'shieling' of Norsemen down by the Lune levels, and there the one long street ends, one fork to the ford of the river, one fork to the church. It is not quite coeval with Gressingham but its church also possesses a fine south door, and is built into the side of a twelfth-century motte and bailey site, now overgrown with trees, but overlooking a Lonsdale landscape of utmost tranquillity and beauty, as fair as any in the north. I know few villages with so many comely dwellings flanking the street, no two alike yet all—even the very new houses, we hope—in harmony. Their builders must have worked with pride, and the first to live in them were eager to carve on their lintels their dates and names. The fronts are good to see and so are their backs, long gardens with dreaming vistas of valley, or fells and far blue mountains.

Whittington, the Whitune of Anglian times, also goes its own sweet way, roadside and scattered this way and that, the line of it decided by the ambling kine returning to byre a thousand years ago. It is still a village of farms and charming cottages, the church benign on a green slope, the parkland, well-timbered, reaching to the Hall. Nothing ruffles the quiet, until local 'ton-up' lads roar through the night, blazing their way through the darkness.

When Arkholme-cum-Cawood was a chapelry folk had to take the Wenning ferry and walk to Melling church for major festivals and burials, and "often times they could not cross without danger of life". Floods were frequent. Now—no boat, and only one bridge between Halton and Hornby. "We might be poles apart," the villagers say. They rarely meet those over the river.

Is there some rivalry here? "Arkholme's on the sunny side, Melling's on the money side": an old saying. Newcomers never discriminate and you find them living happily west side and east.

Friends used to say, to be born and brought up in Lakeland spoilt them for living and settling anywhere else. This is true of the Lune valley. When Arkholme school children played hosts to youngsters from Skelmersdale New Town in 1972, they took their guests to romp in the fields, roaming, and sharing their own particular pleasures. A grand time was had by all, until the visitors began to buy presents for those at home. The village shop—alas!—had no lettered rock, no gifts such as they found in Blackpool or New Brighton. What a place! Later the village children were talking of towns, unable to take in the implications. "If *your* fathers had new jobs in a town you'd have to live there too," they were told. Eyes opened wide, absolute incredulity and even horror in twenty pairs of eyes. Never!

Caton and Brookhouse, Hornby and Melling share in the blessings of country and village life, and look for far more out of it than their grandparents. An infiltration of newcomers with varied interests—'culture vultures', the arty-crafty set and a sprinkling from Lancaster University—has added a zest to life; not forgetting the needs of the low brows. Art, drama, music, if the village wants them it gets them; and even horse riding as an L.E.A. subject!

Caton is particularly energetic. Pulling all together, they won in 1971 the Best Kept Village trophy as runners-up to Halsall—and well deserved it. In 1970 they staged at the old church at Brookhouse a wonderful festival of arts and crafts and it is still talked about. Every December a mammoth village auction is organized, everybody helping, giving and buying, a quite amazing money-raising event. Absolutely 'with it', that is Caton—given its name by Katti a thousand years ago. Centuries before that the fifth milestone from Lancaster was erected where the Roman road crossed over its own stream. Up the Artle Beck thirteenth-century owners of Gresgarth fattened their swine; a century later, worried by too many raiding Scots, they were fortifying their hall. Signs of this pele, massive undercroft walls and machicolations are visible today. Many footpaths climb the green hills above Gresgarth, one up Cheese Banks dropping to the little Conder valley, where it begins to wander on to Quernmore.

Why should there be a Flodden Hill here, and a Flodden Field by Lune banks below Brookhouse? Gernetts of Quernmore Hall told how men of 'Waremore', weary on their return from the battle, rested on the hillside. An old woman once told me in Brookhouse churchyard, "Flodden Field were fought down there," and pointed to the valley floor. The truth was that Lord Monteagle, the victor, gave to the tenants who fought with him against the Scots plots of land below Hornby Castle; here was one piece named with pride by an old soldier.

They fought to end the scourge of the Scots, once and for all. Yet folk did not forget the ravages of the fourteenth century and the terror of the Black Douglas.

Generations of children were chased indoors at bedtime with threat of the bogy man, then hugged and kissed with

> I've got ye, I've got ye!
> Don't fret ye, don't fret ye.
> Black Douglas shall not get ye.

Brookhouse is not as old fashioned as I remember it. There were the tales I had been told by villagers—leaning on the bridge is always good for a chat. Said one, "Romans marched across the brook here. And that stone hollowed out—it were a plague stone, they filled it wi' disinfectant when money changed hands. Horses used to drink from it." The socket stone of a wayside cross was here when the Cockersand brethren set up the fishstones in Caton and the hollow oak was young and strong.

The bonniest bit of Brookhouse was always by the bridge, all around church and ancient hostelry, along Rotten Row—but here are modern intrusions. In fact, more is modern than old until one comes to Claughton with a beautiful little church—and one of the oldest known dated bells. Half of the Tudor hall is on its original site nearby and the other half transplanted and put down far above the clough. What a prospect! Obviously the reason why the half-house was rebuilt here, with enormous labour problems.

Hornby Castle dominates the landscape. Once it dominated the countryfolk too, when Horni lorded it over the serfs from his mound, and Harringtons and later Stanleys over their tenantry. The feudal days are forgotten, the castle now turning its back on the village and all that goes on there. Its role was once important, on a great north–south highroad, now A684. In the Castle Hotel yard are still stables with "POST HORSES" lettered on the walls, relic of busy coaching days. Coaches without horses pass through, from South Shields and Sunderland to Blackpool and the Fylde coast, as do heavy loads bound for Heysham Docks or Liverpool. Not until they come to the right turn beyond the bridge do lorries slow down; Hornby's main road is wide and straight, unlike Melling's narrow crooked street, a frustrating bottleneck to all long-distance drivers.

I put Hornby and Melling among my top twenty villages. Hornby is a winner among the Best Kept, and ranks high also among the most beautiful. Never was its face besmirched by industry, its outlook was always rural; the pretty cottages seem to have an inward look, avoiding what passes their garden gates. And what gardens, as colourful as the covers of flower catalogues —and not contented with this, they have hanging baskets too. Often I stop and sniff the delicious scents. They could be wall-flowers, stocks, lilac or honeysuckle, and in autumn there is the poignant scent of apple wood in the blue smoke from cottage chimneys.

During the day the place seems asleep, so few folk stir. The children are in school—the large Lune Valley school serves a wide area, and the working population is elsewhere. But the evenings wake up, for not only do the villagers come out and show themselves but others join them from the outlying farms of Roeburndale and the valley, west and east. For W.I., Young Farmers, drama society and such activities—especially lively when winter sets in—Hornby has always been the natural centre. It also has shops and a post office, a bank, police and fire station, a public weighbridge—and a better bus service than any of its neighbours.

It also has distinguished names to boast about. Edward Stanley, a younger son of the first Earl of Derby, left his mark. He married the Harrington co-heiress who inherited her sister's estates too, and they became Stanley's. He raised the proud Eagle Tower above the midmost castle keep, and eagle banners floated when he led the Lancashire men to Flodden. Henry created him Lord Monteagle and poured honours upon him after the victory.

> Lancashire like lyons layden them about!
> All had been lost, by our Lorde.
> Had not those leddes bene!

As a Flodden memorial the tall octagonal tower was raised at the west end of the church. Carved upon it is his only memorial, simply: "Lord Monteagle a soldier caused me to be made." When he built the magnificent choir and chancel, with pinnacles and a fine array of grimacing gargoyle waterspouts, he intended his body should rest there; but this was not to be. A pity Hornby folk did not always trust him. He practised alchemy in the castle tower and they crossed themselves when they saw midnight lights and whispered of devil's work. His name was "unhappily famous in the annals of Hornby".

What did the king think of him? "Ho, my soldier!" he would say. "For your gallant towardness against our great enemy the late King of Scots we assure you of royal gratitude for we have good cause to favour and thank you and full heartily we do."

A later owner of the castle earned a reputation for infamy. He was Colonel Charteris, a Scot drummed out of Marlborough's army in Flanders for card sharping. Returning to England he pursued a career of cheating and forgery. But it paid off, and in 1713 he bought Hornby from the Earl of Cardigan. Two years

A facelift for Manchester Corporation cottages near Newby Bridge

Grange-over-Sands primary school

Knott End library

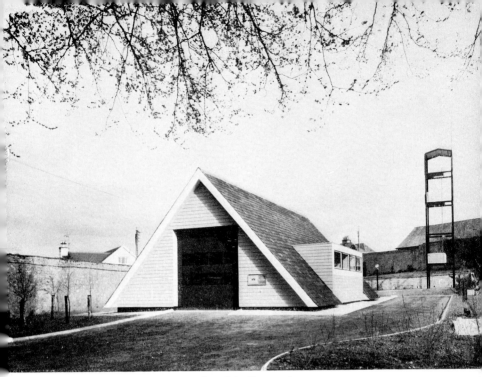

Silverdale fire station

Coniston primary school

Wray 1968, new houses from old

later he brought an accusation against the Jacobite army for leaving his Castle "without paying a bill of £3 6s. 8d. for entertainment", and suggested Lancaster should blow up the Lune Bridge to thwart them.

On 9th March 1730 Peter Walkden, the Hesketh Lane minister, read in the newspaper, "Colonel Charteris was tried. Feb. 26th at Old Bailey for a rape on the body of Ann Bird a maidservant, was guilty and sentenced to death. He is said to be worth £200,000; all forfeit to the Crown." Later he was pardoned and the forfeiture cancelled. Maybe his daughter having married an earl's son helped.

Thomas Gray the poet, here some years later, was shown around by "Mr. Charteris the present proprietor's man" and wrote of recent fanciful additions to Monteagle's Tower, "in the taste of a modern summer house with sash windows in gilt frames, a stucco cupola and on top a rich eagle". Very elegant!

Two remarkable features of interest. The Anglian 'loaves and fishes' stone most intricately carved near the church's west door. Down by the Loyn bridge, a dreaming scene with swans and smooth river, on a gentle slope: one of the 'castles in a hurry' thrown up in King Stephen's dangerous days—wooden keep on heaped mound, ditch and wooden stockade around. What remains is interesting; a place to ponder.

From the days of Ulf and the Domesday survey, the Lords of Hornby also possessed Craven and Lonsdale lands and the lordships of Melling and Wennington. Melling became a rich parish so vast it was divided into four 'quarterings'. One, covering the gentle pastoral valley from Melling itself to nearby Wrayton and Wennington, joined a second quarter extending from Wray into Roeburndale, and the third from Hornby into the sparsely peopled Norse outbacks, the fells of Mallowdale. The fourth, Arkholme-cum-Cawood chapelry, was divided from Melling by the river.

In all these quarterings life follows a slow steady rhythm; however modern they become, lambing, clipping and haytime dictate the farming pattern. Lanes wander into the dales, wriggling into tiny hamlets few have ever heard of, where geese and farmyard fowl flow over the roadway, and dogs lie head in paws, snoozing on hot afternoons, for no cars ever come. Sightseers know nothing of such places, praise be, but property developers are discovering them and one by one old buildings are made new, as

F

at Lowgill and Bottin. My favourite, almost primitive, village pub, 'Rose and Crown', welcoming after our walk over the fells from Slaidburn, is now a local shop.

In Melling people matter, new families soon find their feet and young and old work agreeably together. They tried—and failed—to keep their village post office. The bus service to the nearest is meagre—and, as one old lady sighed, "getting about now is more difficult than in 1900 when I was a child". Now the elderly are dependent on the kindness of car owners, and being a community with the right spirit such difficulties can be solved. The W.I. is a guiding influence in all things, and fortunate in having among its members several whose families have long lived in the parish and cherish a very precious heritage. When there are new schemes to be considered, voices to be heard on T.V., in the newspapers and at W.I. and parish council meetings they are there. Public spirit is a good thing when helpers are needed for Christmas church decorations, Easter flower arrangements, and when there are such community efforts as tree counts—many villages are doing this, to save fine trees—and local history exhibitions—and as here, most successfully—a display of 'family heirlooms'.

When newcomers want to know more about the village they have fallen in love with so completely, there are always others who can tell them. And there is so much to tell—every one of the grey stone houses hugging the roadedge has its own history. Fortunately for them, all have very thick walls, muffling the roar of the heavy traffic. One can almost hear them sighing with relief when there is a lull. There is talk of a by-pass. Let it come soon, they say, each time there is an argument between a lorry, a garden gatepost or a bulging old wall. What care the lorry drivers when they scrape the churchyard wall?

At the church's east end is a high mound, a castle site of the time of King Stephen, or a plague mound raised over a communal burial? In the church, a strong oak chest long enough to hold pikes was probably the parish armoury, weapons doled out when the Scots were on the rampage. The tower stands high, the bells sound far.

Melling church rightly stands out as a landmark. Little Wrayton, an inconsequential hamlet, and big sister Wennington cluster comfortably on the rich valley floor, the Wenning coming near to wash cottage walls; swelling hillocks with short steep climbing lanes between well-kept hedgerows seem to protect them and the country quiet wraps them round.

Tatham too lies low on river meadows, hardly a building visible and peace over all, whereas its past was too lively at times. Until the fourteenth century many people lived here around a fair-built hall and church, but life was dangerous and often men took into the fields bows as well as ploughshares, herdsmen kept their eyes north for warning smoke signals, and even the priest tucked up his cassock and donned armour when it was known the Scots were indeed near at hand. There came a day when the raiders took the village by surprise and all was desolated, Tatham destroyed and the folk compelled to scatter, some into Tatham Fells.

The manor house was forsaken, degraded into a mere farm-stead, the church surviving with Norman south door, twelfth-century walls and under its pavements the tombs of warriors who died fighting in many wars. The nearby vicarage, its green lawns shadowed by immemorial trees, is straight out of Trollope, waiting for croquet players and ladies with parasols and trailing skirts.

The Wenning wanders to meet Hindburn and Roeburn united not far from Wray. Wray, where on 8th August 1967 the heavens opened and down came a wall of water turning runnels into racing torrents, becks into raging floods, sweeping trees, debris and rocks towards the unsuspecting village, blocking the bridges, the pent-up water hurling its might at obstructing cottages. Since it was daylight, all were able to leap into the street as walls collapsed behind them. Bridges were carried away and acres of rich land covered completely by tons of debris.

Wray can never be the same again. But by 1967 it was already changing. I searched for the village craftsmen who in 1952—when I was writing *Lancashire's Fair Face*, were so patient in showing me their skills. One shaped from local alder wood clog blocks, of three sizes, with the ease of cutting through butter. I watched the stripping of oak spales in the wood-yard where they were boiled and made pliant for weaving into spale baskets or truggs. At the wheelwright's men were hammering rims on to wagon wheels, and shaping carts and farm gear. This, in 1972, was the only place still in production. "But it's only sign posts for the L.C.C. now, and sawn timber for house building."

So much lost in twenty years! And many industries wiped out

within living memory. There was a nailmaker's by the bridge; hundreds were employed in the Roeburn bank mills, some spinning China silk imported to Lune docks, others making tall silk hats; and as long as there was demand for cotton weaving, there was bobbin-turning too in 1800.

Wray grew as a roadside village where dales folk met the shepherds from the hills. When one comes out of the wild weather on the Hindburn and Roeburn fells, the tight-packed houses and farms are a welcoming, comforting sight—continuous, cottages joined on to eighteenth- and nineteenth-century flat-fronted houses, and farmhouses with barns, shippons and stables filling in the gaps, as though to keep out the elements. Maybe the narrow ends and bottleneck kept out undesirables too, as they effectively slow down traffic today.

When the villagers had choice of work—industrial and agricultural—they did not neglect the latter. When the former moved away farming went on as before. Farm animals filing along used to claim right of way before buses. Now so many farm buildings are disused one wonders how long before planning applications and improvement grants are allowed.

Few places are so devoid of pretention, so honest to goodness. Wray will keep its simple cottages, cobblestone verges and narrow alleys, one hopes. But no more glass panels with ornamental iron work in cottage doors, no more 'prettifying'—silk ribbons do not go with homespun!

Where cottages were carried away in the floods, the river bank has been strengthened; a terraced site, with paved garden and a stone shelter—built of old masonry and with a line showing the flood level—takes their place. No house replacements at the river edge, but a group of old buildings—those in the photograph (Plate 22)—were restored and modernized to the plans of the county architect's staff, who gave their skills freely, accepting the work as a challenge. Here are pleasant modern dwellings in keeping with the traditional.

It remains to round off the list of villages along this most northerly limit of Lancashire Lonsdale. Tunstall which gave its name to the family of the Sir Thomas who erected and fortified Thurland Castle, within a protecting moat, is a cheerful place, a sun-trap. A pity the proud Perpendicular church in the pastures gave the young Brontë sisters no happy memories. On Sundays the clergy daughters of Lowood School walked from Cowan Bridge to matins here, ate packed lunch in the porch chamber, and stayed for evensong. In spite of road widening near Cowan Bridge, the bridge and the school of Jane Eyre remain intact; a plaque on the gable end tells of the sisters being here as pupils.

Leck and Ireby could be called last outposts—surely the pot-holed and cave-riddled fells above them and their sheep pastures below are just as the Norse farmers knew them. Their becks still rattle over stony beds, all houses are stone-walled, stone-roofed and some stone-flagged.

There are gracious touches: Leck Hall of Lord and Lady Shuttleworth in a tranquil park, and Ireby Over Hall looking as it always was for four hundred years, where history happened but left not a ripple in the pool to show. Ireby hamlet is a happy find. The people say, "We are glad we're staying in Lancashire."

CARTMEL, BY WINSTER, EEA AND LEVEN SHORE

Lancastrians are sad to be cutting the links with Cartmel and Furness forged eight centuries ago, giving us our stake in Lakeland. This is part of the North all feel they share, part of it on the tourist beat—but far more off the beaten tracks, living its own life, untroubled. Here were Norse settlements, 'heafs and saeters', later grazed by abbey stock when Cartmel and Furness Abbey were landholders. All was pastoral; no compact villages here of the English pattern, only scattered family groups. When abbots enclosed large tracts for hunting preserves few people lived here.

The Dissolution brought ownership of mines, iron forges and trading in all its variety into lay hands, Ulverston replacing Dalton as centre in Low Furness, Hawkshead in High. In time this became the industrial area of the North, with almost every community employed in copper mining, iron smelting and scores of woodcrafts, and in the early water-powered stage of textile spinning and weaving.

Steam power and the need of coal caused a vast evacuation of the Lakeland valleys; quiet fell, but gunpowder-making, charcoal-burning, bark-stripping, the making of hoops, kegs, tools and bobbin-making for the Lancashire mills—all these continued until this century, some activities until the First World War.

Now—none remain, even bobbin-making killed by plastics. Signs of old industry remain, in ruins and old hearths in lonely places. The villages, once industrial, are now non-productive; but farming goes on, and new tenants are eager to move in.

I must write very little of Cartmel villages so soon to be divorced from Lancashire. Let it suffice to tell a little of those not to be missed. For the rest—my book *Curious Traveller Lancaster to Lakeland* does Cartmel and Furness justice.

The Winster river about to enter Morecambe Bay is the county boundary and little Lindale the first village—charming, but gashed by major new roads, and the brow-foot dwellers are so shaken by heavy lorries roaring down, everything in their homes a-shake and a-shiver they often think their last hour has come. But off the highway some charming corners remain, and as every householder—mostly in the vintage and veteran classes—is a keen gardener, the place is ablaze with bloom.

Nothing much ever happens here, they say; but they like life as it is, and if they hanker for culture, why, Grange is near and a full programme of activities, even more in winter than in summer.

The Winster valley Cartmel Fell area population adds up to no more than that of a sizeable village; it is still nothing but scattered sheep farms just as in Cartmel Priory days when it was a primitive outback of swineherds. Never having many public amenities natives do not miss them. They used to walk to St Anthony's Church on the fell, or women rode pillion behind husbands; now there is a car rota for church and a mini-bus for Cartmel Fell children going to school.

In the valley nearer Cartmel Town, life is different. Even tiny hamlets like Seatle, Ayside and Barber Green are not quite out of the world, whilst High Newton bestrides the busy Newby bridge highway. Cartmel Town is a treasure chest of precious things, several times champion among the Best Kept Villages—it happens to be about the most beautiful too, immaculate in spite of a constant flow of visitors. All is in harmony. The setting is perfect—as it should be if divine intervention decided where the priory should stand—"between two streams one flowing north, one south", according to a local legend. The two clear streams do just that, washing the garden walls of old cottages and defining the precincts of the priory.

Cartmel grew round the monastery of the Augustinians sharing in the trade which naturally followed the constant passing through of oversands travellers. The humble found lodgings at the guest house by the west gate, the great and noble were entertained at the prior's table—even Scots princes at times. By this hospitality the prior hoped to buy immunity from damage when their object was raiding, loot and pillage.

Not till the Dissolution in the 1540s did new buildings of the expanding village begin to flow into the once-sacred precincts. Gracious new houses were erected against the old walls, and because the villagers had always worshipped in the monastic church, it was still theirs, saved by Henry VIII's order that it should remain "unpluckt".

Population increased, trade grew, but until the eighteenth century the neighbourhood was still "primitive, cut off by mountains and woods, no roads better than cart or pack-horse tracks and twice a day cut off by tides. Farms grew oats, rye barley—and the only root crop, turnips. Travellers expected no fare better than oatcake and salted or pickled meat." Still they came—and the first Lakers, the first trickle of tourists. The flow has never ceased.

The priory is superb, a source of constant delight in its changing beauty, the masonry stained with the splashes of colour from stained glass, or pure, cold silver or glowing primrose—according to the time of day. Worth coming far to see and enjoy, a farseen tower as welcoming now as in the Middle Ages.

Holker too is a worthwhile goal. Prestons—who had so much to do with bringing the priory back to seemliness and completeness after the Dissolution—and Lowthers and Cavendishes who followed, also left their mark on Holker. Their village, a little gem, was planned picturesque, replacing a "huddle of thatched farms and humble cottages round a common", pre-1880. All were improvers, agriculturists, tree planters, reclaimers of old mosses and road builders. They banished dobbies and will-o'-the-wisps and the rheum when drainage was accomplished. They could use carriages on their new roads instead of relying only on horse transport.

Now, the grass grows lush, cornfields wave by Leven shores, stands of new trees grow tall, sawmills whirr where felled timber is stacked. No waste land here; from Holker Park to New Park and Frith Hall everything flourishes.

Like all great houses, the Hall too must pay its way to survive. The Cavendishes, all collectors of works of art, all men of culture and learning, share with the great British public the garnered treasures of many generations; and how grateful we are. No hint of funfair, no wild animals roaring, not a steam engine or any tourist gimmickry until the balloon went up in 1973!

The village is less interested in tourists. Being fairly affluent, the folk of Holker and Cark have no need to make money from them. One can takes one's pleasure here—and wander at will, anywhere.

Both Cark and Flookburgh—though at first glance no one would guess—are coastal villages. Follow the Eea stream down from the Engine Inn—James Watt's steam engine installed here names it—to the interesting terraced houses, former workers' dwellings near a long demolished mill, and on to the old farm by the bridge. Just beyond—the salt marshes, the shining expanse of Leven Sands.

Here, or at Sandgate where Flookburgh's long street becomes a narrow lane hurrying to see the sea, oversands travellers waited for sands guides to shout that all was well for crossing; they filled in waiting time in a state of pure intoxication over the magic of the scene, where folk now wonder what will happen if a barrage takes form. In the past those who could afford took seats in long dillies, or shandras, crossed the channel on horseback or were taken over pick-a-back by native porters. Now there is a chance of a place on a former shrimp cart converted into 'Leven Channel Transport Service'—one way of preserving an old cart now that all shrimping is done by tractor.

What was it like before the sea was held back by miles of high banks and reclamation had made of the acres of Raven Winder and Chanon Winder rich sheep pasture and cattle grazing, and by 1810 thirty-eight fields of oats, wheat and barley? Flookburgh was a fishing village. Tides came up to the cottage walls, boats at high tides bobbed about in orchards and sheep grazing the salt marshes wandered into the streets. The tides were not easily held at bay. Old Granny Hill, then 94, told me in 1954 how as a girl she had seen many farmhouses on the Plain one evening; in the dawn all had disappeared, the hard labour of years undone.

Flookburgh has plenty of character—nothing pretty-pretty here but plain, strong fishermen's houses, many with yards behind where their horses were stabled and shrimps were boiled. The folk too are a breed of their own: Norse stock they say, and very much like their counterparts I have met on the quays of Bergen, Stavanger and Gothenburg. Not at all like pretty, flower-embosomed Allithwaite, though that began as a creek settled also by Vikings.

WEST OF THE LEVEN AND WINDERMERE

West of Cartmel the Leven channels take the combined waters of Windermere and Coniston to the sea. Such untold mineral wealth was in their mountains, so much water running to waste in their streams and falls that from the seventeenth century life of the small communities was geared to industry.

Backbarrow, where the Leven's roaring waters tumble into a dark cauldron below the old one-arch bridge, was inevitably an early starter. The first cotton mill here was prosperous, the owners earned a good name. But the child workers from London workhouses, bound apprentices till 21, were like slave labour. Many tried to escape, were chained to their looms, and little ones through sheer weariness fell asleep at their work. When bankruptcy came, it is said the children were carted off to Leven Sands and abandoned before the oncoming tide! The same mill is now the famous cobalt blue works, dolly blue splashes on the stone walls.

I have never seen a good-looking iron works; Backbarrow's is an eyesore. Machell's, for generations chief landowners here-abouts, own much of the property, but are not in a hurry to sell. What a rush would follow if their picturesque tumbledown cottages at Haverthwaite were for sale! John Wilkinson, the famous iron master, was son of a Machell's employee at Back-barrow. Villagers foretold young John would 'go far' in life, for he was born, it is said, in the cart carrying the family's produce to market at Ambleside.

Haverthwaite grows no oats in its riverside cleanings—as when it earned it name. Here is the Leven Valley School; and not far away at Haverthwaite station the enthusiastic restoration of the scenic single-gauge line to Newby Bridge lakeside is a credit to the more-than-local Railway Society. Here in all its glory, ready to purr with pleasure, the original rolling stock, the carriage coachwork polished to a mirror-like surface, the brasswork of the trim engine without fault; all raring to go!

The old village backs away from the widened highway. A place of pretty corners, some tumbledown cottages bedded on jutting rock, boulders for footings, old walls bulging and twisting to enclose tantalizing lanes. Half the dwellings are empty—flower beds overgrown and shrubberies rioting, untended roses spilling petals. The others cared for, renovated, share their neighbours' gentle melancholy.

It was all trim and tended sixteen years ago when I visited the Rhodes at the hall, the Georgian House with handsome gateway, and a splendid example of an early John Wilkinson fireplace in the kitchen. Very few dwellings were untenanted then.

The village is not altogether asleep. A schoolgirl with placards and drawing pins was adorning the local 'notice board', an old barndoor. "Don't Be A Yokel, Join Cartmel Young Farmers' Club." There were dates for dances, outings, local shows, village sports. No shortage of events here in the Leven Valley, or shared with Cartmel or Grange!

Staveley-in-Cartmel is a lovely hamlet, bypassed and little seen. Its curate, Edmund Law in the years between 1693 and 1742 walked eight miles daily to its church from his home, Boon Crag! Such a quiet place, completely aloof, larch and birch woods above it.

As a contrast, Newby Bridge is seen by all, roads meet near the bridge, folk change buses at this local Charing Cross. It always was a meeting place, more so after the dangerous lake-foot fords were replaced by the bridge, and coaches of the Kendal–Ulverston run went by at a spanking pace. 'The Swan' was always an attraction; the modern arts and crafts centre is a great draw today.

On the lake-edge road north (west, former Lancashire, bank of Windermere) are small communities: Stott Park—no bobbin mill now—and Graythwaite of the Sandys family, who have been here from the years following the Dissolution, when they shared with Machells the iron-smelting industry—able landowners too and, from Tudor times to the present, planters of many trees. Archbishops Sandys founded Hawkshead Grammar School in 1588.

The hall is well hidden and so are most of the homes of about 120 estate workers and their families, dotted here and there— farms, lodges, flats—and near the lake shore some charming conversions of charcoal burners' and wood craftsmen's dwellings, all in delicious coppices; none of these for potential weekenders!

Cunsey by its stream, Sawrey Near and Far (according to the distance from Hawkshead town and market) have numerous attractions apart from connections with Beatrix Potter. The only time I ever saw her was in the farmyard at Cunsey, in clogs and sacking apron.

Hawkshead is unique. What was 'this domestic Calabria—this Paradise of virgin beauty' to impressionable early tourists is as fascinating to travellers today. Which of course has its penalties. The villagers have a life of their own in those photogenic alleys, yards, narrow lanes. They are philosophical when cameras click like castanets and strangers gawp into the windows and lean over garden fences. Occasionally they do more; one owner of a most beautiful garden found two strangers already inside, he with ciné-camera and she gambolling prettily between daffodils and tulips.

Imagine summer weekends if you live in Flag Street, Wordsworth Street or Vicarage Lane or in any cottage which comes straight out of a 'Beautiful Britain' brochure. If you are so beautiful you must take admiration with good grace. The place is gracious, the villagers too if not too hampered by too many weekend invaders. No one likes the car park—full in summer, a grey desert in winter. 'The Norsemen' is huge, seats hundreds, but the neighbourhood can hold dinners, dances there off season.

The three Wordsworth brothers had a happy country boyhood at Hawkshead under the free and easy motherly care of Ann Tyson, doing all the bird watching, climbing, nutting and skating village boys enjoy today. Lucky children. Their new school is already about to split its seams, for village population rises and Sawrey and Graythwaite's under-11s come here too. 'Weather permitting' means something here. In winter there is great excitement when roads are blocked, when neither mini-bus nor Landrover can come by usual routes. Men dig the school bus out of snowdrifts, drivers beat storm and flood by taking circuitous ways; there are resounding cheers when the outlying youngsters arrive safe and sound!

It must be very heaven to be a child here, or over the fell in a forest community within Grizedale, where the air is scented with pine and larch and all around wild life beckons. Satterthwaite is especially exciting and Oxen Park, divided by rocky ridges gold-spangled with broom, and above lonely pools on valley floors not yet completely tamed. Ancestors of present-day Satterthwaite folk—the iron smiths, charcoal burners and carters who transported the iron to the Leven channel ports—would recognize the village if not its surroundings. How happily it lies in its sunny patch, dwellings dispersed round meadows tangled with flowers. The church, the 'Eagle's Head' ("leave rucksacks outside"), the village store and post office make up a complete community.

It is a cheerful place. One June day I rubbed shoulders— literally—with Kent schoolboys, students from Birmingham and walkers from Scotland and Surrey—and one Canadian. And why? Here is the fringe of Grizedale Forest with the forest centre, wild life museum, a nature trail and a unique 'Theatre in the Forest'. Here come not only summer visitors but Furness and Cartmel folk —enthusiastic patrons. Where else have remote villages so much art, music and drama in their midst. In 1971–2 at Christmas *Holy Night in the Forest*, in spring, a piano festival, and at other times well-known singers, strolling players and actors with nation-wide reputations.

I remember Grizedale Hall and the German P.O.W. camp—here there was "one that got away". Then, green pastures floored the dale but the Forestry Commission has changed all this. Life is geared to the forest; the male population works for 'the Forestry', planting, thinning, lopping. Native craftsmen of 'the Forestry' care for greenwood and wild creatures, do outdoor work in the 'open' months, in winter—like the woodmen of the Black Forest— turning their hands to wood and horn carving, their handiwork on sale in local craft shops.

Never have I seen post office walls more plentifully covered with notices—proof of a lively village. In addition to W.I., old people's welfare and community and local shows, sports days, garden parties etc. there are a variety of invitations to share happenings in the neighbouring villages. It is nice when folk share their pleasures, as hereabouts.

Oxen Park, a huddled hamlet, changes not at all; nor does Colton with its charming groups of farms, high level between Spark Bridge on the Crake and Bouth in Rusland. From lonely St Cuthbert's Church—a Cartmel cellarer became parish priest in 1536—are views over the original parish, from Windermere to Coniston, "a mountainous district fraught with picturesque beauties". In the eighteenth century all were farmers or wood-craft workers who took their produce to Kendal or Ulverston markets. Now—only farming.

On the same ancient market highway stands Bouth, a true village—roadside and straggling off to the birch and hazel coppices, into the beech woods. Bouth folk have changed. I remember workers, men of many skills, like Ted Inman, grandson of a cockle merchant drowned on the Seven Mile Sands. He had been a tile-layer at Black Beck, where the gunpowder works employed most local labour until 1928. The end was a blow. Many found jobs at Low Wood Powder Mill, Ten Inman also. "I nivver see you now," wives grumbled. "Away from six in t'morning till six at neet. Not by daylight, in winter."

Fortunately, countrymen, being Jacks of all trades, could turn their hands to anything. I have talked to those whose fathers were charcoal burners, who turned to stone-walling, became carriers, lime burners. Bouth has shrunk. The Turnpike Trust began the process in bypassing the village in the 1820s. Now all public transport has disappeared, save one Thursday bus.

The old village store is no more; a new shop now—round a corner, but the 'White Hart's' door is open. The latest addition is a 'commando mound' in a central play area. It is sad to find so few rural crafts remaining. Spark Bridge bobbin mill, sited by the racing Crake, is gone and the buildings have been 'converted'. No longer the delicious smell of the Stott Park wood piles on the Lake Side road. Plastic bobbins have 'killed' the trade.

Nearby Finsthwaite was also a centre for woodcrafts, birchrods and besoms a speciality. Substitute man-made fibre brushes and brooms have invaded the market, but a good besom, ling or heather, 'Finsthwaite made' cannot be bettered for paved or cobbled yards or garden paths. Alas—now only one besom maker can 'oblige', if asked. As for birch rods—they belonged to the bad old days of corporal punishment when they were bought by the score.

Today in the "clearing of Finn the Viking" is an enviable tranquillity, the cottages huddled together in a sun-filled 'thwaite'. My favourite path through the woods is a short cut from the Lake-side road to the village church. This is a beauty. Paley and Austin won an award for this 'mountain church' design, which fits perfectly into the landscape. A century ago many wealthy families lived hereabout and all were donors of church furniture. More recently there have been remarkable communion vessels made from shell cases, shrapnel and the like.

A plain white cross near the south wall was erected a century ago by a Towneley, of the family so deeply involved in the Jacobite risings. It marks a grave previously un-named. When Towneleys followed Prince Charles Edward Stuart into exile in 1746, so did an ardent Scotswoman Clementina Walkinshaw who shared his wanderings. They had a daughter, who came as a young girl to the Pedders' home, Finsthwaite House. Here she died in 1771 and this is her grave. The inscription: "Princess Clementina Johannes Sobieski Douglas"—and "Behold my King cometh."

LOW FURNESS VILLAGES

Just as friends found the quiet, un-tourist villages of Low Furness welcome escape from throngs at Hawkshead, so I have moods suited to its less dramatic landscape. There is gentler beauty 'behind Hoad' in snug green hollows, around Mansriggs, Osmotherley and Broughton Beck. Pure enchantment lies over the land of Celtic clans, west of Coniston Water, around Woodland, hidden away behind Blawith. No madding crowds enter here.

Down the tidal estuary from Greenodd to the tip of Furness and its outer islands two centuries have left their mark, pushed into the past thriving iron mines of 'England's Peru' at Whitriggs. Gone the forgers of fine-edged tools—bills, blades and spades: there is no hammering on Newland's anvils, no ore-laden carts reddening lanes from Birkrigg to Bardsea shore; no boats on Leven channel make for the landings at Bardsea, or tie up at Greenodd, once a veritable 'boom town'.

Low Furness village life began to change for good or ill when Ulverston Canal opened in 1796. This diverted shipping from up-channel quays. The emancipation of slaves was a 'disaster' to Greenodd too, for no more Liverpool slavers unloaded their cargoes of black ivory here—Mr Bolton, a dealer and builder of Storrs Hall on Windermere, disposing of human livestock at £45 per head! Shipping and shipbuilding was Greenodd's life blood.

The Ulverston–Coniston slate and mineral railway of 1859 cut out Spark Bridge and Penny Bridge, each with small landings, but silting had already put paid to them, piling above Greenodd's wooden viaduct. Local linen flax and cotton mills had been forced out of the industrial field, clacking wheels were silenced. Peace flowed back into the small villages, as we know them.

Barrow in the 1860s was an acknowledged hub of industry, its wealth in the iron trade and ship building, though 'out on a limb'. So it remains. The town has good reason to watch the barrage planners. The future development of the peninsula depends on the outcome. The villagers' future, also, being affected by Barrow's.

For the present, communities away from Barrow and Ulverston outskirts remain unspoilt. Pockets of ancient peace? Great and Little Urswick, Bardsea, Aldingham, Gleaston, Dendron, Pennington, not in the least 'precious' but honest to goodness. No one frowns or grumbles unduly at modern innovations. Each has been 'changing with the times' over a thousand years. They cheerfully accept newcomers but will not tolerate patronage from town dwellers, nor will they allow themselves to be swamped by them.

On 'New Cumbria' Furnessians have strong opinions. "They should spend their time on something else—not tearing counties apart," they say. "Leave us alone. We've always been all right in Lancashire." "I'm not keen on leaving Lancashire."

Compared with less vocal newcomers, true Furnessians are friendly folk who overwhelm the visiting stranger with spontaneous help.

In spite of modern trends old loyalties and rivalries are not entirely ironed out, nor forgotten. Here are long memories.

Urswick Tarn—which 'they say' swallowed up Old Urswick— has a tranquillizing effect, with anglers in boats, white gulls above, swans cruising in the reeds, red-legged water hens and bald-headed coots sauntering on the street. The villagers of the Great are still dubbed 'Ossick Coots' by Little Urswick, long-standing rivalry, started may be a thousand years ago, deciding that never the twain should meet! Each argues about age and superiority! But a truce is declared for Rushbearing at Old Michaelmas, when lads hack rushes at the tarn verge, and later with simple ceremony their emblems are borne to church. Children place flowers on all old graves of the otherwise long-forgotten dead, with touching simplicity.

In Norse times Lyl, a stone carver, wrought on a cross for Tunwinni, a memorial to Torthred Lord of Urswick. Early this century a Barrow artist carved in wood St Michael trampling down evil, on the south door, and inside enchanting cherub choirs and a merry crew of little naked boys play pipes, harps, kettledrums, conch shells and bagpipes, and a barrel organ.

One inn, formerly reed-thatched and with beams which had served as ship's timbers—has a new sign, a copy from the National Portrait Gallery of General Johnny Burgoyne, a poet rather than a soldier, whose heart was *not* in fighting the rebels in the War of Independence in America.

The innkeepers tell me the 'jet set' has not yet overrun Low Furness, locals are not outnumbered by throngs of townsfolk. Men are earning good money, there is surplus cash to spread over a wide area. Vickers at Barrow and Glaxo at Ulverston employ the majority; without them Low Furness's working population could not survive.

Newton, Stainton and Algardley are villages near Dalton, where the finest iron-ore deposits were mined from the eighteenth century—in the peak period of the 1880s, one and a quarter million tons of haematite ore were smelted yearly. All suffered when output slackened, early this century, like 'ghost towns' after the 1918 post-war closures. Slowly the old scars were mantled by nature, till now all is semi-rural.

Swarthmoor and Lindal have brightened up former workworn faces, the working village drabness tailing off into new estates and green fields. At Swarthmoor the hall farm stands in peaceful acres, as it did in 1632 when Lawyer Fell brought his bride, Margaret Askew, here. She and some of her eight children were at home when George Fox came to their door. The laughing, dancing children were awed by this 'Man in Leather Breeches'. Their mother came under his influence. "Fox opened us a book we had never opened—the Light and Life in our consciences." Fox found a sanctuary here, tranquillity after buffettings by angry people between periods in jail. He married Margaret after the judge's death. In 1688 he bought land for a Friends' Meeting House— still here, austere in and out, and much visited by Quakers. They sit quietly here, then they walk to the hall—where so much happened, where life was rich and full, a working farm and centre for the Fells' many trading and mining activities also. They take

Holcombe Hunt Meet at Affetside village

Garstang morris men at Samlesbury Hall

Coconut Dancers of Britannia

Stay-at-homes gardening at Edgworth

Out and about at Rivington

Basket weaving at
Mawdesley

A Glasson fisherman
mending nets

old lanes to Birkrigg and the stone-walled enclosure, Sunbrick Sepulchre, where sheep nibble close the grass over the graves of defence against the Scots, in a fertile valley among rich meadows.

Swarthmoor at a glance reveals nothing. Many Low Furness villages are the same—their precious heritage is their own, never advertised. No part of Lancashire is less prone to self display. Some look mildly surprised if you say you think it is ever 'lovely'.

Bardsea always looks inviting, sun silvering its limestone walls, the church spire silhouetted beautifully against sky and clouds; a silver-grey village with background of shining water, gleaming shores and far fells; an arresting prospect and at close quarters a perfect village, close packed near the Ship Inn and the 'Bradyll Arms'. Cottages have stood for centuries (several 'tumbled' for the inn car park) as neighbours to old houses with new face-lifts—as at Bardsea Green, where I often stayed when writing *Curious Traveller Lancaster to Lakeland*. Modern houses have brought in a new element—some using Bardsea merely as a 'dormitory' but the majority anxious to integrate.

It is amazing what a very small community like this can achieve when all work together. Bardsea is very good at fund raising. One highly successful 'Bygones Exhibition' brought to light heirlooms, grandmother's treasures and antiques, more than one might have believed possible.

When the younger are called in to help, their enthusiasm knows no bounds. Like three other villages in Furness, Bardsea's village hall was a former maltkiln—and being commodious, well-built, they make very good communal meeting places. In 1972 it was realized repairs were needed. First of all the old windows needed renewing, so their first sponsored walk raised £70, and cheerfully they set themselves to collect £2,000 for a new roof. There is not much wrong with 'alive' villages like this. A pity the old 'Bardsea Flyer', a favourite bus, no longer plies, and that access by public transport is now so meagre.

Aldingham, Baycliffe (growing rapidly) and Scales' total population adds up to but one sizeable village. Aldingham's few farms withstand the sea wind's battering, but there is a legend that "Low Scales with its old hall and half old Aldingham" is lost under sea and sand. High tides break over the churchyard wall. St Cuthbert's body was borne ashore here on its journey to escape pagan sea rovers. Waves lash the hill foot, tearing at the foundation of Aldingham Motte, a site now deserted except by grazing sheep. Sir Michael le Fleming, an early lord, preferred a place more secluded from gales and raiders, and so did successors, Harringtons, Lords of Gleaston.

A short steep lane, hedged in between rich red ploughed fields, drops into a shallow groove where was "a large, firm castle, defence against the Scots, in a fertile valley among rich meadows, sheltered from the sea by fruitful hills—a most pleasant seat". An old corn mill nearby, its wheel turned by the beck, now is silent as the castle next door—long deserted, its masonry used for farms and barns. Trees grow from fallen towers, shrubs find roothold in gaping crannies, wallflowers bloom on the sills of trefoil windows. And all this is hidden from the outside world— as its builders intended.

Gleaston, like Dendron its neighbour, is a village with no airs or graces, haphazard in plan, varied in architectural styles, the general result very pleasant, new in friendly proximity with the old. If there is cow dung on the road and cows hold up traffic at milking time, no one bothers. None of these villages are tidied up for tourists, or for new residents with fastidious noses. At Scales and Urswick also, farmyard scents and sounds are essential to the scene. "Good fresh air," they call it.

Shelter matters. Old Scales and Baycliffe threw up massive banks against storms, trusting to thick walls for protection. Narrow streets turned away from the sea and cottages crept close together for comfort.

"Nowadays," said one of Scales' oldest inhabitants—'one o't' old 'uns', here over forty years, talking of the new houses with their thin walls and disregard for leeward or windward, their picture windows and wide views—"all need double glazing, central heating—and they've all got their fitted carpets." She pointed to three youngsters in muddy Wellingtons rushing towards her open door. "That they couldn't do at home! Shoes off before they go in! So they all come to me with their pet rabbits and banty hens."

She was a cheery soul, talked of the good life and earlier times when at Baycliffe the jolting of shrimpers' carts going down the narrow ways to Leven Sands told dwellers in the inward-looking houses it was the turn of the tide. Half the men were inshore fishermen then. She talked of rushbearing, egg rolling at Easter and coloured pace eggs ranged in rows on window sills—all commonplace once, and surviving still in Furness. She had heard of strange doings on the outlying islands of the tip of Furness. All the villagers have a soft spot for Walney, and Piel and Roa Island.

Rampside is a scattered village. Half stands by the Conckle Inn, the landward end of the Roa Island stone causeway. Roa's five-acre island cost a London Banker £500, his laudable ambition to "connect it with the larger island of Great Britain"! A train was to run along the causeway; the passengers would then proceed by ferry boat to Piel Island and Fleetwood, thence join the Glasgow–London train. A pity there was no lasting interest in his scheme. Buses use the causeway now. Roa is a windswept community with a distinctly foreign—or Suffolk coast aspect. Gay-coloured houses were homes of pilots who guided ships up Walney channel. There is a strong nautical flavour, not only numerous sailing craft tied up on the shore but boats in almost every back garden. How the winds blow here! I made no headway in a recent November gale walking between Roa and the Conckle Inn. Summer can be heavenly!

At Biggar, a small place on the levels of Walney, heavenly, in summer too: sea thrift, trailing miniature burnet roses and the rare island plant, a cerise pink cranes-bill, in bloom; horses and ponies grazing the salt marshes; sweet cries of sand pies, sanderlings and sandpipers all around. Always Black Combe looks from the north. Low-built houses, crouching for shelter for there is not a tree in sight, are darkly silhouetted against skies of great beauty, turquoise and eggshell blues. What's doing here? "Nothing doing—but all the fresh air and peace you like. And the tele!"

North Scales' pretty houses have been swamped by new. Biggar Bank is expanding, but the village of Biggar is a glimpse into the past. Thorny Bank lane has high, stone and sodded dyke defences against the gales—as when the abbey farmed here. Once there were several farms and vast wintering flocks on the salt marshes. Now only one farm, cottages grouped close and two inns. 'The Queen's Head' is a place for dining out, white walls turned inwards to inn yard, massive pebble-walled barns with red sandstone for corner stones, rows of pretty cottages backed to the winds. The New Inn (1758) stands up to the elements, as if to say "This is no smuggler's den, we've nought to hide." They *are* Biggar.

INTO HIGH FURNESS—DUDDON SANDS AND DUNNERDALE

One stormy day I was crossing Kirkby Moor westwards when the
cloud wrack began to lift, slowly allowing Black Combe to
appear, dark, menacing and looking twice as large as life, a
monster keeping watch over Duddon Sands and Lancashire's
approaches to Cumberland. I was thinking of 1974 when Cumbria
is to burst its old bounds. It seemed that Black Combe, anti-
cipating 'The Day', was about to stretch itself, growl and take
mighty strides across the water, ready to devour Low Furness,
and grapple with High.

On 'The Day' why not a reception committee to wait on
Cumberland, give a welcoming hand and invitation to a grand get-
together at the top of Wrynose Pass at the Three Shires' Stone.
There let Lancastrians North of the Sands and Westmerians
declare their willingness for Cumbrians to join with *them*.

I must say there is something about this region above Duddon
Sands, looking into Dunnerdale and towards the high mountains,
that gives rise to strange imaginings.

Back to the present; and a look at the past, when Scots raiding
coastwise forded the Duddon channels, and peaceful travellers
were glad to step on Ireleth shores. Orm the Viking made his
landfall here in 900, and his settlement was sited where Kirkby
stands now, a welcoming place between salt marsh and moorland.
I like its cheerful people, and homely cottages built to be out of
the wind's path.

Kirkby's beck drove water-wheels, and one old mill with
abandoned grindstones has been completely converted in modern
idiom. The mill cottage, preserving the old proportions of much
wall and little window space, fits the scene perfectly. So do the
main-street cottages, in rows, walls rough cast or 'rendered',
grey, off-white, but with cheerful colour inside door jambs and
window cheeks.

The church is St Cuthbert's—a saint popular as patron of
ancient churches by cross-channel fords or ferries, where his body
may or may not have rested when Jarrow monks fled before
ravening Danes. The churchyard is roughly circular—an earlier
pagan site?—and crammed with old graveslabs. The south door
has a fine Norman arch—but little of this period remains after
rebuilding. The interior, with warm tinted red sandstone walls,

is made more beautiful by exquisite flower arrangements, colours picked up from altar frontal, stained glass and the soft 'Coronation' blue of the Lady Chapel. Lovely!

The villagers tell us they are 'Kirkby Roundheads'. I wonder if the nickname has a link with Civil War events, thick in these parts, or have they round heads? Some are 'marsh grown', many from local slate-quarrying families. Sandsiders say they "live long and die happy". The sea breezes, brisk and invigorating, have made them what they are, full of energy, always busy.

The moors are still intensively quarried for Burlington slates, a dark blue-grey which polishes beautifully, much in use for floors as in many local halls—Holker included. And in demand for export.

Pennington, over the wild moor, on the old coach road from Ulverston, is hidden from the sea, sheltered from strong winds. The villagers are much attached to the place, of equal age with Kirkby. On a round mound, covered by crocuses or daffodils in spring, stands a small church on the site of one for which Hubert carved a winged angel on the tympanum of a Norman door and in runic inscription told that Gamel had set him to the task. The stone is in the newer church, worn by time and dripping water.

Gawthwaite, Grizebeck, Broughton Beck—they are small communities settled by Anglo-Norse before the Normans came and gave away local land to abbot and prior "for their souls' weal". All the fell country northwards rising to the craggy mountain ridges, above the Crake and the Duddon, had monastic overlords till the Dissolution; and thereafter new owners like the Prestons, Doddings, Sandys and Bradylls, Gales and the Dukes of Devonshire. Under them was work for all—in the copper and iron mines, in slate quarries—and wealth for the owners. The remainder carried on as their forefathers had done, sheep farming.

At the outlet of Duddon to the estuary the most important place was always Broughton-in-Furness. It was an early market, a charter town, the lords in turn being the Broughtons, discredited in Henry Tudor's reign; the Sawrays, who occupied the tower long after it was a necessary outpost of defence against the Scots; and until recently the Lancashire County Council was lord of the manor. The photograph (Plate 8) given to me by the county architect shows the square after the county had cleaned the obelisk. This pillar was erected by John Gilpin's widow in 1810 in the old market place, which Gilpin Sawrey remodelled in the London style after a 1760 visit. The county also repaired the damaged fish stones and generally improved its appearance. Broughton has dignity.

This was for centuries common meeting place for the country folk on market days. Duddon salmon were displayed on the stone tables and price fixed by officials. On the obelisk steps the charter was annually read to the assembled populace—giving warning of fines, no longer necessary in the eighteenth century, for any who came to the fairs "bearing bill, battle axe or other prohibited weapons", or looked for trouble in settling "old grudge or malice".

Nearby is Dr Oliver's house; he migrated to Bath, there producing Bath Oliver Biscuits for dyspeptic patients. Here young Branwell Brontë, tutor to Mr Postlethwaite's sons, made himself agreeable to the Broughton ladies, taking tea with them or "tasting nothing stronger than milk and water so that my hand shakes no longer".

There is real atmosphere in the village though its old glory is shed—remembered however each charter day, with the formal proclamation, the informal scrambling for 50p worth of *new?* pence by the children, sherry and biscuits for the guests at the hotel, today as in the past. The Georgian houses are prim and proper, the small cottages have discreet alleys and yards behind. Many old hostelries known to early 'curious travellers' are frequented by dalesmen and locals. Manorial courts and meeting of churchwardens and 'The Twenty Four' were held at the 'Old King's Head'.

The church of St Mary Magdalen stands apart, battered by sea winds. When I was there in Holy Week the Lenten lilies were tossing their golden heads on the old unnamed graves. Beautiful little girls had been sent from the school at the church gate to gather flowers for Easter decorations. The masonry is red sandstone, as at Furness Abbey, part old and weathered like the Norman arch, east window and priest's door; much of it of 1547 restoration. The Bishop of Man in that year consecrated both sanctuary and graveyard, to which were carried the dead of Broughton, Dunnerdale, Seathwaite and Woodland, outlying chapelries.

The best place to meet the natives at close quarters always was

Broughton market or fair. Today the tup fairs in autumn are thronged with tall upstanding fell farmers whose forebears probably ranged the heights above Ulpha from The Pike to Harter and Hardknott, above Seathwaite from Brown How and Walna Scar to Dow Crags, Carrs, Greyfriar and Wrynose Pass, when Norse was the only speech, when the brethren of Furness had only begun colonizing these, their remotest land holdings.

Today sheep matters outweigh all others. At the Sales good tups are bought to improve the Herdwick stock, and for cross-bred Herdwick-Swaledale flocks. As in all pastoral country, where there was little need for folk to come together—except for church, for convivial evenings at the inn, for disposal of produce at market and fair—nucleated villages are rare in the north of Broughton.

The Duddon valley is more remarkable for its scattered sheep farms than for villages, where life is much as it was two, three centuries ago, sheep rearing the be-all and end-all. Cockley Beck takes in visitors to eke out farming; Dale Head Farm (once a youth hostel) is the headquarters of Leeds University mountaineering club; Birks Farm houses youngsters on holiday from Groves School, Market Drayton; Rucksack Club members use the Moss House barn; Long House is farmed by Tongue House; but the rest are working farms. There was some apprehension in 1972 when Newfield inn/farm was sold for £39,500, but all was well when it was known the new owners would continue farming the land as for centuries past.

But—as natives dwindle in numbers and newcomers who are 'mobile' increase, the community must lose many amenities. No post office at the 'Newfield', no bus with terminus at its inn door, no village shop nearer than Ulpha—nowhere to hob-nob. Most serious, and probably setting Wonderful Walker turning in his grave, no resident parson at Seathwaite, for he serves two parishes and now lives at Finsthwaite.

Seathwaite has had no school since it was used for evacuees during the war; the under 11s attend the beautifully-sited school on the green by Ulpha Bridge, very different from the primitive centre of education a century ago, when tarpaulins served as screens agains rainstorms, when children carried from the saw mill supplies of shavings to keep the schoolroom fire going, and when it went out were told to run up the fell and back to get

warm. Fathers worked in the mills in Hole House Gill, turning
bobbins for the Lancashire mills.

Because of the county boundary dividing them, the west side
children over 11 are transported to Millom, and the Lancastrians
on the east side of the river to Coniston. The border has caused
some farcical situations, but few Lancastrians seem happy about
"going into new Cumbria".

The characters in dales villages used to be very thick on the
ground. Where are they all? When I was writing *Off To The
Lakes* soon after the war and *Curious Traveller Lancaster to
Lakeland* in 1956, real dales' characters were at every gate, bridge
and bend of the road. Then I knew everyone I met and everyone
knew me. Most of them are no more.

I remember one old farmer, of whom it was said, "He'd always
driven horses, so when he got his first car he'd shout 'whoa' when
he pulled up at every gate!"

Old Mr B was an old-timer, lived in a cottage with grooves on
the slate hearthstone, used he said for pouring in hot mutton fat
when his mother made rushlights. A crony of his, being the only
one who knew how, demonstrated the tying of corn bands to us
and other willing helpers during 1944 harvest. He drove the
reaper like a berserk charioteer.

Canon Casson told where his mother gathered herbs for making
salves and ointments, at the tarn edge; another gave the reason
for so much sempervivum planted in thick cushions over cottage
doors and on old roofs—a plant efficacious against thunder!

All were great nature lovers and watchers of the ways of wild
things. I'll never forget the summer day on a moor road above
Ulpha and the pride a county roadman had in the sodding of a
new length of dry walling and planting of ferns, mosses and small
flowers. He surveyed his labours. "That'll look bonny as a natural
rock garden when I've finished wi' it." I think he was the local who
said Esk and Duddon were his favourite dales, "Because they've
no lakes. They've no bush rowtes and no towerists nor ivver like
to have."

Bus routes came in 1945—and ended in 1972, and tourists
come in greater numbers than before the 1950s.

The Tysons are legion throughout Lakeland, descendants of
some Norse clan leader who spread his sons like Abraham across
the land. Harry Tyson of Tongue House was a mine of informa-

tion. His father and uncles bridged the Duddon gorge with the lovely high arch on which everyone takes so much delight in dallying. Wordsworth could not see the clear pools "green as liquid emeralds" from here—no bridge! Folk often eye curiously the bird on the rock behind Undercragg, near Seathwaite. Harry Tyson shaped a bird in metal and placed it there, for, as he told me, "First cuckoo always lets on that stone, so I thought I'd have one here all t' year round."

His own recollections went back to the 1860s, and he remembered tales of Dunnerdale told by his parents and grandparents back to 1800. I am glad I knew such as he.

The Tysons must have known Robert Walker without thinking of him as 'Wonderful', and probably met the Wordsworths— William wandering up the valley 'as far as it is finished' to the throat of Wallabarrow gorge, his wife and sister viewing the landscape from some rocky eminence away from the road.

The valley was still in a state of near-primitive simplicity until after the war. The dale-head passes were rough, stony, washed out after heavy rain, the young Duddon fed by numerous small becks, each to be leapt by stepping stones. On Wrynose or Hardknott I met only other walkers, huntsmen with hounds, farmers herding sheep. Change came after wartime damage by U.S.A. army armoured units. When this was made good, the passes surfaced, becks culverted, of course motorists began to discover Dunnerdale. The world and his wife followed.

In any less-protected region what would have happened? How many eager to buy land, seize upon derelict barns and decayed property, how many speculative builders would have bought up any acres farmers were willing to sell? How long would it have taken to fill this enchanting valley with houses?

The 1971 census returns show—as I stated earlier—no change in the population of Lonsdale North. The reason? Planning permission is not given for new houses on new sites. Find your old property, try to buy it, ask for permission to convert—possibly you will be lucky, but only if very careful rules are followed. No alien styles are to be allowed in the Lakes area; reconstruction and necessary alterations must be in character—as the National Trust and Friends of the Lakes as farm landlords have managed with success, carefully, unobtrusively. Harmony of new with old can be achieved—but very few are even allowed to try.

Who knows what changes the future under the new authority has in store for the small communities by the Duddon, and—because they are far less isolated—to villages well established in the Crake valley and by Coniston water. Because they are on tourist routes and Coniston is a 'resort town' and a mountaineering centre, they will share in the benefits and some of the inconveniences of being popular. But farming will go on, quarrying continuing, forestry also. No fear of dying communities or ghost villages here. They buzz with activity: in summer making outsiders happy; in winter 'doing their own thing', whatever it may be, and enjoying it.

So at Brathay, a last outpost of Lancashire since the border with Westmorland was defined eight hundred years ago. From friends' windows I took out on enchanting vistas, and because the other man's grass is always greener, think one needs just to *be* here to achieve perfect happiness. "Inhale deeply—and out comes poetry!"

Brathay folk think the same, but there is no sitting still for them. They organize things in the most efficient way—W.I. meetings, help for the elderly, visits to the housebound, car rotas to hospital. Life is rich and full for those who do something about it.

Many newcomers have known and loved Lakeland all their lives and now they have achieved a lifetime's ambition to have a stake in it. I met many at W.I. meetings, held in a lovely room in Brathay Hall which most people know about. It is a place where young people can pursue many outdoor activities—canoeing but NOT rock climbing—and cultural ones also: music, literature and drama in a quite superb theatre. There are excellent relations between the young folk and Brathay's inhabitants, who give support in productions if only to encourage, approve and applaud.

Native Lakelanders were always realistic, hard-headed unemotional folk. Anyone you meet who is *not* is almost certainly a starry-eyed incomer; always because life was hard they knew where their bread was best buttered, none averse to cash profits. As folk say, "When a young couple marries and looks out for a home there's little chance of being able to afford one; prices are always pushed up by outsiders!" A roofless barn or an abandoned ruin of a cottage costs the earth. True—and usually the owner, who is possibly a local farmer, reaps the benefit. It has never been known for the owner to say, "That cottage? I've been offered £10,000 for it by Mr X. from Manchester, but I've decided to let John Y. and Mary Z. have it for £3,000 when they get wed, because they've always lived in the village."

Money talks here as anywhere else. Visitors have always been welcome since the first flow of tourists two centuries ago; they brought money into local pockets. Newcomers who settle are welcome too if they bring something into the village community, active participation—after suitable weighing-up period, if they mix in but do not meddle with accepted standards. If they express opinions too freely, throw their weight about, or show a hint of patronage—'they've had it'! Every man has always considered himself as good as the next in these communities; nowadays this is even more true.

3

Lancashire Villages of the Middle Belt: Rural England in the Ribble Valley

Being a child in the old borough of Clitheroe made me familiar at an early age with a dozen villages within a five-mile radius, and, when wanderings took us farther from home, with many others by the Ribble, Hodder and Calder. And all these completely rural communities coming in 1974 into the Ribble Valley Authority, Yorkshire Bowland villages included, will have Clitheroe at their centre.

This will come quite naturally, for many were manors belonging within the Honor of Clitheroe in Norman times, paying their dues to the De Lacys, then to the Crown, at Clitheroe Castle. The countryfolk always made for Clitheroe's markets and fairs in the old days, and they throng the streets every Saturday and market day today.

A century ago, when outlying parishes and 'out townships' came within Clitheroe Union (for better administration of the Poor Law), the borough had 7,000 inhabitants, whilst the combined population of the rural communities was 20,000, thirty-two villages united—and eighteen of them in Yorkshire!

It was never easy to 'tell t'other from which' as far as two counties' loyalties were concerned; mingling in the streets the folk from Gisburn, Bolton-by-Bowland and Slaidburn were indistinguishable from villagers of Twiston, Downham, Hurst Green or Chipping.

THE WHALLEY STORY

Of all the villages, Whalley is most proud—and with good reason—of its importance, history and community spirit. In fact, my friends find it difficult to believe it is a true village. It seems to possess every amenity of a small town. But a village it is, the 1972 first prize winner among the Best Kept Villages in the 'larger' class, a success made possible—after years of near misses—when the by-pass was finally completed and some of the peace and quiet, so long desired, flowed back.

It is not a *beautiful* village, though it has pretty bits. Church Lane is all it should be. Near the bridge, where the pseudo-Gothic architecture was intended to be in keeping with the 'modernized' bridge and the new turnpike, a few of the interesting old houses still stand, and low-profiled cottages, some with oak panelling from the abbot's dwelling, lead on to the four inns crowded at the old Town Gate. The tall Georgian buildings of King Street are very handsome, the older, gable-to-the-street inns very picturesque. But—at the heart of all, the usual eyesore, a large concrete car-parking lot crying out for a screen of trees.

Always I bring my friends from overseas to Whalley church, where Christianity west of the Pennines really 'got going' and one can trace the carvings on stone crosses put up with utmost reverence as sign of their new faith and to show this faith was renewed over several centuries. If ever a village church was living history, every page filled, here it is. Compared with it, the Cistercian abbey next door had but a short time to endure—little over three centuries and it was gone. The church—thirteen and a half centuries, and like to outlast as many.

The chain of events which led to this? Pope Gregory seeing those angelic young Angles in the Roman slave market, started it. He despatched St Augustine to introduce Christianity to the Kentish folk. The Kentish king's daughter, bride to the pagan king of Northumberland, carried her new faith to York, taking Paulinus with her. Paulinus in due time baptized Edwin and his pagan priests and was ordered to spread the gospel beyond the Pennines, newly conquered country. So in A.D. 626–7 the clear Calder was scene for a mass conversion and baptism.

The deans of Whalley, the 'Mother' church of half Lancashire —a region bordering on Bolton, Rochdale, Bradford and Halifax, Gisburn and Mitton—possessed sole power given them by bishops too far away in Lichfield, then Chester, to take personal responsibility. In Pope Nicholas' valuation of 1291 Whalley parish was among the wealthiest in the land.

About this time Henry de Lacy, Earl of Lincoln, Lord of the Honor of Clitheroe, offered the unfortunate Stanlaw Abbey monks the parish of Whalley. They accepted with alacrity, arrived and took over the powers of the old deans, equal to a feudal baron's.

Along Birches Lane, Turton Bottoms

Rivington, cared for by Liverpool City Waterworks

Holcombe Brook, a narrow byway

Winter at Higher Mill, Helmshore

Hoghton Bottoms, a quiet backwater, its mills closed down

Withnell Fold—industry departed

They owned serfs. Abbot Gregory was able to sell their freedom to "Our native John, his wife and children" for 100 shillings. Settled in, and abbey building progressing, the abbots undertook land reclamation around the Pendle fringe, where all had been scrub or moorland waste; new villages grew in areas newly colonized.

Over Adam Huddleston's new Calder bridge came agents and clerics from outlying monastic estates and chapelries to give account. Travellers from the highways through Bowland and Craven converged nightly on the west gatehouse and none was refused lodging. Queues of poor folk waited for bread doles at the porter's door. The noble guests were entertained at the abbot's table.

From the Middle Ages Whalley was thronged with travellers, and on feast days, when all came to Mother Church, Whalley rubbed shoulders with many and so became less inward looking than many a village. It could have developed into a prosperous market and trading centre when monastic shackles were removed in the 1530s and all native skills freed for the use of laymen. Nothing came of it. Whalley settled down to agriculture and to spinning and handloom weaving.

Strange that the first rumblings of the Industrial Revolution, when many forward-looking merchants saw prosperity dawning and turned to sources of water power at Barrow, Lower Hodder, Low Moor and Primrose near Clitheroe; and when new turnpike roads brought speedier traffic through the village—eyes were averted! Local powers acted like ostriches. Most vehement leader and spokesman of the local anti-manufacture protestors was the vicar, Dr Whitaker the historian, his feet planted in the past. Industry was spurned—one local manufacturer had to go across the Calder to build his new mill; but the village caught the backwash, polluted waters under its bridge, smoke from Billington's factories carried over on the prevailing south-west wind. In 1830 villagers still handlooming were lucky to earn 5s. a week, poverty was here; young folk kicked the dust of Whalley from their heels and were off to the new towns. The parish had now shrunk. Now it was only "30 miles by 20, with one borough in it, three large villages, 47 townships. 18 steam engines were working in the parish"; but not one in Whalley.

There was never much work for the villagers. Now there is

H

none apart from staffing of two large hospitals at Calderstones and Brockhall.

In Victorian times its reputation was for the historic and antique and for the beauty of the surrounding countryside, escape and freedom for the thousands of industrial workers in nearby towns. In the 1970s? It has certainly learned how to harmonize ancient with modern. A new county library, a night club—certainly 'modern'!

The very oldest in Whalley? One can trace the carvings of artists who shaped three churchyard crosses when Christianity was new and fresh. One shows Celtic influence—scrolls and convolutions; another the blending of Norse-Anglian symbols when Nordic gods were being replaced by Christ; a third, weather-worn and almost indecipherable, was last to be put up. Inside the church artists and craftsmen wrought most wonderfully for the joy of creation and love of God, the woodwork of screens and the amazing array of misericords (made for the monk's choir in the abbey) worthy of study.

The abbey was vacated by the Cistercians in the 1530s. The Asshetons made their great house from the abbot's dwelling—this is now the Conference House of Blackburn Diocese. On the site of the high altar is a new plain stone table where open-air communion has been celebrated, the Bishop of Blackburn officiating. The only part rising two storeys with roof intact, the lay brothers' quarters, serves a new use, as gathering ground for the Roman Catholic bingo sessions and social occasions.

Abbey Fields, approached by an avenue of splendid trees—the children's playground on the grassy space between—became a modern housing estate, built on the canals feeding the monks' fish ponds. Above the west gateway, "restored at enormous cost", was a 'guest house', then a grammar school room. The newer eighteenth-century grammar school accommodates a multiplicity of village societies. The senior citizens have their own 'garden room' for meeting.

THE MOST BEAUTIFUL?—DOWNHAM

When I heard a visitor to Downham declare as he slammed his car door, "I've never seen a prettier village," I felt as pleased as though I had made it myself! Of course my forebears, paternal and maternal, have had strong links with the village, and my own interest began in childhood. I find here perennial satisfaction.

For its visual attractions, pictorial vitality; as a genuine living community, no museum piece, visited by many yet remaining its own sweet self, not exploiting its role as a beauty queen (placed fifth in a nationwide newspaper competition), Downham deserves all the praise it gets. Its setting is a major asset, among the rounded limestone coral knolls which gave its name, 'Dunum, among many hills'; Pendle with a watching brief to the east. The brook flowing through decided the first settlers to dig in here; their flocks and herds defined the many tracks and lanes out to pasture.

Last year in a B.B.C. interview I found myself leaping from the Rocky Mountains—the canyons of Arizona, where Man can never hope to overcome Nature, unattainable from the day of Creation to the end of Time—to what is best in our tiny homeland, a humanized landscape where for a thousand years and more man has worked hand in hand with Nature. So, inevitably, to Downham, where better than anywhere else the end product is perfection.

Successive manorial lords—those who built the first hall and the early church, the Dinelays who were succeeded by the Asshetons in 1559 and are squires today—made the village what it is. Single ownership means harmony and unity. Tudor rebuilding in stone kept to the old plan, top end by church and inn, down the brow to the brook, round the green, along the old Clitheroe–Colne highway. Two William Asshetons, father and son, did much to improve the village in late Georgian and Regency times; the desmesne walls, the hall façade, the church (1810), the vicarage, the National School (1830s) were of this period—when every villager had his place in the community, worked on the land and was part-time spinner and handloomer.

A living village must renew itself. This was one of the first to have piped water, a pioneer when electricity was introduced in cables underground not to spoil the visual attractions. The Asshetons have always been vigilant in protecting the beauty their forebears created. The new garages are inconspicuously sited; one completely new house behind the inn is in keeping; the retired schoolmistress's cottage by the stocks is so seemingly converted it might well have stood a hundred years. As for the home farm cowsheds, which make Downham a true working agricultural community, I doubt if one visitor in a hundred even notices them. The fine coloured cattle one sees in the fields are members of an elite pedigree Ayrshire herd founded just before the war.

No industry ever came nearer than Chatburn, and one small cotton mill at Twiston, long since disappeared. The Asshetons decided to keep their estate rural, pastoral. Especially so remain their limestone hills, Worsa, Gerna, Ridge and Crow. Look at the depth of rock revealed in the bypass as it cuts through the hall desmesne. How the quarry owners, who have blasted away the limestone ridges just to the west, would like to get their hands on all the rest! Lord Clitheroe sees the future differently.

Downham seems to me like a beautiful lady with perfect profile, equally photogenic from all angles. Take a look from Worsa Hill; down below the light rests softly like a benison on the village stretching out in the sun. From the ridge of Downham Green, where the Roman road strides purposefully *en route* between Ribchester and York, one sees it clustered in a sleepy hollow, lovely in the evening when blue smoke spurting from cottage chimneys tells of warm home-comings. But where the lane drops in from Pendle End one looks at a village tilted against the hillside, like a picture held up to see it the better: the brow-foot cottages, houses around the green, and those rising from bridge end to church gate and inn door, a perfect whole.

Everyone is so envious of Downham, as people always are when they see perfection but cannot own it. Heaven on earth, they sigh. But better not come on Sundays. The world and his wife and his children with paper bags of bread and car boots stuffed with deckchairs and folding tables, picnic kettles and baskets of food, take possession of the lower village, where parking is possible. The bags of bread? To feed the ducks by the brook!

Pendle has long been notorious for its subterranean waters, bursting out in waterquakes, 'gillbrasts', as in 1580 and 1699 when torrents issued from the hillside, tore up peatbeds, unearthed rocks and boulders, uprooted trees, and, tearing deeper gullies in the western slopes, flooded the levels, doing tremendous damage to Worston, Twiston and Downham—even setting the streets of Clitheroe awash. But the most recent disaster fell from the storm-blackened sky in the evening (providentially before cottagers had thoughts of bed) of 8th August 1967—no waterquake but a cloudburst which devastated a belt from Calder to Lune. Downham caught the full force; in a short time all was a raging flood, the deluge still descending like iron curtains. Naturally the lower parts suffered most but now that cottages are repaired, gardens remade, bridges rebuilt, new defences made in case of other such 'acts of God', tons of debris carted away—one would never guess.

A June morning in Downham; ash trees still bare, dark buds unopened, the limes budding, every oak a gay new green and every sycamore a great sheltering dome; faint and far curlews from the pasture, larks overhead and blackbird and thrush in competition. The village smiles in quiet content; everyone smiles, and the burly hairy-chested council workmen, as they cut the grass of the green, whistle away. A band of sixth formers from Preston come in at great speed geological hammers protruding from rucksacks, halt in their tracks, ask the best way to Twiston Clough and race up the hill. College students, each supplied with enviable equipment including the most sophisticated cameras, draw near and sit down on the seat with me as I sketch. They are 'investigating' the reason for Downham being so beautiful. What did I think?

The morning advances, the birdsong is stilled, the grass-cutters are silenced and the workmen wander up the hill; I see them later tip-toeing round the church, speaking in whispers, interested in the Assheton memorials; and they agree the view from the porch 'can't be beaten'.

The village is now astir, for the children in colourful crocodile process from school to village hall for dinners. The ducks, disturbed, squawk loud as they pass, as they do at all who invade their domain, speeding traffic compelled to pull up as they parade on the highway. "You wait for us. We were here first," is their attitude!

There is a great deal more to Downham than sitting in deck-chairs between ranks of cars on Sunday afternoons, eating ice cream.

For instance? Look around for the oldest, for crinoids or fish bones fossilized, every walling stone and gate-post encrusted with them. Find the Roman soldiers' grave to the left of the hall gates, a boulder protruding beneath the wall and on the line of the Ribchester–York military highway. Look at the wrought iron of the gateway with Lord Clitheroe's cipher, erected after he was

raised to the peerage in 1953. Looking along the avenue of beeches
—nearly 250 years since planting—snowdrops, crocuses and
daffodils making a spring procession beneath them; survey the
green tranquillity beyond. Is any prospect more enchanting?
Unless of course you gaze across the green dale to the north.

Every village should have an inn near the church gate. This
had changed names, and character, down the years. Rent day
dinners were an event here, hunt suppers, carousings of local
sporting characters. The splendid escutcheon of the Asshetons is
new, very splendid. Near both church and inn, village stocks—
placed so that most could cast scorn on the miscreants. Here a
venerable sycamore casts its shade; near here the vicar years ago
kicked off the free-for-all football game, having kept the football
in the pulpit during service.

It may be very old, but there is nothing old-fashioned about the
school. The children like it so much they returned in large
numbers to enjoy the first 'holiday school' last summer, for walks,
talks and hobbies. Enthusiasm so unbounded it could become a
custom.

Architecture interests you? Late Tudor—the Lower Hill Farm
hidden away and by the brook; Well Hall near the bridge, a perfect
gem of local building of the same period. Around the green typical
eighteenth- and nineteenth-century weavers' cottages.

The most modern amenity in Downham is the up-to-date village
hall, the older part of which was a disused Wesleyan chapel.
Here everyone gathers for numerous social occasions, musical
evenings, trad and pop, the W.I. meets here, the farmers young
and old; and the parish council with Lord Clitheroe as chairman—
for, in spite of his seat in the House of Lords and work as Lord
Lieutenant of Lancashire, he takes village affairs concerning his
tenants very seriously.

ON PENDLE'S WEST-FACING SLOPES, TWISTON TO WISWELL

This goes for Twiston and Worston too, with Asshetons as owners
for centuries. Twyseltune, a boundary where streams meet and
almost in Yorkshire, in the 1861 directory was a township of
dispersed dwellings where lived 141 souls. It is little changed
today: greystone cottages on the climbing lane towards Pendle,
greystone farms of great age, each with sheltering windbreaks

of beech or sycamore or ash. At Red Skye is a Quakers' Sepulchre, where lie local Friends, early followers of George Fox. He 'saw the light' and a vision of what God intended for him on Pendle summit overlooking this countryside, in 1652. Many local families lived and suffered as Quakers.

All is pastoral, with sheep-bitten fields enclosed by walls of limestone slabs, a worked-out quarry or two, and long-disused lime kilns. Industry did get a foothold down in the hollow where the Moorbys built an early cotton mill in a place of utmost beauty, Twiston Brook filling a large mill pond for power to turn its wheel. Raw cotton was carted from Liverpool docks and here was 'broken up'. A native recalled the story of two nameless Liverpool urchins who arrived with the cotton and how kindly weavers took them into their families. Young Joseph was given the surname 'Amongham'—'Amangam'.

When the mill was burnt down nothing was left but pond and mill dam, now an enchanting bit of scenery in a secluded hollow where anglers brood on still water.

Larger-scale cotton industry and major limestone quarrying, as Bold Venture and Ribble Cement, stopped short at Chatburn, a sizeable village which endured full impact of through traffic until the making of the by-pass. A good self-contained village with one tragic event in its long history: the destruction of houses—and life—in the heart of it when a German 'plane made a direct hit on a passing oil tanker early in the war.

Worston is held securely in the cleavage of two limestone knolls, surrounded by the same sheep pastures where Worsa's followers turned out their stock in the seventh century, away from prying eyes. Nothing much has ever happened here. Maybe a possibility that Old Mother Demdike's forebears had some connection with Crow Hill Cottage—facing the 'Calf's Head'. We believed this true as children, and glanced apprehensively over our shoulders, half afraid a malevolent face would be looking out from its wheel window. The cottage is fifty years later than the days of the Pendle Witches, but parts could be older. Mrs W. told me of a clay image stuck with pins, found hidden in the roof!

There used to be rumbustious merrymakings at the inn—much more important than a 'village pub' now—and rowdy gatherings on the green when bullbaitings were everyman's favourite local sport. One of my forefathers inserted the bull ring in the stone.

There are no events now in the year's calendar; 'nowt happens now', and no-one cares.

Routine was a little upset back in 1961 when a film unit set up in the lane to Downham, worked on *Whistle Down the Wind*, a macabre tale about a murderer in hiding. The producers hoped for wild Pendle weather, in keeping. But all that February the sun shone. Local children ably supported the star, Hayley Mills.

The opening of the Whalley–Clitheroe by-pass on New Year's Day 1971 was welcomed in every place which had suffered for far too long from A59 traffic. Peace descended—but not on Worston. The roar of speeding coaches, cars and heavy pounding lorries came under its very walls. Natives were shocked. Newcomers felt cheated.

The infiltration of 'commuters' is about the only other change. Worston never had many public amenities, so only few miss the axed bus service. The small 'mission church', a conversion from a mid-village barn, gives the place the 'centre' which a true village needs.

In 1861 only eighty-four souls lived here, and nine farming families accounted for most of them. The Asshetons were chief landowners then as now. Worston was combined with Downham when Nicholas Assheton married the Greenacre heiress. He penned part of his famous diary 1616–17 in the room over the porch of the old hall. Old it is, with monastic masonry in the garden walls and gateposts and shields of abbey patrons inset above the door.

The next Pendle-foot village has lived under the same landlords far longer than Asshetons have been at Downham. Pendleton is a complete village which has borrowed Pendle's protection for a thousand years, being old when the Domesday Book surveyors wrote: "King Edward (the Confessor) had half a hide." In the thirteenth century the Aspinalls arrived, and in 1311 two brothers, John of Standen and Thomas, are named in De Lacy charters as of Great Peniltune and Standen. Over Standen hall was built near the Roman road, away from the village, rebuilt in the seventeenth century and given a most handsome façade a century later; and a perfect picture of grace and dignity it makes in a pool of light at the end of a long avenue, tall trees arching like a tunnel. What a sanctuary it must have seemed to the French *emigrés* who joined the Marquis de Serrant here, all refugees from the Terror and the threat of the guillotine.

The pace of life has varied very little throughout the centuries of Aspinall ownership—Starkies of Huntroyd were landowners too. It is as placid and unhurried as cows ambling to the shippons; no mad rattling stampede of milk floats starting off to connect with the milk train at Clitheroe station, as some remember in the old days—the Milk Marketing Board collects from farm gates now. No hurrying for the bus either; Pendleton fought for and lost its public transport.

Native villagers still outnumber those who 'live in the country' but are not of it. The by-pass is near but affects the village hardly at all. Heavy traffic has not yet invaded the narrow ways flanking the brook, because Pendleton lanes are not short cuts to anywhere special. Neither have drastic changes taken over. Modern houses are sited away from the village proper. All else is stone-built, seventeenth- and eighteenth-century, with a touch of Victorian Gothic in the dwellings' top and bottom end. Much as in 1861, when the church, National School (1837), the 'Swan with Two Necks'—and one beer shop and two village shops which are no more—and twenty-one farms are named. The high population of 1,446, however, included 'Sabden Bridge' over the Nick of Pendle. Then, farmers turned their sheep out on the common of Pendle Moor—paying 'Duke's Rent'. Patrons of the 'Swan' talked of the man who there sold his wife to the highest bidder; and Little Ellen of the post office "had never seen, and years later boasted she had never been on a train".

There is a splendid new village hall, used with less enthusiasm than it deserves, a very good conversion job of a barn facing the pub; and a Bronze Age burial recently discovered in a back garden!

When the new by-pass diverted the Burnley–Whalley highroad, little Wiswell was 'saved by inches', but, as at Worston, traffic noises came closer than ever before. Once over the wide road and on the old lane by Shay Wood, silence returns so completely a dry leaf sounds like hurrying feet; pleasant pastorale. Wiswell Hall farm's lambing pastures, sun twinkling on mantling ivy and the leaves of tall hollies—a pleasant welcome to the village. In the early hall a son was born, John Paslew, destined to be Whalley's abbot, the last. The cross in the Shay marks the point where funeral processions long ago halted before proceeding to Whalley church.

Anyone who thinks the sleepy look of Wiswell means 'no

change' is wide of the mark. Architect planning has converted one three-storey building into Orchard Cottage, and culverted the brook under its patio and paved garden. Vicarage Farm facing, sixteenth century but modernized some years ago—a priest's hide and secret escapes revealed at the time—is satisfying in its comeliness. The nearby inn should be too, but the 'Freemasons' has gone the way of many old pubs, more interested in town night-outers and money-spenders than the villager, his pint and game of darts. Old cottages hidden away in folds are in some cases modernized—as are the houses along the through road— most attractively.

When the village school was sold and turned into a private house, nothing was left but war memorial and parish council notice board to give Wiswell a feeling of 'place' and community. Nowhere to meet! Gone the village entertainments, evening classes, lectures, W.I. meetings—folk must go to Whalley or Barrow now. The only place for a gossip or natter, the confined floor space of the tiny village shop—and that has gone. This is sad for the old residents and for those newcomers who want to identify themselves.

I turn to the pages of the 1870s directory. What then in Wiswell? Eighteen farming families, one grocer, one shopkeeper, two keepers of beerhouses, one innkeeper. Here were a national school, an independent chapel. Of the population of 465, those not employed on the land worked in the Wiswell Moor quarries or at the mill in Barrow. It was considered a very poor place a century ago.

What now? Moderately affluent, some charming homes of professional people, many commuters—and the street often so quiet a group of youngsters under the old chestnut tree, a rider stopping to water her horse at the trough, is an event.

About the Pendle-foot villages the planning unit has its own ideas after taking a close look at 'potentials for leisure purposes'. The decision? It would be *unsuitable* for large numbers of cars to invade them, but small-scale recreational development with car spaces and picnic sites could be sited near the Nick of Pendle— which already has the Wellsprings all-the-year-round ski club. Sensitive approach must be exercised, narrow roads banned to cars. "Why improve them merely to allow motorists to stop to eat sandwiches and look at the view?" The A59 halts or disused sections of the old lanes at Four Lanes End would be more suitable. So far, so good.

The planners continue. Population growth is possible: Clitheroe's 12,000 could expand to 25 or 30,000, and there might be limited increases at Whalley, Barrow and Chatburn, as so many townsfolk find the Ribble valley and Pendle foothills "residentially attractive, preferring to live here and commute to work".

Here is the pattern of things to come. What changes are to be thrust upon the Ribble valley's still green and pleasant landscape?

SOME NEW MEMBERS, 1974

I have been asked to go-slow on the villages of Cartmel and Furness because they are being taken out of Lancashire, so I think I am entitled to say a few words about the Yorkshire villages 'coming into Lancashire' as part of the Ribble Valley Authority—which, as I said before, will come naturally, for common sense has turned the steps of their countryfolk Clitheroe-wards for centuries. I am particularly pleased, for several 'belong to me'—the places where my father's maternal and some of his paternal ancestors were born, married, lived and were buried in quiet churchyards.

Gisburn has a wide street designed for country markets in the past, many old-fashioned inns and others for the eaters-out, a café or two, antique shops and, to fill up, some very attractive cottages built between the sixteenth and nineteenth centuries. Few twentieth-century houses as yet. The church is dark and ancient, the burial place of the Listers, a family here from the fourteenth century and of the blood of the Plantagenet kings. The last of them built the mansion within Gisburne Park, the first of the line at Westby Hall—now a farm off the lane towards Rimington.

Rimington as long-drawn-out, simple, unassuming, sometimes ordinary, more often very pretty with some excellent renovations of old barns. Very old in history; known the world over where folk sing John Duckworth's tune, "Rimington" for "Jesus shall reign where e'er the sun". The chapel where it was first sung is now a private house; so is the nearby village school at Stopper Lane.

The specially-loved village for me is Bolton-by-Bowland, a

beauty among Craven's best, not a visible flaw in its setting, its architecture or in local life. If a church should be at the heart of a village, here it has the finest site, central with a green westwards, the 'Coach and Horses', coffee house and butcher's shop looking on, and the hoary stump of a market cross in the middle; and eastwards a long green screened from the highway by trees, the village school at the top end, the old Bowland Court House on one hand—a very commodious private house since modernizing; and on the other the green tranquillity of the park—where at quiet times one might see deer feeding.

The church where my grandparents worshipped has the long nave typical of many in Craven; within the founder's arch the enormous lid of Sir Ralph Pudsays's tomb is Craven marble, otherwise grey Dentdale limestone of great beauty, and carved deep upon it a complete Pudsay family portrait gallery—father, three wives and an assortment of sons and daughters, soldiers, priests and ladies in pointed headgear of Henry VI's time. This poor king was their guest in 1464—in hiding from the Yorkists.

Over the fells within Bowland, three Hodder villages will be the most remote in the new-Lancashire. Slaidburn is so perfect the whole is scheduled for protection. It lies snugly in a deep hollow—you must always climb to get in or out of the village— exciting heather-clad fells above and pure enchantment in the lush green meadows and pastures below. The grammar school of 1712— the present primary—and St Andrew's stand side by side, two fine buildings. Church street runs direct to the meeting with Chapel Street by the 'Hark To Bounty' and youth hostel, formerly the 'Black Bull'. The same gardenless cottages toe the street and take it down to the green and the river—and every yard a pleasure. Newton and Dunsop Bridge are as happily placed.

Grindleton runs on a strenuous course uphill from Ribble to the high fell road. West Bradford as a contrast uses the contours parallel with the river, whilst Waddington, considered the most perfect village, is given added beauty by the brook running through, gardens on both sides and always flowers tended by keen local gardeners. Here is the perfect plan, village by brook; the old hall (now a private home for the elderly, but a piece of history in its own right) looks over the stream at the church of St Helen, the cottages and several inns share the picture, the almshouses keep quiet round the corner.

These and Newton-in-Bowland, Dunsop Bridge and Whitewell in the Queen's own duchy lands, Bashall and Mitton have all shown considerable good sense over the years, for each of the W.I.s has been in the Lancashire Federation.

How we will go on in 1974—we must see! Ours will be the largest authority in size, but with small population and low revenue. But the countryside—and the people!

AROUND LONGRIDGE FELL

Between Whalley and Longridge, Macadam's new road of 1826 was as much an achievement and caused as much local stir as the modern bypasses. Primitive communities sited deep down in narrow cloughs to be near the wheel-driven mills, came up as it were to look at the great wide highway, and—like Hurst Green and Dutton—stayed there.

On the old winding pre-1826 road were simple hostelries, wayside inns catering for the locals. They were rebuilt if the new highway coincided with the old: the 'Mitton Boat' at Little Mitton became the 'Aspinall Arms'; and the 'Three Fishes', 'Shireburne Arms'; 'Eagle and Child' and 'Punch Bowl' went on from strength to strength, still carrying on today, but serving a very different kind of patron, winers and diners for the most part. Times change and entertainment with them.

Hurst Green began to look up when Sir Nicholas Sherburne of Stonyhurst called upon teachers to show his tenants the skills of spinning and weaving, keeping apartments in his hall for them and "as many as could spare time from their families became in time proficient". Then Sir Nicholas "provided each with yarn and looms whereby the countryside around began to prosper".

The Sherburne male line ended, Welds inherited, and they in the 1790s handed the house to the exiled Jesuit school from Liège, and henceforth the village had the college Fathers for landlord. "Hurst Green's always bin a turrible place for parsons." I often met contemplative priests in black walking the field paths, and college boys running, skating on Crawshaw pond, enjoying the countryside. The neighbourhood is geared to the college estate, the Jesuit Fathers always innovators and up to date in indoor and outdoor improvements. They installed during the 1830s the first gaslight in the district. As a very enthusiastic native recounted after seeing the switch-on, "Dayleet's a fool to it!"

As a school it is among the most modern, yet the boys live in great halls surrounded by priceless works of art. Stonyhurst College is one of the ancient houses of England, fair to see—especially come upon unaware, from the end of the long drive. At the gate, the Shireburne Cottages are a post-war rebuilding of Sir Nicholas' early eighteenth-century almshouses, sited on the top of Kemple End; now occupied by outdoor workers on the estate. So many are needed for the efficient running of Stonyhurst that staff recruited from a large area are brought in by 'bus. The college owns most property, including licensed premises, and provides most employment—a good thing, for industry has moved out of Hurst Green.

When I first started writing I had fascinating letters from Dr Rowlands, a much-travelled brother of Stonyhurst Observatory's famous astronomer. He remembered the old mills down in the Dean, two turning bobbins for spinners, one worker being Polly Cross, who taught school but was bobbin-turner in her spare time, and also produced pop-guns for small boys! He also knew the sandmen, Sandstone Billy and Dickey Wells, who from Sand Rock—a hollow in the enchanting glade higher up the Dean—dug out the red sand for sale to thrifty Lancashire housewives to scatter on their stone-flagged floors, before the days of cheap linoleum.

Macadam raised a high embankment above the Dean to carry his wide, curving highway. Below this, in the 'bottoms', was old Hurst Green of the busy little mills, rows of workers' cottages, and the sound of rushing water always in their ears. One house has a long waterfall plunging down to the edge of its lawns. Naturally, house hunters have always had their eyes on this pretty spot. The very shabby cottages have been modernized, made gay, and somehow everyone has contrived a plot for a garage and lead-in for a drive—the essentials of modern living even for 'imitation countryfolk'.

The new council houses are nicely sited too, just off the main street, and the village hall—the pride and joy of the community—was built with voluntary village labour, apart from plumber and electrician, from weathered masonry to blend in perfectly with its neighbours.

The bridle paths and footpaths are a constant joy. One day I watched college boys, who had given up part of their summer holiday to crippled children, wheeling them down to the Ribble at Dinckley foot bridge so they could splash about in the river. How they shouted and laughed! The boys are helpful to old folk too, leisure-time service.

On the highroad Knowl Green, Dutton and Dilworth string along towards Longridge, but each has 'secret places', out of sight in their own special solitude, each with a derelict, ruined old mill of the water-powered age, all with cottages 'prettified' and converted with all mod cons. Their first tenants drew water from old wells, brought up large families, a thrifty breed of weavers, warpers, wood-turners, bobbin-makers, who when their landlord said their rents were to be raised to 6d. a week threatened to give notice!

Perhaps Longridge of today does not warrant a place among the villages; although it has chosen to become part of the rurally orientated Ribble Valley Authority, I always feel it turns towards Preston and will have more town-minded than countryfolk in its growing population.

A century ago it was a village, mentally and otherwise. Of the old Longridge the top end High street was intact, from the Dog Inn to the 'Quarryman's' and the entry into the then famous Tootill Heights stone delphs. The railway had come from Preston in 1848 allowing the hard freestone to be carried by horse-drawn wagons on the tramroad to the railhead and thence to Preston and building sites—Liverpool's docks, the art gallery and museum at Preston, Hansom's St Werburgha's church among them. The village prospered, growing out of its simple pleasures. The old-type weavers, stonehewers and masons knew hard work and also played hard, could down their pints with the best, dance to the fiddle on merry nights and share the festivities of St Lawrence Day— when, running races, horse races and the like, they used the long street as their course.

Now, some of the most interesting cottages, with steps to their doors—and many with eighteenth-century date stones—have been demolished; the 'Quarryman's' is renamed 'The Berries' and very busy it is on kart racing and stock car racing days. New sports nowadays!

One interesting row of cottages is fortunately protected. In

March 1793 twenty men formed a club, paid a guinea a month, and in May purchased land near the 'White Bull', 120 yards by 30, intending to build thereon "on a voluntary or spare time basis" over ten years, twenty houses with "necessary and coal-house". On completion each was balloted for. They are still standing, provided with "internal modern conveniences, sanitation, bath and hot and cold water". Club Row looks good for another 150 years.

THE CHIPPING STORY

What makes a village perfect? Its setting and the way it adapts to this, building styles and materials of a kind, the happy siting of cottages—along a curving street, around the church—the inn, the village store, the school and the village hall at just the right places, where one expects them to be; and, tucked away down alleys, hidden away where one never expects them, the 'best bits', completely unconcerned that the world hardly knows they exist? Or are associations, the role the village plays and has played for a thousand years, the way it is adapting to the present and facing the future, more important than visual attractions?

Chipping is perfect, and beautiful with it, a living story book. I have known it all my life. I still think of it as 'one of the best'.

Envious neighbours used to shout, "Cuckoo" and, "Whittle to t'tree", after Chippingers, reminders that once it was only a poor place with one communal knife, and so gawmless folk tried to wall in the cuckoo to keep perpetual summer!

In the Middle Ages this was *the* Chipping, the market for the Vale of the Loud and Leagram Chase, to which great families who were royal officers—Hoghtons, Sherburnes, Welds and Stanleys among them—travelled to the parish church for mass. In later years it was centre of a rich agricultural, pastoral countryside which was turning to industry; farmers and local weavers, wood-turners, chair-makers and iron workers meeting on common ground. Chipping brook until a century ago turned many wheels, Tweedies foundry and Berry's chairworks the most important and longest lasting until today.

St Bartholomew's church is at the heart of the village, a dark yew tree, seven centuries old maybe, at the east end; a seventeenth-century sundial near the south door. On two north arcade capitals

Worsthorne high above the Calder valley

Whalley, ancient village by a historic highway

The bridge over Sabden Brook

Pendleton west of Pendle

Newchurch-in-Pendle in the witch country

Wycoller, perhaps about to come to life

stone carvers cut a portrait gallery of local labourers, the ass which worked with them, and what seems to be architect's drawings of window details. There are some fascinating brasses; and, to show how the church adapts to a living community, the newest chancel furniture was work of Berry's craftsmen in wood, whilst fine hammered iron screens were made by men from Tweedies. The south aisle window is brilliant modern glass incorporating symbols of the industries long essential to the life of the village.

Everything in Chipping is good to look at, from the seventeenth-century buildings given by a local lad who made good—John Brabbin's grammar school and row of almshouses in Windy Street and the modern primary school round the corner—to the neat houses hemming in Talbot Street. Especially refreshing the inns, none over-modernized or 'with it', and simple cafés, for Chipping does not neglect its many visitors. By the bridge the old corn-mill is being restored by local people and will open as a restaurant, where one will be able to sit within sound of the splashing of water over the old wheel turning.

Berry's Kirk Chair Factory uses water power no longer—as in the 1840s when new—but one can wander down the hill to the brook, past the piles of timber sending out delicious scents, and discover in the older mill by the mill pond men at work, rebottoming old rush-bottomed chairs, sunlight splaying on piles of rushes, and gold dust in the air. The nearby cottages used to be rented at 1s. 6d. a week, and are still for workers only.

There is nothing phoney about the village. It does not hide its council houses, it shows no signs of spurious imitation or gimmickry. It enjoys all the activities geared to the young, the women, the pensioners, a modern village must have; it has been champion several times in the Best Kept Village competition, and shows a lively interest in what its neighbours are about, collaborating as it does with Goosnargh for the great summer show etc. Hesketh Lane, part of the parish, shares all.

As for the past, it certainly knew how to enjoy itself, with fun and games, ritual and old custom up to the last century dictating the pattern of a score of purely local happenings, from the cradle to the grave.

A child is born. Neighbouring goodwives attend the laying-in, to celebrate with rum and tea drinking; and all attend a 'shouting',

I

a merry night with the family. When the mother is strong and able she invites all to a 'shilling tea', proceeds for the infant.

A lad and lass start courting. Friday is forbidden, for every house-trained lass is too busy on that night for walking out or sitting in; Saturday is the favoured evening. No outsider dared to trespass in Chipping's limits, knowing if found chasing a Chipping girl he would be tied unceremoniously in a sack of flour!

The wedding bells ring; small boys tie the church gates, refusing to unfasten until the bridegroom throws out 'hen silver'. A race follows to the bride's house, the winner sure to be the next at the altar.

The passing bell tolls; all men are 'bidden' to the funeral. Two women in black stand at the house of mourning, handing spiced ale and funeral biscuits to the mourners; and into the chief mourner's hand, if poor, a shilling is given. The poor walk to church bearing the coffin, singers and musicians going before. At Roman Catholic funerals the mourners always knelt and repeated the *Deo Profundis* at the sites of early wayside crosses.

Fairs and festivals. Candlemas was servants' hirings, the village full of stalls like a fair day. An orgy of pancakes lasted through Shrove Tuesday. Pancake tossing caused great hilarity when the pancake fell when being turned, and the unfortunate one who was last to finish his pancake was carted to the muck midden or his face blackened with soot. Local farmers bred fighting cocks for their landlords, to fight at the Shrovetide cockings. The schoolboys shared the sport, dicing for cocks. Frottis Thursday followed Ash Wednesday and all ate special cakes. So they did on mid-Lent Sunday, when it was simnels, with spiced 'braggart ale'.

Eastertide. On Good Friday small children begged door to door for cracklings. Easter Monday meant horseplay, one day men lifting the girls, the next day the girls retaliating.

Spring and the rising of the sap. A boy in a sack, playing 'Old Ball', ran wild through the streets, wearing a horse head of calf-skin with a mouth which snapped open and shut and scared the children. April Noddies and May Geslings were made fun of on the appropriate days, and young girls arose early to go May-dewing in the cool fresh fields. All May horses were bedecked in braid and flowers, whilst boys adorned with ribbons trooped behind Jack-in-the-Green in and out the houses and yards, like a

North Country version of the Helston Floral Dance without the music.

Club walkings on Ascension Day, perambulation of the township boundaries, sheep-shearing, haytime and harvest, and so to Michaelmas, when the curfew rang once more. In October, Chipping great fair, and, on the last night in the month, All Hallows, the faithful at prayer for the souls in purgatory and a girdle of fires on every hilltop.

LOWER RIBBLE, SAMLESBURY TO RIBCHESTER

Travellers leaving the motorway at the Ribble Valley bridge see their first Lancashire village, Samlesbury. A true village community, Samels-burh dates from pre-Norman times purely pastoral, agricultural, on the richest alluvium of the valley, happily scattered over a wide area. Ancient church, village school and adjacent farms make a pleasant Ribbleside picture, near the old highroad and ferry, and a 'potters' ford' on a medieval through route to Scotland. This proximity brought unwelcome attention from David the Bruce, who, during a ferocious raid of 1322 laid waste the valley and left Gospatrick's Hall a smoking ruin. His family rebuilt far enough away from this hot spot.

Their newer hall was built from great oaks of nearby woods—finally cleared for Samlesbury aerodrome. This splendid fourteenth-century black-and-white Tudor hall is open to the public, and is part occupied by the Lancashire branch of the Society for the Protection of Rural England. The hall brings many visitors, and, if it should become a centre for country arts, crafts and general culture, should attract even more.

In May 1969 we had protested with success against the Lancashire New Town spreading up the valley towards Hothersall and Ribchester, the 'Longridge Spur'. In 1970 this equally quiet rural area was shaken when an application was made by Whitbread's, supported by Preston R.D.C. and Blackburn, to build a large-scale brewery on the Samlesbury pastures. This was refused by the inspector for ten very good reasons. Chief objection was "a gross intrusion of industrial development into a pleasant rural area, a necessary break between Preston and Blackburn". Soon afterwards his decision was overruled by 'the Minister'. "A juicy financial catch for the brewery", cried one paper. Another praised sky high the "quite breathtaking silhouette of Preston and most impressive views of Lancashire" Whitbread's were about to desecrate. This area *is* pleasant, historic, but not scenically outstanding.

Whitbreads had their way, but, being known as 'lovers of the English countryside', they have been obliged to prove it by 'landscaping', erecting high banks of earth excavated from the 55-acre site, planting hundreds of trees to screen it. Eventually it will be well hidden.

Here are ghosts at large—not displaced farmers and cottagers bewailing their lost homes, but from an earlier time when the Southworth family, very staunch in the old faith, were caught up in religious persecution. The hall had secure priest's hides, rarely without a tenant, for itinerants new from France were received here. They held forbidden masses and, when celebrant and worshippers arrived by night, ghosts were a good cover for strange movements, whether white ladies or grey monks, or 'Lady Dorothys'.

Did Lady Dorothy "whose Protestant lover was slain by her fiercely bigoted brothers, and died of a broken heart" ever exist? The Southworths produced one priest who influenced an epileptic teenager of Samlesbury to tell of awful things she had seen in the woodpile at the 1612 trials, giving evidence of witchcraft against Samlesbury women. The chief victim was Jane Southworth, Sir John's much-hated Protestant daughter-in-law. Another priest John Southworth also, a late candidate for martyrdom, who cared for London's poor, was arrested and executed—and was among the saints canonized in 1970.

The Ribble-edge church is full of fascinating seventeenth- and eighteenth-century dated calf box pews. Near the south wall a local witch, who on her deathbed swore to haunt her husband 'if he wed again', was buried under a heavy graveslab. Cracks appeared, so iron bars were riveted down—to keep her below ground! Cracks and rivet holes are visible today.

Samel's contemporaries, Osbald and Baldhere, possessed rich manors a few loops upriver, tilted, wind-raked farmland, from highway A59 to the Ribble. The tranquillizing rural landscape of today comes from a thousand years of farming, "peace dropping slow" over the valley at Balderstone Hall, over Oxendale Woods, to Mellor's moorland pastures.

Industrial changes did little to alter the gentle rhythm of living. Incomers have modernized old and built new homes here because this is what they like. Some families a century ago left to find work in the mill towns, others emigrated, among these an Osbaldeston, when sons of the ancient landowning family had come down in the world and were scattered over it. He was granted land in Canada by the Hudson's Bay Company. With an axe and spade he faced the future in the far west, so his great-grandson told me one summer night over a camp fire in Jasper National Park. "He was offered a shack," he said, "so decided to write to an old sweetheart in Lancashire to join him."

"Did she come?" I asked.

"Like a shot. They were married the day after they met. The next morning my great-grandfather took her to buy a wedding gift, to a hardware store. 'Choose a good hoe,' he told her." Then, fully equipped, they faced the future together.

When Osbaldeston Hall had a ferry boat—destroyed in a flood and never replaced for public use—it was but a short distance to Ribchester. Now, four miles roundabout to get there, they are poles apart.

After the 1969 New Town Public Enquiry, Ribchester, freed from fear of being trapped within the Longridge Spur, breathed once more. Now it takes renewed interest in itself. The keen curator of the Roman Museum started a local history society. The R.A.T.S. are making a name in amateur theatricals. The village continues in its efforts to win the Best Kept Village competition. In a desire a rejuvenate its age-worn face, plans are made to landscape the river frontage. There is even talk of a car park, the only way to prevent congestions of cars—a major problem by the river, near the church—but some fear improvements might encourage too many visitors! In the summer they have little privacy, for Ribchester is about the most visited 'touristic' village in the valley. Its attractions: a Roman museum, Roman remains, places to sit and enjoy the peace, and a few shops making an effort to please visitors. It is rather late in the day to discourage them. We are not living in the last century, when hooligans thrust broom handles at visitors' horses and were as likely to chuck stones as welcome them. Some say dislike of strangers started with the Roman occupation in A.D. 79!

Ribchester folk have always been a 'special case'. They keep themselves to themselves; intermarriage was once common. "Mind what you say, they're all relations i' Ribchester. Slap one on the backside, and they all smart!"

Two centuries ago numerous Roman finds brought a spate of eager antiquaries. They quizzed the villagers hoping to buy 'souvenirs'. Some looked for Roman noses! None had so rare a find as the truanting schoolboy who kicked up a Roman bronze ceremonial helmet which now has pride of place in the British Museum. Roman temple pillars dug from the Ribble bed were too large to be carried away. Look for them in the 'White Bull' porch, the church gallery, and at Stydd Almshouses.

Anglian 'Ribblechester' grew up around Roman Bremetanacum. Fifth-century Picts and Scots destroyed the fort, seventh-century Anglian settlers took possession. St Wilfred's church used a temple site, the 'White Bull' was built near the Roman well and bath house and the very streets follow (approximately) military highways. The Longridge road is that of the legions to Lancaster, Stonygate to the Great Wall, Littletown road the eastern route to York.

Archaeologists are constantly at work, doing nothing by chance. Frogmen dive, searching the river beds for finds. During thirteen centuries the Ribble has changed its course, wiping out one-third of the fort—therefore careful investigation here.

Spinning, stone quarrying, farming, then weaving, were local employment a century ago, but of two cotton factories built on the outer edge, only one is still working. Fortunately, the good, well-mannered Georgian architecture was unaffected, the highway by-passing Old Ribchester, where at times our footsteps echo in the silent village streets.

There is so much to see, several history lessons at once for anyone so inclined; an excellent museum and a perfect 'living' church.

Ribchester is a most remarkable village, no other in the county sitting so squarely on a piece of old Rome. In Tudor times Camden wrote: "many signs of Roman antiquity are commonly digged up"; in Georgian times discoveries multiplied, according to Dr Stukely who reported the "Ribble's inroads eating away a third of the Roman city—and people talk of whole houses and the inn washed away, and once the bank gave way and part of an orchard fell into the river"—and apple trees went on growing therein.

We can enjoy much of this at the Roman Museum; there is a

good section of the granary behind, a section of 'city wall' and a fragment of the north gate. When I was a child we could pick out grains of corn 'burnt by the Picts and Scots' and carry them home as souvenirs! Once I took a number of lads to see the antiquities —and they evaporated into thin air; I tracked them down in a neighbouring apple orchard. Discoveries far more to their taste!

The simplicity of the church always affects me deeply. The interior lines are uncluttered, the walls unadorned—apart from a very faint mural—which I know is St Christopher carrying the Christ Child upon his shoulder, his strong hand clutching a staff, but anyone seeing it for the first time would have difficulty in identifying. The masonry of the twelfth-century nave and thirteenth-century chancel and tower is beautiful local stone—from Buckley delphs?—the tall pointed arch, the slender lancets of the choir, the arcading of the north chapel—all fine workmanship. Who worked the Roman temple pillars holding up the gallery? Who knows, but some chiseller smoothed them too effectively after centuries in the river. Perhaps the timberwork is even finer: enormous girth like the great tie-beam of a nave roof, and the delicate carving of the screens of the Hoghton chapel of 1405, and the Dutton chapel. The pulpit (Jacobean) needs a story to itself.

Out in the fields north of the village, Stydd church has all the strong simplicity of a barn—yet it is the oldest of our churches, with Norman door head, early transitional work—and an atmosphere poignant with age. Midnight communion on Christmas Eve was celebrated in 1972, the first for many years. It has no light, no heat, so use is restricted.

4

*Mid Lancashire Villages of the
Industrial Belt*

In the 1770s Blackburn was described as a town in a bottom or valley among hills, becoming prosperous because of an overflow of manufacturers from Manchester. Land was cheap hereabouts, so manufacturers arrived. 'Calicoes' were printed and fields whitened with materials bleaching. For generations local looms— every farm and cottage had a pair—had produced greys or checks of linen warp shot with wool. Chapmen gathered up the produce from cottagers in all the nearby villages.

Within its orbit, linked with church and market, were villages like Witton, Livesey and Feniscowles, Little Harwood, Wilpshire and Ramsgreave—each destined to be enclosed in the town's boundaries—and Darwen, Rishton and Great Harwood which were to become towns in their own right. Small rural communities—Over Darwen, Eccleshill and Tockholes, Mellor, Salesbury and Osbaldeston, Billington and Langho—have grown, but insist they are villages and separate still.

Those north and south of Blackburn, their people, the village 'look', are as different as chalk from cheese. Those south in the bleak moors, with small-holdings and rough pastures were first to turn to the textile trade as more rewarding than farming; excellent springs of water, abundance of building stone and much coal hastened their participation in the Industrial Revolution. By contrast, the rural acres into the Ribble Valley north and west, where richer land was amenable to husbandry, became providers for the growing towns—and they still supply milk, eggs and poultry. The rural district north of Blackburn has 'opted' for inclusion on the new Ribble Valley Authority in 1974.

The ups and downs of Blackburn's trade had repercussions in the villages. In the boom time, 1801–21, the tide flowed to town. As Blackburn mushroomed the villages, which fed their young people into it, dwindled. For example Mellor's population (with Eccleshill) dropped from 1,839 to 198, and Tockholes from 1,077 to 646. Darwen also drew in the workers from outlying villages.

In the 1830s the handloomers' hatred of the new mills and the machines in them—culminating in smashing of new 'Jennies' and 'mules' and the destruction of mills—led to an exodus of 'capital'. No manufacturers were eager to invest money again in Blackburn factories. When traders returned, their interests were in the town as a weaving centre. Spinning was concentrated round Bolton.

Improved roads, new canal, the railway—in that order—brought changes to villages like Langho and Billington on new road and railway, and Cherry Tree and Feniscowles on canal and railway—and to other small communities, each to have one or two mills. As industry never got out of hand—always green pastures against the mill walls and larks, cuckoos and curlews to be heard overhead—there was no "dark Satanic" future ahead. Blackbird and thrush sang as cheerfully as though no mills were there.

Industry does not threaten them now—but few mills are working. The fear is that too many people want to live in these now residential areas and that therefore new estates and developments will eat up the remaining countryside around them.

Take Mellor, enviably placed on a breezy hill ridge, Blackburn southwards, where most villagers and new residents work; looking over a wide expanse of the Ribble valley to the Fylde coast and the sea westwards. Romans had a site on the moor top, near their Manchester–Ribchester military road, smoke signals by day, beacon fire by night. Apart from the farmers no-one produces anything now, mills closed and stone quarries silent. Apart from scenery, folk find fresh air and numerous other advantages living here; one hazard, snowdrifts during bad winters! So, as many new houses follow the road, Mellor draws near to Osbaldeston and Balderstone, to Salesbury and Clayton-le-Dale.

The Bishop has fine prospects from Bishop's House in Salesbury, a village of great charm. Many townsfolk find the rural amenities so persuading they buy houses in the parish, decide a country school is best for their offspring, and here they enjoy the best of two worlds.

Commons and open spaces *make* Salesbury and Copster Green, once a goose green with handloomers' cottages ringed around it. Unfenced lanes trail across the common, and paths trodden by children's feet run in and out of hollows, around gorse bushes and bramble patches, a place to jump, leap, stare, listen and shout! How sad so few enjoy this delight of childhood, trailing home slowly from school. Parents come in cars to collect.

Once powerful local families dwelt at Salesbury and Lovely Hall; the Talbots, who arrived as Lords of Salesbury in the early Middle Ages, only died out, in the female line, a century ago. Their park extended from Ribble Edge to Parkgate (now an inn name). The head of the family dwelt at Salesbury Hall, had sons at New Hall (a sorry place, derelict, with hen huts as focal point in what was a most beautiful scene) and at Dinckley Hall—this the only Talbot house with any signs of the family.

Salesbury is an alive place, with clubs, sports ground, institute and care for the elderly. Dinckley is too small to do more than preserve its ancient place; it becomes smaller—197 folk in 1801, now only 90! It is a completely farming community, never caught up like its neighbours, Langho and Billington, in industry.

These two with the A59, A666 and the railway shaping them, had to change. Old Langho—a pretty hamlet with sixteenth-century church, school and stocks on a green—was replaced by a new highway-side village, where Spring Mill provided work for local weavers. At the same time the early handloomers from slopes of Whalley Nab at Painter Wood moved down from the old road to the new turnpike where work waited. Two mills; Solomon Longworth erected the 'Judge' Mill on Calderside—Whalley refused a site across the river, and Abbey Mill was sited on the new road, this last survives in full production, and advertising for weavers! Three mills now reduced to one. The two villages have no other work for the parishioners, but two local hospitals employ large numbers, and there are world-famous engineering and electrical works within easy distance. The moor quarries of good stone are worked out. From these were built the old cottages and nineteenth-century terraced houses also. 'New York', was a community of stone-getters, the Lord Nelson Inn giving a clue to its age.

The parish (with its two villages never seeing eye to eye) was in the ownership of Hackings, Shuttleworths, then Walmesleys and the Petres of Dunkenhalgh. None remain in the parish. In the 1940–50s the Petres allowed sitting tenants to buy their farms. Selling has continued, farmland diminishing rapidly. In fifteen years five farms have passed over to housing development.

The green acres dwindle and the population doubles.

What contrasts here! Stonebuilt Victorian terraces—named from millowners, Clayton, Longworth, Birtwistle—inns recalling old families—'Judge Walmesley' and 'Petre Arms'—these taking the place of simple, low-built seventeenth- and eighteenth-century cottages and humble hostelries on pre-turnpike roads. The wide gaps between them are narrowed by bungalows and modern house in-fillings. Meadow and pasture lands have disappeared under new housing; newcomers are eager to live here, buying bungalows which were £2,000–2,500 in the 1960s for £5,000–5,500 and houses under construction for £15,000–17,000! There are old folk who remember when old cottages recently offered for £4,000 were rented at 1s. 6d. per week!

As yet Wilpshire, Langho and Billington have green fields dividing them and miles of sign-posted footpaths and old bridle paths—horse riding *very* popular and several riding schools in the area. When the need is for gentle landscape one may wander over to Dinckley or Hacking and Ribble banks; when breezy heights are more inviting, then up to the moors and Whalley Nab or Cronshaw's Chair, splendid viewpoints, to watch swift clouds and sunshine chasing over hills and dales.

In Lancashire we realize how lucky we are: climb any hill and there is the sea westwards, the 'cloud capped' bulk of Pendle northwards, a pointer to the higher highlands of Craven. If you are a countryman you can survey valleys within the folds, filled with sprawling towns—as from Billington Moors one looks on the Calder. If you are a town dweller you gaze on the fair country outspread, pick out a favoured village—and to sweetheart or spouse say, "What about looking out for a cottage?"

TOCKHOLES ON THE MOORS

South of Blackburn and on the slopes of Darwen's moors are villages quite unlike any northwards, Tockholes being typical—a straggling lane-side community which has in recent years not changed its shape, only closed its gaps. Bog Height, Moorgate, Gib Lane, Brokenstones and Hordern Rakes once echoed with the clatter of clogs as weavers trudged to Tockholes' Top and Bottom cotton mills, lanterns flickering in the darkness of "six o'clock in't morning".

Some of the Tockholes handloomers' cottages of the period, 1790–1830s, are intact; look for them near Lower Hill, the chapels and the church, at Higher Hill, and Whalley Terrace on the top road. Redmaynes and Hollinheads employed local weavers and 'imported' many from Livesey and Mill Hill. Their mills are long demolished—a Tockholes man told me that as a boy he watched the chimney at Ryall Fold being 'felled'—there is no employment in the village. Had there not been a return to the 'home town' of their great-grandparents by scores of young families, Tockholes could now be a dreary place. But back they come, improve old property with grants, sometimes with over-exuberance so that one fails to find traditional features intact. There is a great desire to add garages—quite naturally; to build on porches to defy the elements—with which one sympathizes; to knock out the old sash windows and replace by overlarge plate glass picture windows or the present 'rage'—rows of Georgian bows. More unfortunate, though understandable with growing families—addition of dormer bedrooms; and patching up of old stone-flagged roofs with an assortment of alien materials, assorted in colour.

No one has ever considered Tockholes as a beautiful village with architecture worth protecting. Only recently has public conscience been stirred. I doubt if any parish has so many historic buildings so outrageously neglected; the oldest and finest, Ryall, the Lower Hill manor house of the Radcliffes and Crow Trees, a perfect gem of a yeoman's homestead of the seventeenth century, almost past redemption.

When Radcliffes, Southworths and Osbaldestons owned the moor, moss, turbary and waste and very little land fit for farming, their tenants dwelt in long cloughs below the moors—one, Tocca's Hollow, so old its church had a seventh-century cross at its door. When the population grew large in Victorian times, it was rebuilt—a draughty barracks of a place to hold a thousand—and this in turn was pulled down and rebuilt half the size on half the old site, a completely modern bright and welcoming place of worship.

In the 1660s Tockholes became famous in the annals of Nonconformity, fierce in dissent with an early Congregational chapel and numerous breakaway sects, all of whom had freedom of worship.

A most remarkable vicar arrived soon after the victory of

Waterloo "and never left Tockholes during the rest of his life". He had been chaplain in Wellington's army. The village remembered tales long told, how when he opened a Sunday school, he himself rounded up defaulting youngsters from their play and drove them before him. When any in the congregation drowsed in the warm closeness he banged his bible on the pulpit edge, roaring, "Wake up, there'll be plenty of time for sleeping in Hell."

His great pride was in the National School in the church yard, built in 1834, as the tablet tells. It has an unusual outdoor pulpit used in annual sermons in the summer, but a new village school was erected in Rock Lane. And this is the place to see the hope of New Tockholes, at playtime or hometime, when bonny young mothers, pushing prams with apple-cheeked infants, converge upon the gate awaiting the 3.45 stampede. Out pours a flood of bright, boisterous small sons and daughters, all glowing with health.

"We wouldn't live anywhere else. It's always so fresh up here." Stinging rain, winter snowstorms, nothing bothers them. This is a village with singing telephone wires, screaming peewits on March days, kestrels and sparrowhawks hovering, from the high pastures curlews calling, and above June meadows, cuckoos. Lift your eyes to the hills, or turn west over woods and valleys to the distant lowlands and the sea—as all say, "There's nowt to beat it." Why, townsfolk come from miles away just to enjoy it all.

It is a happy place, the people content; and all feel they belong. But changes are imminent. Plans are in the pipe-line for large-scale housing schemes. "Tockholes is not going to stand still. But is it going to go forward? That's what we'd like to know."

I talk to Mrs Rossall, who remembers Tockholes of Victorian times, "when we never had time to be bored, there was always something doing, parties, efforts, sales of work, concerts, always something to work for, church or chapel, and it kept us all together". But nowadays, she was sure, was much better. In her young days there was "no piped water, no electric, no sewerage, no buses"—and no Women's Institute, such an enlivening part of village life, and no old people's welfare.

I have known old Tockholers who could tell of bad times when weavers at the two mills never saw their families by daylight during the winter months when the working day was "six in t' morning to six at neet". When the mill owner Brock Hollinshead,

The Friends' Meeting House at Crawshaw Booth

Seventeenth-century Newchurch

Newchurch-in-Rossendale

The quarried moors above Whitworth

White pointing at Broadclough on Irwell

Moorland houses at Leavengreave

seeing down-at-heel mill lasses with holes in their stockings, threw down money and ordered them to buy more; when those in the know could buy cheap whisky produced in secret stills near Rocky Brook and Engine Bottoms; and if you wanted cheap coal you took your donkey up the Step Back track to the moortop coalpits and paid 6d. a donkey load. On the way they passed 'Old Aggie's', a lonely beershop frequented by colliers and stone getters over a century ago, and one night the scene of a dastardly crime—the murder of Old Aggie herself by men with blackened faces, who stole her money; their arrest came later when, spending the money in a Darwen inn, their grimy skins gave them away. On the same route stands 'Fine Peters', 1757 on its date tablet, with a window through which night travellers reported seeing ghostly duellists, drawn swords and white spectres. Preston court records of the 1790s tell of a forger of bank notes whose workshop was in an upper room here but who escaped the death sentence when the incriminating evidence was removed before the constables arrived.

Like the best villages Tockholes has its share of folk-lore, remembered tales and local 'trivia'.

It is fortunate in its surroundings and miles of footpaths, through woodlands towards Feniscowles, by old stony tracks— part of the pre-turnpike road system from Rocky Brook to the Belmont-Abbey Village road, and by the man-made lakes land- scaped by Liverpool in its ambitious water undertakings of the 1840s. Best of all, climbing paths to the moortop—enchanting in summer evenings with countless swifts on the wing and cotton grass fluttering. It is every Darwen child's first big hill to be climbed, very popular for sponsored walks; a challenge!

OLD COMMUNITIES ROUND DARWEN

Down below sprawls Darwen, a 'new' industrial town in a valley, attracting the village folk on the hills of Over Darwen into its mills, print works and bleachworks. A scanty population of around 600 people in 1720—by 'active and successful industry' and the 1797 construction of the Bolton–Blackburn road over Turton Moor to replace the ancient road, originally Roman—by the 1801 census was 3,587. A pity it had developed when building styles were at their ugliest and no-one cared about it. By 1871

K

the new town stretched in a narrow two-mile belt along the highway; there were no less than thirty-six mills by river and road and railway, and over 21,000 people in it.

Eccleshill and Blacksnape, Waterside and Hoddlesden in a dip between hill ridges, Belthorn, Yate and Pickup Bank beyond, were each villages with long histories which bred folk of independent spirit. Many were firm chapelgoers, with a Spartan streak which helped them to overcome adverse conditions—hard labour, hard times and wild weather. These villages string out on storm-lashed skylines. And what wide landscapes their windows frame, east and west, reaching to distant moors and valleys—even to Pendle and the Craven mountain northwards. "I never knew England were that big," declared a stranger taken to survey the view. The immensity can be breathtaking.

There was a time when the hill folk forgot their neighbours' surnames, knowing them only by nicknames. When I asked a Belthorner whether any were used now he said, "They were once, but they're all dee-ad now." I am glad I was in time to collect nicknames once in current use: Dolly Mop and Duchess, Cock o' Nicks, Neddy Wapp, Dick o' Pill John's, Cock o' Ned's and U o' Kissers.

I was fortunate to talk twenty years ago with natives in those places with evocative names, Pinnacle Nook, Drummer Stoops, Temple Baron's Fold and Grimehills and Jackamans, before new families arrived on the scene and modern improvements took over. I doubt if any could find life palatable without their central heating, double glazing and a car in the garage! 'Soft,' the natives would call them.

The newcomers are a different breed from the rough, tough types who clung to their hilltop homes four generations ago, and who told tales of characters before them. 'Jemmy for Turton', a fighter ready to challenge any fair day champion, had a trio of sons—Nelson, Wellington and Blucher—all redoubtable pugilists. A neighbour, James o'Temple saw off a son to Liverpool and did not see him again for seven years—he was press-ganged at the port and forced into the navy, but as he refused to take orders was kept a prisoner in the man-o'-war.

During Sough tunnel-making days cockfighting was common near Whittlestone Head, and illicit whisky always available. Up here in lonely places like Deadman's Clough and Cuckoldman's

Rough, gamblers gathered in illegal 'schools', when better men, like Jeremy Hunt of the revealing *Memoirs* of village life of the early nineteenth century, were teaching the illiterate weavers and mill workers of Hoddlesden and Pickup Bank, and by example raising their minds to higher things.

Jeremy, son of handloom weavers, was self-taught. Parents around Pickup Bank paid him £25, raised by a collection among them, to teach their children. All were half-timers in the mills; half came before noon, the others after, and at night their parents battled with the three Rs. At Lower Chapel other adults assembled at eight on Sunday mornings, as eager to learn. Still tireless, Jeremy was off on Sunday afternoons to conduct a singing class at Ebenezer Chapel. And, with unbounded optimism, he raised money in eleven years to build a new chapel at Pickup Bank; his three halfpence weekly, and coppers from the workers—average wages little more than 10s. weekly—made this possible. The site was on common land, and every able-bodied man quarried, carted and shared in the building, which was completed in November 1835.

A man at Jackamans told me how he set his own leg in splints after a fall, preferring Nature to the local doctor. Gazing over his gate at the moors he said, "I reckon nowt o' towns wi' their noise and chatter. This suits me better, nowt but stones and watter."

NEAR CHORLEY

It is obvious, watching the crowds in Chorley's main street and round the stalls in the open 'Flat Iron' market, that folk are not there just for the shopping, but for gossip and meeting friends. It must have been the same when Chorley—though 'a mere village'—held weekly markets and four annual fairs, for the benefit of the neighbourhood communities rather than for its own good.

In 1800 the population of the town and its parish combined was no more than 4,316. But change was on the way, and when it came, increases were rapid and prosperity kept pace. Local weavers of wool and linen cloth left their villages to work in waterside mills by Yarrow, Chor and Lostock. When steam power took the place of water power and cotton had ousted wool and linen, there were no fewer than twenty-six muslin-manufacturers, five spinners, fifty-seven calico-printers and two bleachers, in and around Chorley, ready to employ them. Some had not far to go; every village had one or two 'on their doorsteps'.

"Coal in abundance is found in the parish, the quarry in the declivities of the hills yield excellent flags, ashlar, slate and mill-stone—and the canal passing within half a mile is excellent medium for conveyance of these heavy goods," wrote Baines in 1824, when he estimated the population "could not be less than 9,000".

In fact, the population of the twenty-six parishes within Chorley Union (so grouped for poor relief purposes), 4,316 in 1801, was 13,130 forty years later. Where there was factory, bleach works or print works in a village, its population had doubled: Euxton from 830 to 1,560, Withnell 760 to 1,700, Wheelton 580 to 1,300, Whittle 1,300 to 2,300. Even Croston, way down the Yarrow, had increased from 900 to 1,500.

Within a hundred years, pits abandoned, quarries reverting to Nature—until motorway and by-pass making required their slag, shale and stone. Hardly any village mills remain—some, like Bagganley, White Coppice and Crosse Hall, demolished; others used as warehouses, or for battery hens!

By the 1951 census Chorley town had over 33,000; in the 1971 returns 31,600, a loss which has possibly passed into its rural area—around 27,000 in 1951 now risen to 37,879!

Wheelton was a typical Victorian mill village, everyone working in the factory which, until destroyed by fire, overshadowed the stone houses of Victoria Street. None find work here now, nor at Brinscall over the hill, tucked in a rift below the moors and alongside the Goyt, which channels Liverpool's higher reservoirs at Tockholes into those at Anglezarke and Rivington. The old is rather depressing, the new sprawls in all directions.

Neither has ever become a 'depressed' area—in fact the folk are cheerful, the local council on its toes; but Abbey Village, 'a model' of the 1840s on the Preston–Bolton turnpike—a planned community round a 'family mill' where everyone worked, master and weavers interdependent, mutual respect shown for each other—became the heartbreak village of 1971.

I often heard parents warning of the danger of having every member of the family working for the same master. "When trouble comes," they said, "all are out of work, no money coming in." When news came on the radio, out of the blue, that the mill was to shut down, 240 folk were shattered. It seemed that Abbey Village, "Mill For Sale or To Let. Large Labour Force Available", would have no takers. But after a sad winter, in March 1972 there was a gleam of hope: glass-fibre panel manufacturers decided to take the mill, train a few in new skills and eventually employ "well over 250". But the mill's fate was again in doubt in late 1973.

No fear of a 'ghost' village now. In fact in the 1972–3 winter every one of the terraced houses after 150 years is being completely modernized, with improvement grants; the folk naturally are a little put out by the upheaval, in temporary homes until the conversions are completed. "But in the long run, it'll be worth it."

Considering Lancashire villages are interested in sport, not to have mentioned cricket or football must be thought a serious omission. Almost every community has some field where the local lads kick or bat a ball, but none can equal the verdant oasis backed by toppling moors where folk gather on summer afternoons to watch the White Coppice eleven. The village is no more than a few cottages, well cared for and improved, originally weavers' dwellings when the rushing brook powered two mills. Unless you are a cricket enthusiast with eyes for nothing else, you will leave White Coppice loud in admiration of the gardens, the flowers, the ranked daffodils and tulips of spring, the superb summer rose displays. Every cottager is a dedicated gardener. Where are the sporting types with time for cricket? It is counted such an honour to play for the village that men can be called upon from the surrounding area to make up two elevens.

In 1950, when writing *Lancashire Landscape*, I often talked with Mrs Croasdale, then over ninety and sprightly with it, who spoke of her childhood as if yesterday. She was born in a cottage with a flurry of water against its walls, and at 7 years old started work in the mill, so small she "needed a plank on bricks to reach the loom". Her tales were vivid. Every member of the family worked in the mill. All wore clogs, so every weekday table legs "wore stockings" as protection from kicking feet. Every Saturday night the sanded flagged floors were swept clean, the 'stockings' removed, for Sunday meant shoes, and all to chapel, following granddad in flowered waistcoat and grandma, resplendent in a three-cornered lace shawl and with pansies in her lace-trimmed bonnet.

Twenty years ago this was an old-fashioned place—but lively, for the village school was full, such apple-cheeked youngsters who always insisted on "doing things proper" and brought into the classroom little lambs, piglets and farmyard fowl when acting nursery rhymes or dressing up for concerts. An ancient lady ran the youth club, organized village affairs and "did the cricket teas". The Women's Institute and local groups used the school therefore when it closed down, so did social activities. The children now are carried off by bus to the bright modern school in Brinscall. "No school, no trains, and we never had a 'bus. Not many young folk, it's too quiet for them. Place would die if there weren't new folk coming in. Of course, you've *got* to have a car."

One year Withnell Fold was in the list of villages I was to judge as one of the Best Kept competitors. It was a pleasure. This is a very special place, self-contained, the pride of long-standing land-lords whose paper mill was built on the canal side in the 1840s. The green grass in the squares, the stone-built houses in terraced rows on three sides, their gardens, hedges and sidewalks—all were faultless. So were the school, the institute, the tiny Co-op shop—a pioneer in the movement—the mill approaches and the sports ground, so perfectly cared for I could find no fault in them. Withnell Fold was an eye-opener for any who expected an industrial community to be dark, dirty and depressing. Beauty encompassed the village; in June tree shadows, perfume and flowers, and swans cruising in the still water under the paper mill walls.

Ten years ago its days were numbered. When the end came a complete village was for sale, auctioned and partitioned. Sitting tenants had first option on their homes. Many left to find work. Newcomers came in—and, inevitably, desirable plots on the approach lane have pleasant new modern houses. The fate of the mill is uncertain, but as a residential 'village in a fold' its future is assured.

Next best after bridges over rivers I like leaning over canals. Top Lock Bridge near Lower Wheelton was always a favourite, especially good for meeting oldsters who knew this 'cut' before the First World War. Chancey work, they used to tell me, but good when there was plenty of freight—mostly coal, before horses had been driven off by motor-driven barges. Then stables on the tow path were full every night, and horses were grazing in the crofts ready to take over. Two men were kept busy day and night working the lock gates, and queues of boats waited below the Johnson Hillocks' seven staircase locks at busy times.

The top Lock-keeper remembered his father, "stepping on a barge here at his own front door, down to Liverpool, and on a big boat for America without setting foot on dry land". I would like to watch his reactions now, at changes to Top Lock. The British Waterways have provided a comfort station here, and the toll keeper doles out fresh water by the pailful to those who tie up nearby. "It's all for pleasure now. Nowt wrong wi' that, but it were a lot nicer wi' horses." I stood by a native, looking on scores of gay craft, multi-coloured, and reflected—as a bonus—in blue water; a gay, happy sight. A very enthusiastic boat club with 240 members is responsible for this marina, undertaking the upkeep of this very pleasant length of the canal. They organize popular events, boat trips, dinghy races, skin diving, and happy families set out for gentle voyaging on peaceful waters.

Down 'Copster Brew', below the canal bridge, transformation is taking over Lower Copthurst, a pretty collection of cottages by the hump-backed bridge of the little Lostock river. A century ago the hollow was thronged with print and bleach works, local coal pits too, every cottager a worker, and more than one cottage a beershop. House hunters have discovered it. Conversion is at work!

I doubt if any of the new folk know what made the old Copster tick. From their new doors they step into cars, and away. Their predecessors trudged up the brow, laden with bolts of cloth of their own weaving, and, because safety was in numbers, joined forces with others, all bound to Chorley market. Any who returned alone were at the mercy of footpads, who lurked at the crossroads on Huggart Brew. The broad motorway cuts through the hill now but has not obliterated the Robbers Graves. Tradition has it that men caught cloth stealing or waylaying 'with intent', were hanged just here, and stakes of quick-thorn hammered into each heart to prevent their evil spirits walking. "And each stake struck—a row of twisted thorns!"

Turn towards Brindle and you come to a hamlet, two rows of quarrymen's cottages sturdily built from the delphs just behind them; many have unusual design in mullioned windows. Plans are in the pipe-line to make Denham Hill with its superb views and exhilarating breezes, and a worked-out quarry designed for the purpose, into a country leisure park.

But what changes face Brindle village—a community with vitality, community spirit and a recorded history which goes back eight hundred years? That tall perpendicular church tower, landmark and focal point, has seen history flow by. They say Roundhead snipers picked off Cavaliers riding by, firing from the battlements, and men reported movements of Parliamentary armies massing to march and intercept King Charles II's army in August 1651. Church, vicarage among trees, the inn, the village school down the lane, old white-walled cottages which are one with the place, and a few new houses which are not yet, make this a village complete and with few flaws. How long can it remain so?

The sand delphs seem to be exceeding their bounds and throwing up ugly prison-like fences on the approach to Brindle. This could be nothing compared with plans to develop, for housing and industry, 400 acres between the M6, M61 and the Brindle–Clayton Green crossroads—this first site, a pool of houses needed for the key workers for pioneer construction engineers of the Central Lancashire New Town. Just 'a starter' they say! Protests and public meetings are planned, residents perturbed.

RIVINGTON VILLAGE

In the 1860s Rivington was centre of an uproar, concerning Liverpool's water-gathering grounds: Pikists v. Anti-Pikists. The Pikists won, whereupon gangs of labourers moved as an army towards Anglezarke, upon Rivington, their aim to drown a quiet valley and change the age-long pattern of living.

Andertonford's farms and halls, the cattle grazing of the upland 'airdh' of Anglezarke and much of Rivington below church and grammar school were submerged; Liverpool took the village in hand as new landlord, improved, rebuilt, put everything in its place, walled in and fenced so efficiently it might have strayed into a public park. It remains a true village community nevertheless.

The Pilkingtons of the hall had long departed. One built the church; Bishop Pilkington founded the grammar school in 1568— with a very detailed code of conduct for the boys, no street brawls, haunting of ale-houses or brandishing of daggers in school! Gone too the Levers, Breres and Andrews who acquired the Pilkington lands when financial troubles forced them out. Mr Andrews was highly delighted with his surroundings and urged his guests to the hazardous ascent of the Pike, coaxing them upwards with promise of splendid prospects from his new Tower and refreshments provided. Erected in 1724, this landmark and goal for thousands has with difficulty survived the assaults of modern vandals and, of course, the slogan daubers. Once the only landmark, it now shares the skyline with the towering I.T.V. mast and radio controls.

Having so many outdoor attractions, the Pike is well visited. It is the motor cycle scramblers' venue; and the archaeologists'. The exciting grounds of The Bungalow, built by Lord Leverhulme a Boltonian who loved the place, almost reverted to Nature in the last decade but were the more fascinating for that. The extensive acres of Lever Park were a gift of the wealthy soap magnate who set skilful masons to reconstruct from plans a replica of Liverpool Castle on the lake edge. Naturally crowds converge on summer weekends, and young outdoor lovers all the year round.

Quite naturally this has been looked at carefully during Environmental Improvement Year by Bolton Corporation. In principle a plan to make of it a 260-acre country park has been approved and work is afoot. It has been a leisure park, unofficially, for over three generations: "just ready-made for the job" folk say. The villagers say they are 'worried already' by too many visitors from towns too near! Fortunately many who come are quiet appreciative folk who enjoy the green peace, midweek, midwinter, the type who enjoy pottering in the churchyard, reading the stones in the Unitarian chapel graveyard and just wandering around.

The active vicar keeps in the stableyard a minibus, to bring to church those of his widely scattered congregation who could not otherwise come. He helped me decipher the curious symbolic stones in the churchyard, subject for controversy. Were they from a drowned Pre-Reformation chapel called Lady Hill, hospice of a crusading order? The stones not only show badges of local Andertons, their 'bolts' the legs of Man of the Stanleys, but also some very odd marks of Crusading orders. Once a Black Boy Inn was standing below the church bank; was it originally the 'Saracen's Head'?

Ghosts and hauntings! A ghostly horseman rides a long-eroded lane now within the vicarage garden; nothing but his head floating through the air, his ghostly body and spectre horse hidden by the non-existent sunken way! Was another searching ghostly apparition a Lady Hill priest who forgot where he hid his chapel's silver and gold altar vessels from Thomas Cromwell's despoilers?

Today many are non-productive, but villagers a century ago were yeoman families of farming stock, or quarrymen, or miners in the moor top coal pits, or the lead and barytes miners below Anglezarke moor. Some of their names are on tombstones.

Talking of memorials, the most impressive is Lord Willoughby's of Parham, local landowner and sometimes benefactor. It dwarfs all else in the Unitarian chapel—this is a little gem, outstandingly beautiful compared with many Non-conformist chapels. The Willoughbys traced their descent through the Plantagenet kings, the Angevins, back to the Conqueror and Emperor Charlemagne, and to Edgar, King of the English.

Relics from Rivington's past? Two ancient cruck barns with old timbers several times enclosed by newer walls. Great Hall Barn is the local 'fun place', for dances, parties. The adjacent hall is eighteenth-century with a bit of sixteenth in the rear. The grammar school scholars now share with Blackrod's the new buildings nearer Horwich, only the young attending the old school. The old tethering post remains, relic of days when children arrived on horseback. On the green, not far from the two-seater stocks, a stone trough is filled with clear pure Liverpool water—nothing stronger on tap in the village!

Local names are evocative. Two Lads on Winter Hill and Scotchman's Stump near the I.T.A. mast—scene of an unsolved murder in 1838—Pike Stones, Danes Dike and Edgar Hill, Round Loaf, Standing Stones Hill and Devil's Dyke. There is a secret hollow in Noon Hill where local Non-conformists gathered to worship in the 1660s. Down below, the farm where Moses Cocker, inventor of a flying machine, intended to take off from the Pike but, discouraged by friends, instead leapt from his barn roof and made a safe landing in the muck midden!

AROUND BOLTON—VILLAGES ONCE INDUSTRIAL

"Bolton upon Moor standeth by cottons and coarse yarn; divers villages in the moors about Bolton do make cottons," wrote Leland in 1540. Also, "fairs and markets held at the ville of Bolton are for the amusement and good fellowship of the neighbouring people, a holiday sort of folk". Town and country long inter-dependent, their trade, industry and well-being linked? The moors, "waste, uncultivated, without roads or thinly inhabited, with morasses, destructive to mortals", surrounded the town and allowed the countryfolk to eke out but a meagre living, subject to their manorial lords.

The change came in the 1790s, when 250 acres of this waste-land and moorish ground were enclosed at the town edge, bringing small folds and hamlets within the expanding town.

In 1800 demand on land within Bolton was so great values rocketed, forcing the town's bleachers of cloth, the 'whitesters', to look elsewhere for their needs. Thefts were so common from the town 'crofts', they were eager to move out; so came an exodus to places like Wallsuches, Belmont, Egerton—wherever there was a pure-water supply, extensive open spaces for their bleaching, and land at a fraction of the cost.

By 1800 hardly any of the old landowning gentry remained to oppose change. New owners, of the manufacturing class, took over land, houses and village labour. Opulent bleachers and manu-facturers like the Ainsworths had replaced the ancient families of The Smithills, Kays were to occupy Turton Tower, Ashworths were to be the big name at Eagley, and Deakins at Belmont—and Egerton, Thomassons and Horrocks, the last to become a name of world-wide fame, at Turton and Edgworth, Ridgways at Horwich. New families made their fortunes in the villages. Small communities, no more than minor townships in Bolton parish, grew steadily between 1801 and 1821.

Everything necessary for manufacturing was found around Bolton, from Blackrod and Horwich over the moors to Sharples, Belmont and Longworth, Egerton and Eagley, from Entwistle, Edgworth and Turton to Bradshaw, Harwood and Walmsley—copious supplies of soft water, lime-free from the peaty heights, unlimited quarries for building material, coal pits scattered across the region, the native skill of the country people. There was also the considerable business acumen of local chapmen—merchants—for generations suppliers of raw material to the cottages—who had traded in the markets of Manchester, Bolton, Blackburn, where Lancashire's yarn and cloth was the chief commodity from the late seventeenth century.

In the late twentieth century—what changes? Of these villages how many are now mill villages, working communities? Very few have any industry at all; mills are turned to other uses or demolished, coalpits closed down, and model villages like Barrow Bridge and Eagley, purpose-built by early industrialists, no longer house workers with work on their doorsteps. The older villages—especially those north of Bolton, in the moors—are set to become pleasant residential areas, for those who work elsewhere; and where they are in open country their amenity value is to be shared by others less happily placed.

In 1972–3 environmental improvement is taking hold, a wide swathe of country leisure parks envisaged—and some partly completed, from Rivington to Darwen moors, and within the Bolton area a large expanse between Bromley Cross, Turton Bottoms, and the Jumbles, where work is well advanced around a new 'lakeland'. Not only these 'pockets', and smaller areas between them, newly landscaped and about to be planted with thousands of trees—the Men of the Trees interested and helpful and donors of twenty native types—but surviving historic and 'traditional' local buildings around Chapeltown-alias-Turton, have led to this being designated as a conservation area.

The townsfolk who have chosen to leave Bolton to "share in the smile of earth and sky"—boosting the urban district of Turton by 2,000 in the last decade—must be prepared to allow those remaining in the towns to share the restored green landscape too. The 75 per cent government grant for 1972–June 1973 to remove and improve eyesores is to benefit *all*. I have always found country folk happy to share their advantages with visiting townsfolk—until vandals struck, or cars at weekends crammed their lanes and took over village greens. Live and let live, share and share alike, are mottoes less appreciated by newcomers playing at being villagers, and afraid of invasion of the privacy they believed they had bought with a house in the country.

If the splendid plans take shape and all pipe dreams materialize, what a cheerful world the villagers will share with all comers; especially in outdoor sports, for centuries a speciality. They have followed the Holcombe Harriers for over three centuries. On the moors north of The Smithills and Belmont, in the days of Hultons, Radcliffes and Bartons, they heard the sound of the horn in rocky ravine and along high 'scout', from Tiger's Clough to Longworth.

A Sharples of Sharples saved a Barton within an inch of death one hunting day and claimed thereafter a yearly gift of a gilt spur and six days' freedom of Smithhills' wine cellars "to drink their fill and be merry" each year.

Those were the days, when deer still roamed the moors from Winter Hill to Holcombe, where wild boar had been common and Plantagenet kings had been supplied by Horwich foresters with young falcons for the royal mews. This was the wild landscape, "all precipices and crags", which made early travellers recoil. It bred a rough breed of men, who worked hard, played tough, were addicted to clog fighting or 'purring'—often lethal and made illegal—and indulged in gang fighting—which gave Turton Fair a bad name. They enjoyed cock fighting, dog fights and blood sports round rat pits in lonely places round Edgworth well into the last century.

Future plans includes fewer bloodthirsty sports. There is nothing pleasanter than blue sailing days at Delph or on Belmont reservoirs, yachts skimming on bright water, or quiet afternoons with anglers quietly meditating around the Dunscar and Eagley lodges, or a cricket match on Egerton's immaculate sports field. Almost every sport, indoor and out, has its place in village life. What they have the local sports councils intend to hold; to fight, if need be, building threats against Eagley's highly valued works' recreation and sports ground—65 valuable acres long devoted to football, hockey, cricket, tennis and the fishing, provided for their work-people by enlightened mill-owners. The local golf courses covet enviable acres to be protected against development.

Soon the sports council hopes every known outdoor activity can be enjoyed. Clay pigeon shooting (in the Lancashire tradition, a Lancashire 'vet' in Garstang won the Mexican Olympic gold medal) takes place on the moors near the Toby Jug. 'Peggy', another local game, was revived at Turton in 1972. Only target archery and canoeing are lacking, and these are to be catered for in the new country park.

All this shows how the wheel has turned. With a final twist in 1974! Most fierce protest against the new pattern of local government has come from residents in pleasant rural or semi-rural areas threatened by take-overs by large towns. Parts of Cheshire and Merseyside Lancashire cringed at the thought of their villages and parishes being included in Greater Manchester or Greater Liverpool. Ulverston and villages thereabouts are horrified at any connection with industrial Barrow of the grimy image. My own part of the Blackburn rural area chose to turn from the new county district of Blackburn towards the new Ribble Valley Authority and a future combined with Clitheroe, Hodder and Bowland—a pleasanter prospect, a brighter image! The countryside, their land of heart's desire!

Turton Urban District, comprising many 'true' villages as well as outgrown villages, and having celebrated its council's centenary in 1973, has been victim of an extraordinary carve-up, a Solomon-like decision to cut the area in two.

South Turton nearest to Bolton has naturally lost more of its rural character. Bradshaw, Harwood, Eagley and Egerton, fastly growing residential areas with over 18,000 people, take a revenue of three-quarters of a million pounds into Bolton. North Turton, comprising the smaller part of its about-to-be-dismembered body— Belmont, Chapeltown (alias Turton village), Edgworth with Entwistle which have kept their rural individuality, with a population of 4,000 passes as a rural unit to Blackburn. The only links— the up-and-downhill ridge road the Romans defined in A.D. 79 and the Blackburn–Bolton railway line with 'ghost stations' and a skeleton service of trains which only stop because the folk of Edgworth and Entwistle have fought strenuously to keep them. The main road over Bull Hill is well away from each of the North Turton villages, Belmont as 'detached' being on the direct Bolton– Preston highway. Organization from Blackburn will be remote control—far, far away, after years of local government from Turton Tower and the Bromley Cross office.

Community spirit has been stronger in the Turton villages than anywhere I know. The future will be interesting. Such strong identity cannot be destroyed easily.

Now for a brief survey of the villages—as they began, as they are.

SITES OF EARLY INDUSTRY NORTH OF BOLTON

When Leland wrote in Tudor times, "Bolton burnt sum canel but more se cole of wich the pittes be not far off. They burne turfe also," he referred to places like Horwich and Blackrod. Peat is still cut from the mosses between them and stacked as in Ireland. Coal pits are numerous; the small, privately-owned

Mountain Pit in upper Horwich till recently produced a fair coal, but Blackrod, from which 1,000 colliers laboured in local pits until 1939 and around which acres of open-cast coal were excavated during the war, has turned from mining. Seams of coal underlie that long dark hill alongside the A6, which looks so dramatic at sunset, church tower, the rooflines of its long street—which follows prehistoric track and Roman road—silhouetted against the west. Coal Lane, and White Hall Lane dubbed 'Coal Street', for it was the miners' way to the pits; Black Row and 'Scotland' have flooded mines beneath them.

Beginning as a village, Blackrod became an important stop for travellers in medieval times and later for Manchester merchants, who came weekly to the 'Leigh Arms' (now demolished) to dole out yarn to the local weavers. An old man listed for me numerous other inns—Church Inn and 'Ringers Arms', 'Travellers Rest', 'Royal Oak', 'Red Lion', 'Victoria', 'Shoulder of Mutton', 'Horse-shoe' and New Inn, 'Cock Tavern', 'Beehive'—and these not all! But the 'Leigh Arms' was the chief hostelry, with stabling for twenty horses, pack horses and coaches drawing up at the door. The old mounting block is useful to rest shopping baskets nowadays, as women gossip with friends.

Local pride in Blackrod showed itself in John Holme's founding of a grammar school, not to be outdone by Bishop Pilkington's at Rivington in Tudor times. Now the two are combined in newer buildings. Blackrod U.D.C. occupies the eighteenth-century school in a quiet courtyard off the main street—very dignified.

A most historic community is this, but much of the old is demolished, the light has been let in, and cheerful folk live in the many new houses, sanguine people with far prospects from their front doors. They would not live anywhere else, they say.

Blackrod and Horwich looked up in the 1790s when the brothers Ridgway left Bolton, where they had problems in their bleaching grounds, seeking new pastures. They pushed a cart past the 'Blundell Arms' towards Horwich, where the wheel fell off, and "where it comes to rest there will we buy land," said they. A tradition? So was Wallsuches 'born', a pocket of industry, where new bleaching methods were used, a 10-horse-power Watt's engine installed and cottages built for the crofters' families. The several buildings needed for the bleaching processes are now used for warehouses, stores, light industry. The green slopes where

Ridgway fattened prime beef cattle—slaughtered at their own Shambles, the meat sold to their considerable labour force drawn from Blackrod and Horwich as well as Wallsuches—are still as green and lush. The cottages overlook the pleasant valley, the dreaming lakes and over to Ridgmont Park, where the Ridgways once lived, kept hounds and surveyed all that was theirs. They started a school at Horwich for young workers, half-timers, they opened a truck shop so that their employees could have good bread, good food. At Blackrod the colliers brought out coal for their use from Ridgway pits. Pioneers in their time, enlightened employers. Some old folk remember the last days of the bleach-works, but their numbers dwindle.

Wallsuches never grew into a complete village, but shared church, chapel and school with Horwich, which expanded into a small town with the coming of industry and work in the railway engine sheds.

Its neighbour beyond the intervening moors is Belmont, a true village, also concerned with bleaching. Bleaching, dyeing, printing were important processes around Bolton. Lancashire cloth had to be sent to Holland for bleaching in the eighteenth century, or was bleached locally by painfully slow crofting or 'grassing' methods, as at Horrocks Fold in Belmont. Here is still to be seen the old bleach house, a culvert channelling soft water, and a long croft, where sunlight—a rare commodity on these often mist-shrouded moorlands—was a slow whitening agent.

At the end of the century, urged to experiment when output of cloth now increased a hundredfold, a French scientist, Vallette, tried out new methods at Bolton. They succeeded, three weeks of laborious work at last reduced to one hour! No need for Dutch bleaching now. In 1820 twenty-six steam-powered engines were bleaching six million pieces a year, in and around Bolton. Then Belmont grew rapidly and the wild bare landscape was changed into a new 'land of lakes' as at Wallsuches—all printing, bleaching and dye works impounded water in necessary reservoirs. Now that all is over—come and gone the bleachers from Sharples, Longworth, Egerton and Eagley also—the blue pools are frequented only by anglers, or yachtsmen and sailing clubs—and possibly in the future, water-skiers? On quiet days swans cruise unconcerned.

Belmont was astride the old road to Bolton, turnpiked in the early 1800s when it was no more than a few farms and cottages.

In the 1840s, the bleach works, printworks, and weaving mill working full out, Belmont (included within Sharples) was bursting at the seams, 1,000 villagers crammed into the small houses, several families to each dwelling, as we have found recorded at Dolphinholme and Helmshore. Fire closing the cotton mill in 1867 'killed' the print works also, until new owners, the Deakins, restored life to Belmont a few years later—another case of a textile community's dependence on the manufacturer-mill-owner. Hereabouts were many good humane employers.

Egerton across the clough, along the parallel highroad, Darwen to Bolton, gave its name to a Cromwellian family destined to become great, but their hall was demolished and the site used by Mr Novelli of Manchester for his new French-style mansion. The village with its roadside inns—the 'King Billy', 'Cross Guns' and 'Globe'—is made up of long rows of stone-built cottages, designed for workers in the local mills and many now 'converted' very satisfactorily. All is extremely pleasant though much grown.

Novelli started a large cotton mill, whilst the Ashworths in 1840 built a mill in the clough to the west, with a long sough and a 60-foot wheel. Once silk spinning was intended and mulberry trees planted. Now industry has departed, so have the old families, their mansions adapted to other uses—an old people's home, a licensed hotel—and their extensive grounds now developed, many large modern houses among tall trees.

At Belmont and Egerton the 'new' villagers feel they share the benefits of town and country and there is general satisfaction, a buoyancy in the air.

But Eagley? It is not long since Eagley at a stroke died a sudden death. On 23rd June 1972 the 4.30 Friday whistle sounded for the last time, a final gesture ending a long tradition. All who knew the village are saddened.

Eagley Mill began work in 1799 and the new village was part of the set-up. Here was a family mill, where all, from the owners, the manager to the youngest worker, worked in harmony. Everything was designed for community well-being. Pleasantly situated too, in a deep hollow by a brook, handsome buildings by a sweeping road, well-built dwellings—trees and birdsong. From the open windows after working hours came music from a water-powered organ; brass band music also. There was "something for everyone", good life for all the village: social clubs, sports of all

L

kinds, a recreation centre—and good working conditions under some of the 'best bosses in t'world'. The end was sudden, unexpected.

There was no reprieve; closure was final. But Eagley workers, who had always prided themselves on their adaptibility, found they were wanted by other employers. "If a man can work at Eagley, he's good enough to work anywhere." Many of the redundant have gone to other jobs. The old stay on. And everyone wonders what the future holds. Maybe it will contine like Barrow Bridge, highly commended by Prince Albert during a royal visit, today without mills but sought after because it is a pleasant place to live.

Barrow Bridge was a model village of the 1850s, on the New Lanark plan, where the owners chose a beauty spot for their mills and reservoirs; very beautiful these are, especially in daffodil time and in autumn, with lawns of modern houses reaching to the water edge. They provided a school, an institute for leisure hours and lectures, a common laundry, a communal bakehouse. They sited their workers' homes on terraced slopes from brook side to high level, with good effect. It has given pleasure to Boltonians for generations. The future? The village wholly conserved, the old laundry—a museum.

Life in such places, as Cooke-Taylor wrote to the Bishop of Dublin in 1834, was totally unlike that in industrial Manchester, where too often homes were slums and the workers degraded. Here, around Turton and Egerton, Eagley and Belmont, the operatives were well situated, the master known to each; there was mutual dependence and interest. The gardens and paths around the mills and mill lodges, at Dunscar too, they were free to enjoy—not debarred as in the town. These are included among amenities of a proposed country leisure park. After years of disuse mill ponds, sluices and streams are the botanist's paradise, known to Bolton's keen field naturalists.

Cooke-Taylor came to Turton as guest of a prosperous manufacturer at The Oaks. He met a nonagenarian who had woven 'cottons' when weft was woollen, and who had been "put to work as soon as he could crawl". He found cottagers in the many folds still spinning and weaving for local merchants, and listened to their fears of the powerful steam engines, the end of home industry. Leaving Turton he wrote, "I never felt air more balmy than when I left this morning." In the train his fellow passengers were two lads "full of life and spirits" and a manufacturer who "could not resist the smile of earth and sky but laughed as merrily as if he had been a denizen of the Garden of Epicurus".

A pleasant picture of Old Turton! Chapeltown, Edgworth and Entwistle have plenty of lively and high-spirited folk today. When I phone friends and there is no reply, I know they are out walking, gone blackberrying, cutting bulrushes for decoration or at a W.I. meeting, helping with Meals on Wheels or an old people's luncheon club, doing a count of local trees, gathering material to be used in a new local history, at a Civic Trust meeting or discussing how best to compete and win again the Best Kept Village trophy.

Their success in 1971 was the result of tremendous local effort: the young men, youth club and scouts cleaned up grave-yards and unsightly waste places, the able and willing shared painting and decorating of old folk's homes. The gardenless houses were provided with window boxes, darkened walls were cleaned.

In 1973 there is an added feeling of urgency, so much to do before centenary celebrations and 1974 dismembering. A pity ancient units with a shared history cannot enter the future united.

WEST OF WIGAN

Of course Billinge is a village, all insist, surprised at any doubt. It was a settlement of Bill the sword wielder's folk in the seventh century, coupled with Winstanley, Ulstan's leah and coeval, and Birchley's dwellings by the mosses and now rapidly joining up. Yet Billinge feels separate, as any true self-respecting village should.

I remember it as quite detached, and the impact of the hill-top church against a stormy sky, the old 'Stork', a coaching inn, permanent on bedrock, close-linked Georgian houses by the road-side. All charming, one with mullioned windows, dated 1674, nodding at a tall house, dated 1740, with lowly stone cottages clutching at its skirts, along the highway steeply downhill. The number of inns was surprising, until one realized the road's importance and how convenient the 'Labour in Vain', the 'Odd-fellows', the 'Stag' and the 'Stork' for travellers' halts, and for local stonehewers, coal-miners and nailmakers.

The first man I talked to the other day I recognized as a miner, crouching on his haunches—a most comfortable posture they tell me—waiting for the bus, rod and Mawdsley-made basket at his side. Keen anglers every one, and numerous mining flashes within reach, promising good sport with coarse fish, roach and bream. He wore a leaping fish, the Stag Club Angling Association badge. "Don't fish flash out, Bill," admonished a crony cheerily as he passed.

Billingers, as villagers ought, always have time for a crack and talk easily to all and sundry. Like their village they have character. What is being done in the name of progress they view with resignation. "It's the penalty of being on a main road. Widening, widening, tekking off corners so traffic can go through twice as quick." Irate drivers queued up as bulldozers turned round to charge once more into old houses, leaving one more gap choked with crushed rubble. "And that's another stone house they've tumbled as shouldn't have bin!"

Away from the din I fell into step with other Billingers. One talked of local pits, good house coal once got from each, but now only one left; and a clay pit. No nailmakers either. Rows of cottage workships were knocked down near Birchley, where craftsmen hammered out square, pyramid-shaped heads, and produced iron work used by Liverpool merchants to barter for slaves on the African coast. I remembered the nailmakers of Atherton not so far away, who one November hammered tools into bills then marched behind their redoubtable minister from 'Chowbent' to Preston to defend their country from the Jacobite highlanders of the '15 rising.

One talked of multi-coloured stone quarried on Billinge Beacon and how recent excavation had threatened to spoil the contours of this their local landmark. Cromwell, they say, "fired his cannons from here to Upholland church". People claim theirs is the best place for viewing the coloured landscape of the west, and North Wales. They cried 'stop' to the desecration, stage a 'demo' and marched with banners, "Save Billinge Beacon." The quarryowners promised to restore the contours by infilling and to hide scars by tree planting.

Billingers have long memories. A 'pensioner' talked of a dean, Father Powell, who had built for the poor some cottages I was admiring. They stood so pleasantly above long dewy wet gardens, reddened with windfall apples; a robin vigorously attempted to beat the traffic noises. "He died a poor man. Every Friday he'd watch poor folk coming wi' their baskets to the butcher's cart. When they'd chosen their bit of meat he'd say, 'I'll pay for that'. He died over sixty years ago—and folk still remember!"

He bought a neglected Tudor hall, encouraging the occupants in restoration. Birchley Hall was a secret 'mass house' in penal times, where Roger Anderton set up illegal papist printing presses. Mr Bernard Wood who lives here now is also a printer of books. His wife showed me the historic wing with secret hides for travelling priests. One was a narrow squeeze hidden in the schoolroom wall's thickness next to a secret escape contrived within the granary, a chimney breast offering a getaway into nearby woods and the corn mill.

Papists came to the hall quietly to avoid suspicion. Now they arrive openly. The combined efforts of the Woods family, scraping off old plaster and doing remedial work, cleaning and decorating, completed the restoration of the old granary in time for the chapel's three-hundred-and-fiftieth anniversary as a place of Roman Catholic worship. The beautiful pillared reredos, painted white, has flanking curtains of gold; a moveable altar is placed before it. Paid towards the cost was £100 'fishing money' contributed by local anglers using the hall pond!

In these parts we recognize 'character' but do not expect charm. But it is there. From a friend's bedroom window filled with sky I looked over a gentle swelling landscape, cornfields, grassland, rising in smooth lines from Moss Bank to the woods of Windle. A footpath runs along back-garden fences, and it must proceed, untouched, for "it was there in the Domesday Book".

Upholland, reached by way of Winstanley and Orrell, equally changed by roadworks and the country gashed by the M6, is also a village full of surprises. Where now the charm and the strong character it once possessed, in a fine sweep up to its church and Alma Hill, and in a plenitude of ancient houses perfectly in harmony? Too little remains. I cannot see what Upholland has gained in demolitions of the last twenty years. Its historic quality was worth keeping.

Every year Wigan seems nearer; and as for 'Skem', where is it going to end? The top road gets busier every day. I have enjoyed walking on windy days, up beyond the windmill along the ridge way to Ashhurst Hall and the Beacon. What a view! In 1670 Roger Lowe wrote: "As we were going we looked up and down, stood on a hill and saw the land round about. It is the pleasantest place that ever I saw, a most gallant prospect. . . . We got wimberry."

New houses—of raw red brick—outnumber old stone buildings, growing naturally it seems from the hillside; raw red goes ill with darkened walls, especially in this hill country of excellent building stone.

Old Upholland *can* be found—There is a high wall hiding the Conservative Club car park and behind is Priory House and a fragment of masonry heavily mantled in creepers—all that is left of the priory dorter. The massive church tower was scaffolded, when last I was there, prior to strengthening.

Upholland is proud of its parish church, and rightly so. Early in the fourteenth century the Benedictines built their priory here, the present church their chapel. Much of its beauty is intact—the delicate soaring nave arcade pillars—but the hall of the Hollands has gone. Good Sir Robert, the close friend of Thomas, Earl of Lancaster, annually fed the poor on St Thomas the Martyr's Day; and at Christmas too, 240 were bidden to the feast, whilst the overflow were given doles of meal. In the same vanished hall, Edward II held court in the fateful years which saw the overthrow of Earl Thomas and the Hollands. History wiped out!

Upholland ought to live up to its history; its site is equal to it and modern buildings could be in keeping. Special places like Upholland need special treatment, and watchful care.

The old street abuts against the churchyard, full to bursting after centuries of burials. Backing into it is the old court house, where Lovells, then Stanleys who received the Lordship from Henry VII, did manorial business, the Legs of Man on a stone shield at the back, and the 'Brid and Babby' at the front; not so good as I remembered it, now converted into a private house with modern windows out of keeping. Neither have demolitions adjoining the Owl Inn improved the high street, a gap as obvious as a front tooth missing, where it shows most; for a car park, of course! Another case of the oldest inn in the narrowest street with most traffic congestion destroying old cottages to find space for patrons' cars.

Upholland folk need no prompting to tell of their native Robin

Hood-type robber. George Lyon stole from 'haves' and gave to the 'have nots'. The bread he was carrying away from the Owl Inn when arrested was probably for some hungry old soul! Perhaps she was waiting in one of the aged cottage doors opening on the main highway, or in a humble dwelling through the archway by the old grammar school (derelict).

Miss Weeton's *Journal of a Governess* is a good and lively true-story book reviving the 1800s in Upholland. From her window— she lived in a "pretty white house" facing the church tower—all prospects were "pleasing, romantic and beautiful". She watched "children disporting themselves in the churchyard in harmless frolic, people gathered in small groups before their doors enjoying the serenity of the evening".

Talking of what? Of hauntings and apparitions, nightly ghostly visitations to Mill House when the wheel was set a-going and the spinning wheels spinning and every bit of furniture, even the firetongs, danced to the merry din? Or of imminent catastrophies, as in the autumn of 1807? As the hunter's moon rose over Upholland that year everyone wondered, would it be their last? Rumour had spread like wildfire. A mermaid had told the captain of an American ship which docked in Liverpool that all within 20 miles would be swallowed up by an earthquake. But 29th October came and went—and Upholland and all south-west Lancashire still stood where it was!

BETWEEN DOUGLAS AND YARROW

Upholland, like Billinge and all villages on hill ridges where the oldest roads ran, well away from the mosses, was an early starter, whereas lowland communities were small and well scattered. The River Douglas—Celtic 'dark river'—which "creepeth and stealeth along quietly" between Wigan and the Ribble, was of little importance until mine-owners, looking around for cheaper means of transport, saw that it could be canalized. The river was deepened, horse-drawn barges moved along to the estuary and the sea; stopping places with provision for men and horses punctuated the slow miles. Later, when James Brindley was planning, and John Gilbert carrying out, canal schemes, the Douglas Navigation was engineered, "increasing materially the prosperity of all towns and villages lying near its banks".

Dalton and Newburgh were already 'on the map'; Parbold, Shevington and Wrightington too. Water transport brought into being new villages like Appley Bridge, tight-packed around its mills and warehouses.

The history of industrial Lancashire was here in the making. Out towards the Ribble went heavy-laden coal barges to supply coastal communities and towns with cheap fuel. Inwards came lime, bricks from Tarleton, slates from Wales and north Lancashire, for the new houses of spreading towns. Corn came from the Fylde and west Lancashire, where windmills turned merrily and the grain markets reaped rich harvests, financially, as never before. Now—the effect of the canal is negligible.

The old high-level communities grew at a slower pace. Until the people of Wigan, outward-looking, decided to live in nice new houses on those sunny slopes beneath blue skies, where larks carol over the golden corn and bees hum among the heather. Near the new are pockets of older buildings; in green fields stand interesting old farms. I have had pleasant surprises expecting little, charmed and delighted at the bygone rurality at Roby, an adorable up-and-down place one hopes will never allow itself to be over-'improved'.

At Tunley was founded one of the very oldest Congregational churches of Charles II's reign, this beautiful building and the nearby farm making a small pool of quiet off the beaten track.

On High Moor and Harrock Hill I chance upon many authentic pockets of the past, still rural. Newcomers enamoured of this countryside, walk these windy hills to take the air and watch the sensational sunsets. Some are more addicted to country walks than the natives.

MAWDESLEY, ECCLESTON AND EUXTON

Mawdesley, a most complete village although scattered over many acres, gathers up its population from many winding and haphazard lanes. The only cohesion is modern: much gap-filling by assorted styles of houses and bungalows between the beetle-browed thatched cottages and white-walled dwellings, left-overs from the eighteenth century.

I can excuse Mawdesley almost everything for, in spite of its changing population—the newcomers all willing to merge with the native—it retains old manners and loyalties and welcomes innovations. The women are the prime movers, I think. What a thriving W.I.! At my last visit I watched lucrative business in sale of 'good as new' garments and a very sensible turnover in good but outgrown children's wear. Sensible people, and also fond of a measure of culture. That month drama was the thing, two home-produced plays written by a member, one introducing a local ghostly happening, playing to full houses for a full week in the hall—authentic staging for the spectre once walked here.

Mawdesley's hall—the pre-Tudor central part half timbered, its flanking eighteenth-century wings, one of native stone, one of hand-made brick—was there on its red rock when the village took shape. The Mawdesley family dwelt here, and later the Nelsons, a link with a tradition that "Nelson billeted his men here"; *a* Nelson, not Horatio.

The highly successful play resurrected the local ghost who walked where the audience actually sat, her wonted beat being, so they say, from inn to hall. Or has time confused the old lady's ghost and the bottle spirit once kept at Hell Hob Inn? The troublesome apparition after the rites of exorcism was imprisoned in a bottle and hurled into a nearby pit. For a money-raising gimmick the landlord, "a majestic man with a wibble-wabble in his gait", discovered the bottle and allowed his gullible customers to handle it for small 'consideration'.

The inn has improved its appearance in the last decade, new patrons doubtless knowing it by its name 'Black Bull'. The old still prefer to call it 'Hell Hob'. A giant poker, 16 pounds weight, is probably like the original one of the sixteenth century, when the fireplace was in a wide inglenook "and needed a poker big enough to stoke the fires of Hell". This was Hell Hob? Or was the inn name 'Hill in Mawdesley'; or more like 'Hell in Mawdesley' when drink and the Devil set men at each other, struggling to wield the poker—no mean feat—and creating such an uproar the villagers believed all Hell was let loose. Each Sunday morning "the landlord picked up a bucket full of noses and ears". No one in his right senses—and Mawdesley folk have their heads screwed on the right way—would have these wild times return. Nor that the bad old days should be repeated when local papists were forced to worship in secret places—as in Lane End House at the Black Moor end of the village—and priests in hiding crouched in the attic. John Finch was a local martyr, and another John Rigby, Gentleman of the ancient Hall of Harrock.

There have always been Finches at Lane End, an imposing roadside farmhouse so clad in creepers they appear to hold the fabric together, a handsome eighteenth-century building of old warm-tinted brick, a spacious yard behind enclosed by capacious outbuildings.

At my first visit—when writing *Lancashire Landscapes* in 1950— they used pump water and rainwater collected in huge cisterns in the roof. Within the roof, and lit by the greenish glass of low dormers, was the chapel—small, dim; beneath the altar, a glass case holding the 'martyr's skull': Other ancient relics of value were here too: a fine silvered pre-Reformation cross and a wooden box, the library of Cuthbert Haydock who was first priest to serve the local papists. And now—restoration of the best kind, the once-shabby attic a beautiful little chapel.

Exactly a century ago Hewitson, cocking a critical eye on the community, was scathing about the "tumbledown thatched cottages, emaciated huts and degenerate wigwams" which housed people who deserved better. Basket-making employed those not working on the land or in the stone quarries, a vital trade with good remuneration to all concerned. "Thousands and tens of thousands of baskets are sent all over the country every year." Benthams, Mawdesleys and Cobhams were chief names, growing buff, green and white willow used for basketry, in the local mosses. A revival in red-willow growing was begun some years ago near Clyde and on the levels nearing Rufford. Basket-making continues locally, in and on the village outskirts, and pigeon baskets are made at Parbold. For shopping I use a sturdy Mawdesley basket bought from the large modern showrooms; the same can be seen in the very best London shops—and chairs, carry-cots, baby baskets, the most attractive woven articles.

I have already said that this community, with a shot in the arm to give it impetus, is certainly forward looking, and completely 'with it'. The old stock are willing to admit that the newcomers "know more than we do", and borrow their 'know how' for the public good. Take the ambitious schemes for a village hall to replace the Comrades Hall called 'Th' Hut', being two army huts knocked together by service men demobbed after 1918 and used to capacity ever since.

Mawdesley is on the best terms with neighbours, the men having get-togethers, discussion groups on farming and local matters, and since 1971 money-raising efforts with their help for a brand-new village hall. In 1971 over 3,500 watched the first inter-village "It's a Knock-out", the local team winning by a short head, Scarisbrick and Hoghton joint second. In 1972 on August Bank Holiday Monday many more watched rival teams bombarding each other on crazy bridges, pillow-swinging stalwarts hurling opponents into watery beds, girls captive in cages balloon-bursting, sack races with two lads and two lasses tied up in each, Bickerstaffe, Halsall, and Parbold competing with 1971 winners. In 1973 they hope to reach their target—£5,500—and with all their energy directed towards it, surely will.

"There's nowt wrong wi' village life when it's like Mawdsla," they say; and I agree.

Eccleston's attitudes to native inhabitants and incomers are similar. There are more of the latter, for in recent years the village has expanded considerably, with far more impetus than the change brought about when Messrs Smalley started their weaving mill here early in the last century. The mixed population now, with rural and urban origins, work together, several times winning the Best Kept Village trophies. The older part—the ancient sandstone church on Yarrow banks surrounded by a churchyard impossible to fault, immaculate lawns, flower beds, old graves tended carefully, the mill by the hump-backed bridge where the wheel turned and all local corn was ground once upon a time—not only well kept but beautiful.

In 1872 Hewitson described it as "flat, rustic, unsophisticated, with a moderate number of inns, many apple trees and an eternity of gooseberry bushes". Today there could not be more flowers or fruit trees to the square yard; it has certainly a pleasant, cheerful, welcoming aspect.

Apart from church, mill and bridge, there are few clues to its age. It was here over 1,000 years ago, Norman barons owned it, and later many distinguished families—Gernetts, Dacres, Molyneux and Wrightingtons and Dicconsons. There were a few prosperous parishioners who remembered the poor: a Rigby of Harrocks' gift of 1629 for yearly "laying out of bread, grey coats and gowns"; and Hugh Dicconson's in 1683 for buying "six blue coats annually for six poor persons to be lettered with H.D. on the sleeves". The bread used to be handed out after reading of names by a church official. Now the loaves are left on the table to be claimed whether any poor need them or no. On the surface everyone appears happy and prosperous.

In the beginning 'Eukeston Burgh' flanked the Roman Road; now a wide modern highway runs through. Euxton has adapted to great changes. The greatest upheaval was when large-scale armaments factories took over its richest farmlands during the 1939–45 war, when displaced persons occupied the site afterwards, and a vast industrial estate took over. What comes after? Early signs of the new town? A prototype, the 230-acre site in Astley Park—a new town 'village'.

It is the fate of roadside villages to be overlooked by those who travel in haste. A pity. The church on its elevated site is a piece of history. Once a chapel of ease to Leyland, it was built by the Molyneux as Lords of Euxton—they succeeded the Hollands and before them de Lacys and the Barons of Penwortham—and passed to the Church of England in the eighteenth century. It is not so large or grand as Eccleston's venerable red sandstone church; just a small building with west-end bell turret, origin obscure, probably fourteenth-century with door and buttress which could be earlier—Norman?

The pulpit is a handsome three-decker which came into the news in 1854, when *Preston Guardian* reported that apparatus for distilling of whisky had been found under the said pulpit floor; it was capable of making 6 gallons a night. The Rev. John Williams was completely innocent one is glad to know. The sexton it was who was found out.

Like Whittle-le-Woods down the highway everyone wonders how the future Lancashire new town will affect them; all will oppose any move to 'swallow them up'.

CROSTON VILLAGE

Among all the villages by the Yarrow and Douglas, that of most ancient importance I have left till last. Croston—unique, the postmistress told me, the only Croston in the U.K. The cross in the early settlement was set up about 651 by Aiden's missionaries—this the centre from which the light was spread from tidal Ribble to wild moors where the two rivers begin, the parish "almost the size of a diocese". It was so large it was divided into four quarters, three of which I wrote of in the Preston and Ribble estuary pages: Hoole, Hesketh, Tarleton and Bretherton.

Eventually the small chapelries broke away and became parishes in their own right. But until this happened all journeyed to Croston, come wind or weather, storms and floods, especially to the Festival of St Michael, which, being held at Old Michaelmas, the first week in October, often coincided with the end of the equinoxial gales and before the setting-in of wintry conditions.

Considering its early importance, Croston has retired into a fairly quiet old age. Crowds converged upon it for the annual fair and Feast of St Wilfred, its weekly markets drew the farmers from all the Leyland Hundred—whereas now the only annual junketings are the Coffee Feast and Croston Wakes, pale shadows of what once was. By all accounts it is better so, for the modern public would not take kindly to the rowdiness, ribaldry and drunken revelries which ended the day. After a procession in which various clubs walked with bands playing, the villagers keeping pace with them, the participants adjourned to the inn of their choice—Croston had several—imbibed freely, and when they joined the innocent revellers dancing and merrymaking in the field in front of the rectory they were ready for anything. Too ready, so the rector's lady said; she would have no more such spectacles within sight of her windows.

Preparation for return of exiled family and friends meant the baking of large quantities of Wakes cakes—large round 'biscuits', always stacked in piles. Now the feast is a happy family occasion.

A newer Croston, developed round cotton mills, brickworks and railway early in the last century, is quite unlike the old. One might expect to find the mother church at the heart of the early village; and so it is, the tall tower slightly out of true seen from afar. It has survived nine centuries, repeated Yarrow floods—some of which overflowed into the graveyard, into the nave and under-mined the walls. Floods also demolished the schoolyard walls, small children carried away down the raging river. The school had John of Gaunt as founder in 1392, but John Heit in 1660 gave it a free school endowment—he was ejected two years later, during the Commonwealth.

Town Bridge (strongly built in 1682) has stood up to the storms of 300 years and traffic of markets and fairs. Farmers drove cattle this way, one with a ferocious bull which lowered its head and tossed a boy from the parapet into the river to his death.

Many cottages which followed the curving river—very prone to floods—and from the back doorsteps of which, "We could take running jumps for a swim when the Yarrow ran high," have been demolished. So has the corner shop, Yorkshire House built in 1813, a period piece worth saving, with large bow windows.

5

East Lancashire Villages of the
Pennine Moorlands

Witches are popular, stories about witches favourite with children, witchcraft fascinates adults; and as long as this is so Pendle people will pander to it. Cornish piskies, Irish leprechauns, Pendle witches on broomsticks, the shops are full of them, good selling lines! What does everyone want to know about at Barley, Newchurch and Rough Lee? That they are pleasant, even pretty villages, each with a very interesting history of its own, worth looking at for their own sake is hardly noticed.

Over the years—apart from reading all the authentic records of the local witches of the seventeenth century, and the trials of 1612 and 1633 held at Lancaster Castle—I have sought out all the spots in Pendle associated with them—because my readers wanted to know about them. The walking was good too, up and down and around the hill, and I filled sketchbooks with seventeenth-century and late-Tudor farms which in their time knew the Demdikes and Chattoxes and the rest of their group. It was all good fun.

That an attempt to make a film of the Pendle witches, with my script, proved disastrous—to begin with all the film turned out blank; that every time I was due to give lectures on witchcraft, Old Nick and such like there were thunderstorms, tempest and floods; all this was rather amusing, but hardly worth mentioning.

I collected a whole packet of purely oral traditions from the villagers. When an old man of Newchurch stared me straight in the face and said, "Believe i' witches? Of course I do, so did mi mother. She used to say 'How can you say you *don't* believe when one has fixed you wi her evil eye?' " The secretary of Barley W.I. once pointed out the corner of a fouled field, frequented by the Demdike crew and henceforth never mown "because it were poisoned", as an old wife at Under Pendle farm had truly believed. Near Huntroyd an aged barn was haunted "by a man who hanged himself wi' his galluses because he thought he'd been witched".

M

And recently a farmer at Barley talked of a neighbouring farmer who "were witched and just withered away and died". Folk have pointed out a table-topped tomb in the churchyard—a witch interred therein; and at Rough Lee the wide hearth in the fireplace where the housewife scribbled strange hieroglyphics "so as Old Chattox can't come down".

On Hallowe'en the Pendle Hotel makes a showing of witchery. The landlord in witch gear stirs a steaming cauldron of 'witch's brew'. At Newchurch, flights of witches four inches high dangle in a shop window, and for 5p inserted in a slot the 'Witch's Kitchen' becomes animated, leering hag cowering by her pot, fire burning, contents bubbling!

But do not be misled. The three villages have a life of their own, the inhabitants keep them immaculate—and frequently win the Best Kept Village awards. Newchurch is flung high on a breezy hillside so the dwellings hug each other for protection. Barley sheltered and out of the wind's way follows a prattling brook which later flows under the old mill walls of Narrowgates. Rough Lee, down the same stream—which can be a raging monster in floods as disastrous as that of 8th August 1967—is a long, narrow village, at the waterside and huddled in small alleys off. Once a booth in the royal forest, like Barley and Newchurch, it had its share of water-powered industry like them. It also draws modern witch hunters. At the Tudor hall at Whitehough, upstream, lived Bulcocks, suspected of being witches; at the end of the village is Rough Lee Hall from which they took Mistress Alice Nutter to stand trial—though she was a wealthy woman "of good repute"—together with the poor half-witted harridans, her associates.

Ask about witches here and you are likely to get nowhere. One part of the hall is the weekend and holiday cottage for a boys' school. The field in front is rapidly growing large modern houses. The old man at the gate is a realist, no nonsense about him. "There's folk who'll believe owt. Tell 'em three bears are coming round t'corner and they'll run!"

The old-type villager in Pendle Forest tolerated curious visitors, but now a new type of town commuter—living in very nice improved cottages, appreciating the quiet life and very rural surroundings—is not anxious to promote tourism. They do not need to.

In literature the villages never had a chance to advertise their gentler aspects. No hint of meadows "a-ripple with mirth", thorn hedges white with blossom, and hedgerows rich with meadow-sweet; or of the soft beauty of April evenings with lambs running races in the nearby pastures; or the crimson glow of the heather on the hill flanks on August afternoons; or the enchantment of June dawns witnessed from the hill top.

No. Richard James in 1635 only wrote of "desert mystie moors which gave poor old wives strange phansies" and put them in the devil's power to contrive the deaths of men and beasts. Cooke-Taylor in 1834 described Pendle Forest: "in the seventeenth century it filled north England with alarm and almost persuaded people that Satan had seized upon the Duchy as his proper herit-age, and installed himself there as heir-general to the Plan-tagenets". Dwelling on the wild aspect, William Howitt a few years later described a Pendle storm which forced him to the shelter of a barn. He found within two girls, little, half-clad, bare-foot creatures to whom "common English was unintelligible, their appearance wild as their speech".

I must say to me, a Ribblesdalian, and to those who live in Downham, Worston and Pendleton, Pendle Forest is the 'backside of the hill', the 'dark side', lashed by fiercer winds from the east, where snow falls heaviest and lasts longest. Perhaps so, but the villagers make up for it in community spirit, warm hearts and roaring fires. "Oh, it's all right living here, if you've bin brought up to it," the natives say cheerfully.

There is more to Pendle than witchcraft, and that is over and done with. After the last round-up of 1633 the poor souls who survived were acquitted, their doings 'rationalized', and slowly the thraldom of superstition was lifted. Better approaches allowed trade and eventually industry to flow in, Pendle's brooks attracted water-powered mills. After the poverty of the 1830s when a family's earning power from spinning and handloom weaving was twelve shillings a week, circumstances forced them into the hated steam-powered factories.

Barley had two brookside mills. The Green was first to go, then Narrowgates complete with weavers' cottages beside an enclosed mill yard, working till the 1950s; now it is a conversion piece—modern house from early factory. Newchurch folk trudged down to Spen brook mill, but Rough Lee had its own, tall and formid-able, near the bridge.

AROUND HIGHAM AND SABDEN

Barrowfield, Higham and Sabden were even more industrialized, and civilized, though their menfolk swelled the plug-drawing, warp-slashing and machine-breaking rioters, driven to this by abject poverty and near-starvation. These tragic days are part of their shared past. And farther back, a common history to monastic clearances of the thirteenth and fourteenth centuries. A medieval road passed over Calder. The Earls of Lancaster and Duchy agents used Ightenhill manor house as their overnight stop, *en route* for York or Lancaster or Pontefract on royal business.

In Higham and Sabden people matter. Each, through sheer native grit and buoyancy, has risen from depressions which might have destroyed less resilient communities. I was in Higham the week North Sea gas and the summer weather of 1972 arrived, together with much cheerful upheaval, neighbourly involvement, passing of keys, and in and out of houses. Being neighbourly is a well-developed local virtue. Without it one could go under, as stand-offish newcomers soon realize.

In both villages there is a hard core of native stock, in old cottages belonging to the handlooming period which, in towns, would have been scheduled for demolition as slum property. Here they are well cared for, with improvement grants raised to the status of "desirable residences in semi-rural areas" and snapped up like hot cakes when for sale—as in Sabden's oldest corners at Heyhouses or in Wesley Street, and Higham's oldest cottages which survived the making of the new bypass. Slum property? Not at all.

"I'm well suited. One up, one down and new flush toilet in the cellar," declared an old inhabitant who emerged with me from the supermarket-alias-village stores and gossip shop. I was told to meet an old Highamer, knock at a certain door, call, "Aunt Maggie!" and walk in. She lived in a street of back-to-back houses (commoner in west Yorkshire), where conversion—by breaching the rear wall of each by a communicating door—has made two tiny cottages into one roomy dwelling. Some are so much improved by the most modern interior alterations they are no longer 'cottages'. But Aunt Maggie's—gas men 'converting' in one room and a blazing coal fire in another—was still a cottage in character, old-fashioned, warm and welcoming.

Nothing old-fashioned about this octogenarian, completely 'with it', interested in everything about Higham—past, present and to come. Of newcomers: "We're glad to have 'em. Some's nice folk, but some want to possess everything. To them we say 'No.' Young couples—they're go-getters. And as for some of the youngsters, there's times you could batter 'em, they're that gawmless!" On the villagers: "Old Highamers cling together. Some think we're odd, like them Manchester gas chaps—maybe we are, but we're happy here. We have plenty of fun. Country life's narrow, but it's a good life."

A neighbour popped in. "Highamers are more thoughtful than town folk. There you could be found dead. Highamers know when help's needed and couldn't stand by and see a neighbour in want."

Seventy years ago to be young in Higham "was very Heaven". Never time to be bored. "School—half time; work in t'mill—some lads in t'pits." And then walking down to Burnley for night school or choir practices for *Messiah*, or music classes and the village string band. Sunday *was* Sunday then, no work done, no washing and no clatter of clogs. William Boothman used to stop any lad or lass wearing clogs. "What, no shoen?" he'd ask, and hand over money to buy a pair.

The Sabbath was a full day. Aunt Maggie was one of nine; four sang in the Church choir, four in the Chapel, and one brother in both. School, morning chapel, then dinner. School in the afternoon, then a walk—lasses in gangs, boys in gangs following them through the green pastures and breezy meadows. Home to tea and off to evening chapel. A typical Victorian Sunday!

Families were in descent from the handloomers who supplied the merchants and chapmen with their weekly output. The derelict three-storey building in Garden Street was an early loom-shop, with a butcher's shop tacked on. Grimshaw's tall mill no longer hums with the noise of looms; bales of cloth woven elsewhere are examined for flaws. Duckworth's shuttle shop is no more, its last tenants a local 'group' who made evenings hideous with pop and jazz practices.

Plenty goes on, something for everyone. A play group, Brownies, Young Wives, Mothers' Union, Women's Institute, Men's Fellowship, 'sausage sizzles' in a local barn, barbecues in the Old Hall. There was an arts and crafts festival in the church, raising £1,000.

The Four Alls Inn, its outside older than inside, is no longer the typical 'pub'—few are—but for those who like it, there are convivial evenings, new style, with organ music, brass and drums.

From the nearby spout comes "best water anywhere, never dries up. Farmers come with kits and carts when their own supplies fail." Not far away, a seat under a tree in a pleasant paved area, good for watching village goings-on.

New street names recall Higham's past role, when halmote courts and courts leet were held at the hall twice a year. These grew from early forest courts where tenants of copyhold met the king's steward and deputies to deal with surrenders etc. of mortgages and leases, the two parties holding a 'surrender rod'. Twelve jurors deliberated over the "soundness of mind, memory and understanding" of the makers of wills. Later the courts were held at the 'Four Alls', on which the sign reads, "I pray for all [the parson], I govern all [the sovereign], I fight for all [the soldier] and I pay for all [the man in the street]."

One road is named after Sir Jonas Moore, a famous 'civil engineer' of Charles II's reign, mathematician and scholar. The Moores were of Sabden Dean, but he was born in 1618 at White Lee, Wheatley. He planned the draining of the Bedford fens, reclaimed the Sussex marshes, had a hand in the new London after the fire, and wrote an algebra.

Sabden's story is similar to Higham's, spanning an ancient route trodden by Bronze Age traders travelling from the Humber to Morecambe Bay. Old packhorse routes met here, so the village was a centre for seventeenth- and eighteenth-century transport operators who stabled their horses here, pastured them on the hillside, and did much business with local yarn and cloth merchants, Clitheroe limeburners and Calder pit-owners.

On Pendle Forest fringe, the cottagers of Heyhouses—older far than Sabden—shared in the witch scares. Harrison Ainsworth made the houses overlooking the brook the scene for a chapter in *Lancashire Witches*, every household bewitched. Today it looks innocent enough, roses smothering the walls and isolation banished by many new houses overlooking. Townsfolk are growing increasingly fond of the new residential Sabden. The weaving industry is finished—gone the mills Richard Cobden founded with such high hopes, giving employment and educating his workpeople and their children to enjoy the fruits of their labours. The buildings are levelled or partially used for small industry, plastics, carpets and fashion ware. The 'White Hart' calls itself the 'Pendle Witch', a local arts and crafts centre trades on the name of 'Mother Demdike'. A retired mariner produces a multiplicity of objects from Lakeland green slate, and a large caravan site puts Sabden squarely in the 1970s. With a practice ski slope on Pendle, and talk of a country leisure park in the area, "things are looking up," as a villager commented, "and we can do with it!"

"It looks bonny," said an old Sabdenner, resting on a bank near the Nick of Pendle. We looked down on the peaceful vale, soaking up the July sunshine, relaxed after the last hay load had been carried. The village is clustered so happily in its own green sanctuary.

MOOR-EDGE COMMUNITIES, WYCOLLER AND TRAWDEN TO CLIVIGER

When the Pendle foresters were breaking out of their isolation and entering the industrial world beyond, so were Trawden Forest folk and the hillmen above the Calder, Colne and Burnley; the ancient trading centres—which for centuries had disposed of their fleeces, hides and livestock—now dealt with their "calimancoes, tammies, shalloons", the yarns and cloth of cottagers from Trawden and Wycoller to Worsthorne, Hurstwood and Cliviger.

Between 1801 and 1821 Colne's growing population doubled from 3,600 to 7,200. Its new Piece Hall had two spacious rooms and many booths for traders and buyers who came from York and London. Burnley too was booming, especially after its turnover in 1800 from woollens to cotton textiles; the stubborn, independent handloomers stood out against change as long as possible.

Baines wrote cheerfully: "A region such as this could not fail to be prosperous, and though adverse circumstances may cause occasional temporary depression there is here sufficient buoyancy to rise above all difficulties". The buoyancy was there, the indomitable spirit of the people tested many times in the years to come. "In this ample tract is much fine romantic scenery, which being far from any of the principal roads is less visited than its deserves," added Baines attracted by Colne's surroundings. In his days its many old halls were all still occupied and the hamlets and villages humming with activity.

Wycoller Hall had been destroyed "by a mad woman setting it on fire." Charlotte Brontë was so impressed by the drama of the ruins she made of Wycoller the Ferndean Hall of *Jane Eyre*.

The Cunliffes had departed, the handloomers were at last being forced out—and down to the valley towns; Wycoller was on the way to becoming a 'ghost' village. Apart from farms which continued as before all became deserted except for two or three occupied cottages, suppliers of teas and pots of tea to happy families who came for paddling and picnics and to ramblers who walked this way *en route* for exciting places, the hardy types to High Withins, Wuthering Heights.

In ruin it was all highly romantic, Time and Nature mantling roofless cottages, and fallen walls with creepers and encrustations of lichens, cushions of vivid green moss. Only the hall ruins, with the care and money of the Friends of Wycoller, were protected and made safe—as ruins. Not only a ghost village but supplied with 'authentic' spectres, of Cunliffes who wined, dined, roistered and caroused after cockfights and foxhunts, full-blooded in life and unquiet in death.

There is more than the wind's whisper and creaking of branches on winter nights. Without knowing it one listens for voices, the beat of horses' hooves, the baying of ghostly hounds urged on by ghostly horsemen. Some hear and see strange things—as did a bonny lass who informed us, conviction in her voice, "On Bonfire night my sister and me saw him, when everyone had gone home, galloping over bridge by t'Hall, with his head under his arm! We could hardly believe our eyes!"

Everyone said, "What a pity Wycoller can't be brought to life again." As there is no good road access, no water, gas, electricity, and the Calder Water Board not over anxious to allow development, any change seemed unlikely. But in 1972 rumour was rife. The public began to take notice. Even Lady Cunliffe, who lives in Lakeland, came into the open, alarmed at rumours. The village of her ancestors to become a tourist attraction, a fun fair?

It was reported: Wycoller had been sold as a complete 'lot'; it had not been sold; it was being sold piecemeal. After weeks of rumour a public meeting was held, the L.C.C. officials putting forward a plan which had unanimous support. If Wycoller could be bought for £100,000 with the government environmental improvement grant of 75 per cent, before it was too late, it might be restored in part, cottages converted into a folk museum, local artists and craftsmen allowed to work there, to become again a living community within a country park.

A tremendous task, a great challenge, but not impossible. Think of the folk museums so popular in Scandinavian countries. There new villages have been created by assembling component parts from demolished old villages—a church from here, farms and laithes, houses and workshops from there, each furnished as in the old days. Here every dwelling is where it was—all it needs is pulling up to its feet and to be given a good reason for coming to life again.

Lanes wriggle out, one to Trawden which, unlike Wycoller in its dean, stands high on a hill, the topmost buildings stark against the sky; and nothing beyond but the Pennine watershed, and the forest which once stretched from its backdoors 'into space'.

It had its macabre moments, a tendency for old hags to seek companionship of the devil or his minions; black cats were common, and on unholy nights bewitched cattle danced jigs in shippons and calves ran up the walls of their pens. But, being essentially down-to-earth folk, the villagers entered into industrial change, applied themselves to water power, then power looms. And its mills still go strong, one bright factory employing 230, village weavers and others 'imported' daily from Colne and Cowling—producing fine shirtings and dress materials. Hope and good cheer fill the air. Once so grim, stone walls begrimed with smoke pollution from scores of Calder valley mills, it has taken to colour, brilliant lashings of it. Trawden does nothing by halves. The long terraces stepping uphill or down, with improvement grants have been transformed. Everyone is 'doing up' or 'breetening up' with exuberance. One home decorator after completion rejoiced in his (or her) lilac paintwork and decided the coal bin should be painted lilac too, to match the front door!

Trawden folk are hard working, enjoy work—and have work to do. The moorland breezes, the wide-open spaces, green pastures on their doorsteps—all contribute to their wellbeing. It shows. So in the highflung communities on or near the old lanes to Haggate, Worsthorne and Hurstwood, where two centuries ago all were merchants, farmers and landowners—like the Eckroyds— or handloomers and smallholders. Inevitably all were caught up in the wave of prosperity which sent Colne and Burnley populations soaring, created subsidiary towns between them, and made of Marsden the new town of Nelson.

Quarrying and coal-mining were important too. Now, no stone-getting; instead the old delphs like Catlows are being filled up by the rubble and waste of demolished factories and houses. The number of pits burrowing into the most northerly seams of the Lancashire carboniferous series, has greatly diminished. The mills are few or turned to other uses, like the foundry at Worsthorne.

I am very attracted to these Pennine-edge communities so near the watershed, with prehistoric and strangely haunting moorland sites behind them—and below, the thickly populated Calder Valley. Such contrasts!

A long switchback hill road links them—historic, every mile of it. Haggate has character and Harle Syke its characters—and a reputation for close-fistedness; even newborn infants are born "with fingers turned in, the better to hold brass".

Real villages—Worsthorne, Hurstwood and Mereclough—stand 800 feet above sea level. The breezes are invigorating and the inhabitants bred tough and able to withstand the elements. "Aye, wind knows how to blow up here," commented an oldster, one of a group standing in Worsthorne's open centre, big as a town hall square. Mid afternoon brought an overspill of youngsters from the school playground. Soon they disappeared and sunny silence flowed back into the village.

Worsthorne has changed. The old hall has disappeared, leaving Wall Streams as example of sixteenth-century architecture. Rows of industrial cottages, Victorian terraced houses, are on the peri-meter—but no weavers work here now. Local mills are no more, demolished or used for other purposes. Cosy cottages with gay touches of paint, and new bungalows follow the roads to Brun-shaw and Burnley, to Hurstwood and Mereclough. The oldest outlet is an ancient church way, a causeway raised above water-logged Swain Lane. Folk who walked this way long ago half expected to meet fairies by the springs, or in storm and tempest find evidence of the devil's doing. A place for superstition, fortunate in local historians like the Tattersalls, who listened to old wives and grey-beards and recorded what they said of ghosts, hauntings, boggarts and witches.

For church, school, inn and shops, Hurstwood folk must walk to Worsthorne, for it is no more than a hamlet with hens spilling over the road, farm gear piled on the verge, more of a farmyard than a village street. But it has had its moments, its outstanding men and homes with histories.

Barnard Towneley, kinsman of the Towneley Hall family and a builder of fine halls, built the large house by the bridge for his 10-year-old bride, Agnes Ormerod, a neighbour's daughter, in 1576. Theirs is the most imposing dwelling. Restored to its original beauty in the 1960s—once it was divided into two cottages and a shop, let at 2s. 10d. and 1s. 10d. a week—the whole is leased from the Thoresby Trust by the present tenants. Lovely it is, the well-dressed interior walls stripped to pale golden stone. The mullioned windows frame romantic pictures of deep clough below and swelling hills eastwards. A near neighbour is another Tudor house.

For so small a place Hurstwood contains a good slice of Tudor Lancashire. Possibly the much photographed Spenser's Cottage was visited by the young poet Edmund, staying with his uncle during the 'long vac' from Cambridge. He wandered though the countryside and had a romantic attachment to the 'fair Rosalinda' of the *Shepherd's Calendar*, who some believe was a Dinelay of Downham, or an Aspinall of Standen. Two centuries later a lad called Richard was born at the nearby farm, Tattersall's Tenement, and his name also became world known. He founded 'Tattersall's' at Knightbridge and Newmarket, where December sales are the highlights of the international bloodstock buyers' year.

They say the Battle of Brunanburgh (King Athelstan leading his Wessex and Mercian warriors v. the rest, A.D. 926) was fought here, on Brun banks. We know that over the bleak moors comes the Long Causeway, a Bronze Age road in use for 3,000 years and for much of its exciting high-level route a link today with the West Riding towns, via Heptonstall, Hebden Bridge and Halifax.

No buses serve Hurstwood now, so folk must depend on offers of lifts in emergencies. Walkers stride out from here over wild heights; girls who have never heard of Richard Tattersall canter by on ponies. As a youth Richard bought a pedlar's nag 'for a pittance' and, after allowing it to run on the same hills, sold it for 'a small fortune'—his first horse-dealing.

The sporting tradition is remembered at lower level Mereclough, at the 'Fighting Cocks' (shades of cockings with Towneleys setting high stakes) and The Kettledrum Inn—named afte a racehorse which won the Derby for the Towneleys a century ago and was grandsire of Persimmon.

Now we are in the extensive parish of Holme-in-Cliviger, its wide-flung borders following the county boundary on the water-shed, following the Brun bank to Ormerod bridges, running south to Irwell Springs beyond Thieveley Pike.

To the highly dramatic Gorge of Cliviger—a place of rocks, eagle crags, witches' haunts and robbers' lairs, feared by solitary travellers—came the Whitakers. Richard married a local heiress possessed of green acres on the valley floor, a 'holm' by the Calder. From the 1330s the Whitaker descent is clear. As free tenants they were as lords of a manor. At Holme they erected a homestead against sheltering hills, facing south to the sun—a fair spot. Sheep pastures and cornfields provided revenue and they prospered, sons fit husbands for Towneleys, Sherburnes and Nowells. Thomas in 1530 married Elizabeth Nowell, sister of Roger of Read Hall and Alexander, later Dean of St Paul's.

The house grew in beauty. In 1603 the centre hall was rebuilt in stone, only a few years before son Alexander (named after the Dean?) voyaged to the New World to become the Apostle of Virginia. He baptized Princess Pocahontas and married her to John Rolfe. Eleven Whitakers were to emigrate in the next fifty years.

To the hall wings were added in 1668 and 1717 and much alteration done by the learned Doctor Whitaker at the end of the eighteenth century, including ambitious afforestation of his estate. By this time trade was beginning to flow along the high-way, industry taking hold—in spite of the doctor's protestations—and the village of Holme firmly set on its course, with coal pits and drift mines, a cornmill which became a fulling mill when sheep replaced growing of crops. From a sparsely inhabited valley—to each man 9 acres of living space, "bleak and bare without a sheep fence to be seen", it was fast becoming well populated, the vale and hillsides divided into enclosures, the bare contours—thanks to the doctor—softened by his 422,000 young trees planted during the wars with France.

At the heart of the village is Holme Chapel, an ancient chantry rebuilt in 1788 by Dr Whitaker and, in very convenient proximity, the old Ram Inn. In due time to this group was added the church school and Church House, all playing vital parts today.

Vitality is the key word, yet in the 1950s all work ended, no mills, none of its drift mines nor pits open, the unemployed—all the 20s to 50s—forced to seek jobs and homes elsewhere, Holme almost 'died'; a dreary 'ghost town'. In recent years the tide has turned, families have returned, all empty houses are improved, occupied, new homes built for eager buyers. You can sense at once the cheerful optimism. But they are here to *live*, away from the town's rat race, in fresh, clean country surroundings, good for them and for their bonny children.

None is anxious about large-scale development. Land is locked between high hills leaving little room to expand, too narrow, too deep. At present the size is 'just right'. The school is full, many children are transported from Burnley by bus; the infants overflow into Church House, which out of school hours shares meetings with the village hall. Think of community amenities: Holme has them all. Ask anyone and the list they give is amazing. The church choir can call upon forty voices. The riding club can muster 150. The Women's Institute is vigorous; so are keep fit and evening classes. On Saturday evenings a full programme of dances—'discos'—are organized by such a variety of clubs the young folk have no need to rush off to town for amusement. It is a good place to live in and play in. Nowhere more friendly folk.

The great event of the year is still the Ram Fair, near Michaelmas. This year to attract the modern crowds a sheep dog trial was included, and a fell race. Old folk remembered well when "the world flocked" to Holme on fair day, blocking the highways, and sheep matters were all important, with stalls and side-shows secondary.

Hill-farmers herded their lonk sheep—the super-active breed with dishevelled fleeces, purpose-bred for Pennine climate and Cliviger heights—offering them for sale in their 'working' fleeces, no combing or attempts to improve their appearance. No auctioning, just a hand-clasp and adjournment to the 'Ram' for a pint and the sale was sealed. Men tell me that full purses led to many 'going on the rant' for the following week. 'Ranters' found their way home up and down steep paths on hands and knees!

Times change. This October 150 young local riders gathered for the meet on Deerplay Hill for a day with the Holcombe harriers. Gone the wolf, the wily fox, the stag and the deer—"only the timid hare remains to kindle the huntsman's enthusiasm and wake the volleyed thunder of the eager pack", as in Rossendale, just over the Cliviger southern border.

ROSSENDALE AND IRWELL VALLEY VILLAGES

William the Conqueror, it is said, found Rossendale a harassment to his destroying armies. All was swamp, waste, without roads, almost uninhabited, among impenetrable woods, perilous rivers and overflowed valleys.

Rossendale's river, 'Irwell Flud', was a clear, sweet stream in Tudor days, when no more than eighty dwellings in small booths and launds were to be found. All Rossendale from Norman times had been restricted to access and development as royal forest and only slowly, after sixteenth-century afforestation, did the tenants with leases and grants set about turning former wasteland into fertile farmlands. The homes they built were the nuclei of the later hamlets and villages.

In the 1770s change came rapidly. It took less than a century to turn the clear Irwell into a "noble work-a-day river with a smutty face winning the children's bread, sole offspring of a sterile, uninviting country". Here "Vulcan's fires ascended, there was now endless whine of spindles and uneasy tumult of looms". An enthusiastic visitor from Dublin, Mr Cooke-Taylor, was full of praise. "Wasteland soil has been sowed by spindle, shuttle and loom," he wrote, "and bleak moors bloom as a garden and desert hills blossom as the rose." And mill chimneys were planted instead of trees!

He was loud in commendation of the new manufacturers who had made these 'improvements' possible. He wrote nothing of the old landowning families, the owners of great houses and green parks that the new industrialists had ousted. The country folk had combined small farming with the cottage industry of spinning and weaving, and every man his own master. To work at another's command went against the grain. Mills were anathema—as they were to hand loomers in Pendle and Calder valley.

> The Lord sent the rain to till the ground
> But not to turn the wheels around.

But the mills multiplied in Rossendale valleys, small streams were harnessed for power, hills torn open for building stone and the carboniferous coal-bearing rocks mined intensively when steam power took over. Bleaching and dyeing found right conditions here, so green acres dwindled under bleach grounds and tenter fields.

The new Lancashire mill-owners were not all cruel taskmasters. The Peels, Grants, Aitkens, Turners, Whiteheads, Ashworths and Kays were men of the highest principles. They watched the morals and well-being of their workers. On hard-drinking Rossendalians (who could slake thirsts at fifty-five pubs and sixty-five beershops) and men of the moors between The Valley, the Irwell and the Roch, to whom "beer was meat, drink and washing and lodging", they enforced abstinence. Their new model villages had chapels, schools, institutes—but never a pub. However, distilling of illicit whisky went on—underground!

Gambling schools were held in lonely places; coin tossing and 'pitching' led to the loss of meagre earnings. So employers like the Whiteheads of Hollymount Rawtenstall encouraged thrift. The weekly 'schoolpence' paid by their scholars were 'banked' to provide lump-sum savings when each reached the age of 21.

The new villages were "model for all villages, an earthly Paradise", wrote Cooke-Taylor. Today one can see something of them and appreciate the ideals of their planners.

The Whitehead brothers had known early poverty. They wanted the best conditions for their Rawtenstall people. Their own houses were substantial, but the chapel (Methodist) built by them was "fit for the Author of their prosperity". Workers' houses—four- or six-roomed cottages—were "examples of neatness".

The three Grant brothers arrived young as Scots immigrants. At Ramsbottom in 1805 they laid out the village of Nuttall, a complex of print works, spinning and weaving sheds, dyeing and finishing shops, dwellings for the workers, a fine mansion for themselves and—being Scots Presbyterians in 1832—the church of St Andrew. The brothers made their fortunes also. They were hard, ambitious men who could pay off rioters to leave their property alone, frown on drinking, yet give their workers weekly 3d. vouchers for ale to be spent at the 'Grant's Arms'! After meeting them in 1838, how much did Dickens adapt for the Cheeryble Brothers? Little of their foundation is left—not even the Grant's Tower, the memorial of their arrival in Lancashire in

1785 remains. The Reverend Mr Carmellie is an enthusiastic collector of Grant memoirs.

Helmshore is widely known now as the village with old mills, and the quite amazing textile museum, Higher Mill still preserving the giant wheel, 'Old Faithful', and the mill dam something of a botanist's paradise today. Here the Turners employed 2,000 workers—and at one time housed many in dark buildings, one an inn—five families crammed into each room, more like slaves than free-born Englishmen.

These mill villages are now enclosed by Victorian towns. But Aitken's Irwell Vale, down the river from Ewood Bridge, remains a small, complete, compact community, in a pleasant pocket of green meadowland (one site earmarked for new houses), and where the river retains some of its ancient beauty. Powerloom rioters destroyed its first mill in 1826, then the Aitkens took over, rebuilt the factory, erected rows of neat weavers' houses around open squares, built a solid home for the family, an equally solid chapel, and in later generations a co-operative shop, a workers' canteen and a sports ground. All this remains—and production of cloth, sailcloth, continues. Not far down river is the pleasant seventeenth-century dwelling of the Rawsthornes, Lumb Old Hall, with green lawns and flower beds on Irwell's rocky banks.

The Industrial Revolution did make a sorry mess of much of Rossendale and places south of The Valley so the more surprising are the villages set in green acres and among uncluttered hill slopes, to delight us by their unexpectedness. Native characteristics survived change also, until the last decade with an influx of town and city commuters, many bringing nothing into the community. "We work in Manchester, we get our pleasure there. We only *live* here." Live? Living in villages is not merely a table, a bed and a coat hanger. If Rossendale's past is destroyed, its future is only problematical.

The old spirit of south-east Lancashire? Men, to survive, had to work hard, endure poverty and lean times. To compensate, they drank hard and played hard. Hunting was in the blood—on foot following the Holcombe hounds. James I, in 1617, gave the local pack leave to hunt in his once-royal forest "for ever". When the harriers were out, weavers left their looms, farmers their ploughs, village schools turned out, master and scholars, to join in. Football too was played hard and often, even on Sunday! The devil once joined in, unbeknown to the lads of Crawshawbooth. A mighty kick, a ball disappearing into the sky, a flash of fire, reek of sulphur—and terrified players rooted to the ground!

Singing put heart into south-east Lancashire folk. They are still a singing people, like the weavers of Dean (a hamlet tucked into moors near Water and Lumb) known as 'Dean Layrocks'. Methodism, strong in these parts, encouraged congregational singing. What a joyful noise they raised to the Lord at every village sermon and Harvest Thanksgiving! At Unsworth's Big Sing crowds reached such proportions that the Primitive Chapel could not house them all; choir and orchestra (Hallé instrumentalists among them) were seated inside, but the rest outside, in 'tents', near open windows. The Rossendale Male Voice Choir is of the old tradition.

Young wives at Weir village told me they liked living there "because of the fresh air and so many good walks". Walking is still indulged in. There is a big turn up for every annual Rossendale Boundary walk over miles of rough moorland. Yearly the Edwin Waugh Society meets at Waterfoot to climb hillways to the poet's well on Fo' Edge, there to sing and recite his works—poems which helped cotton workers to bear the tragic years of the Cotton Famine.

In the 1830s Cooke-Taylor and Dodd could write enthusiastically about south-east Lancashire, painting a bright picture of villages 'improved' by industry, many cottages "furnished with every convenience, with mahogany furniture, a clock, a collection of books". They waxed lyrical about the "agreeable walks" from town to town, pleasing resting places by Irwell banks, always with pretty views to lighten the step. Then, Stand was beautifully sited, the scenery so interesting that opulent Manchester business men chose to build fine houses there. Prestwich was a "retiring village, the nearby clough highly picturesque and fraught with delight". Incredible now?

Returning a century later they might have eaten their words, for here was darkest Lancashire, 'miles of prison' with no escape for the inhabitants condemned to life sentences!

If a perfect village must have a pretty face, small wonder people prefer Downham and Yealand, Little Crosby and Halsall, to Crawshawbooth, Weir or Whitworth. But if people make a village, then the workworn in south-east Lancashire—undergoing valiant transformation, torn by demolitions, rebuilding taking place—still have much to commend them. Here are the warm hearts, smiling welcomes and cheerful firesides.

"Smiles? What have they to smile about?" ask strangers. Here they look well, eat well, ignoring modern weight ideals. "Smile? What do you expect us to do? Cry? Isn't there enough water about already?" Every small courtesy is performed with a ready smile. To ask for help is a pleasure.

Haslingden and Bury for centuries had definite spheres of influence. The first, on the Rossendale Forest fringe, was in the 'alpine district' of farms till 1801. Then the new textile boom took hold and Haslingden's population and its chapelry increased rapidly—1,000 in 1801 jumping to 6,000 in twenty years. Folk of the booths by Limey Water and from the green and fertile Irwell valley west still came to Haslingden markets and fairs.

Bury printers, dyers and bleachers now had work for the men and women of five small townships and three chapelries who before 1800 had been smallholders and cottage weavers. Twenty years later 3,000 or 4,000 rural families had been absorbed in the new mills largely due to setting up of print works by the first Sir Robert Peel, the newcomers boosting the population—2,000 in the 1770s to 10,500 in 1821. And all flocked to Bury's weekly market and three annual fairs.

Rochdale was astride such important 'cross highways' it had to grow when industrial changes came. At the same time surrounding villages—hitherto primitive, bucolic, where the old dialect was the only speech and old ways retained—were caught up. By the 1820s manufacture had invaded the moorland cloughs up Roch and Spodden, "defiling the most picturesque spots and the beauties of Nature" by steam, smoke and forests of chimneys. From fairy dells, boggart cloughs and devil's dens, sprites and spirits good and evil were banished for ever, just as in Pendle Forest.

Such changes also affected the most westerly Rossendale river, Limey Water. Centuries ago traders travelled moorland packhorse roads linking Haslingden, Bury and Rochdale markets with those of Todmorden, Colne and Burnley. Early tracks were monastic links with the mother church of Whalley, when here were only chapels of ease, as at Goodshaw Booth and Newchurch. The most historically interesting buildings survive on Goodshaw Lane, and where rough tracks descended to Crawshawbooth, bringing Friends to the Quakers' meeting house.

What is there now on Goodshaw Lane? The old road disappearing into November mists, a new estate taking shape, and the house where Don Whillans used to look across the valley at Cribden—and dream of Everest.

Up here, on 'Morrel Heights', Dunkirk and 'Church Hill' are Georgian survivors. One fine house was once an inn with outbarn and wool store of a prosperous merchant. Two inns, 'White Hart' and 'George and Dragon', then gave sustenance to man and beast, and Goodshaw Chapel and Baptist Chapel spiritual refreshment. From Dunkirk, Mrs M. came forth with the key to open the church for us; and what a shining, well-cared for interior it is, bright with flowers and obviously a living part of Goodshaw today; this is mother church of the valley. Crawshawbooth's is far younger.

In the church we saw a stone from the long-disappeared chapel of ease, naming local yeoman, Thurstan Birtwistle, Omerod of Gamelside, and others here in the thirty-second year of Henry VIII's reign. Once there was a three-decker pulpit—from the older chapel. The stained glass is new, the east window a memorial to a Brooks of Crawshaw Hall, which recalled the link with Brooks of Whalley—one an early 'unofficial' banker whose two sons prospered, Samuel as partner in the banking firm of Cunliffe-Brooks, who bought land and developed growing Manchester, Brooks Street and Whalley Range, whereas his brother took to manufacturing and large-scale quarrying in Rossendale, built the imposing mansion at Crawshawbooth and became Lord Crawshaw. Descendants still live in the same mansion, neighbour to the very handsome Diocesan House.

November is not tempting to linger over churchyard tombstones, which was a pity, for at Goodshaw Chapel are fascinating epitaphs, one phonetic example beginning:

> Halt a foot and cast anie
> As you are now so wonce was i . . .

In a valley where population rose from about 2,000 in 1801 to nearly 8,000 in 1861—in spite of emigration to the towns—where sheep farming and cottage handlooming had been the sole occupation from forest days, in 1861 were deep quarries, a score of factories, and tightpacked rows of back-to-back workers' houses.

Before all this, and surviving all demolitions—the Friends' meeting house.

George Fox's teaching found ready ears in these parts, when Stubbs and Dewsbury came preaching in farms and cottages. Rossendale Friends had no meeting place save homes of members until 1715, when this plot of land was bought, a quiet spot in Crawshawbooth, convenient for bridge and moorland paths, along which Quakers came walking and riding on their asses and horses. Thereafter and until the present day it has remained changeless in a rapidly changing scene.

First Day meetings ended at two on winter afternoons to allow folk to return to their scattered homes in daylight. Monthly meetings were timed according to the full moon, but so many attended from distant places they stayed overnight. There was stabling for six mounts under what is now the cottage, the sleeping places in the gallery over the ante-room. In 1735 the high-roofed meeting hall was added, lit by tall mullioned transomed windows, still containing the original leaded lights today. In fact, very little here is not as it was in the old days—floors original, wooden, high-backed and narrow seats, a far older refectory table—gift of a Friend of early days, its foot-rails much worn. Through wars, rebellion, industrial revolution and modern resurgence—no change. You can still sit through the 'quiet hour' and *hear* silence.

In the valley north of Rawtenstall, in Crawshaw, Goodshaw, Dunnockshaw, Loveclough and the Higher and Lower Booths in the Haslingden chapelry, a score of cotton and woollen mills and print works have dwindled to a handful. Half the indigenous population has moved away, out of Lancashire.

One day of strong winds, swift-moving clouds, and smoke blown horizontally from the chimneys of high-placed farms, we sought for Old Rossendale. Such conditions gave beauty to landscapes grim on dark days. The sun came—and all smiled and exclaimed, "How lovely!" The sun hid behind grey rolls of cloud, and all was gloom—derelict cottages, ruined farms, abandoned pits and derelict mills.

At Weir they said, "The empty barns and buildings? Oh, owners are hoping someone will offer a few thousands and convert them." The completely new houses are too often alien to the landscape, red brick and sharp angles, where their neighbours are typical stone-built, roofed with Haslingden flags, emerging after sand-blasting from a century of grime as a warm golden gritstone.

Now that the local coal pits and mills from Irwell Springs to the valley have closed down the villagers must find work in Bacup or Burnley, the councils see the future role as residential. And new residents build as they wish, 'commute' by car and ask nothing of the community. But wives are left at home, and what is there for them? The cutting of bus services has 'killed' the once thriving Women's Institute, the best of all village social gatherings —and this one rather special. I once talked with old 'natives' who had walked over the moors on dark winter nights with 'guardian hounds' protecting them until the lights of home appeared. One, very old, had know a farmer's wife who changed herself into a black cat to raid neighbours' dairies—the Weir Witch.

It was good to see signs of industry at Broadclough, a village gripped close between the knees of toppling hills, and the Irwell noisy in leaping down a rock-step staircase, hidden under rose bay and elder blossom. Here the Finishing (Cloth) Company Mill is providing work for the villagers on their doorsteps.

So too is Cowpe, close and cramped in its own solitudes across the valley—south of Bacup, approached in the narrows of a clough, crammed with works and before that with bleaching crofts and tenter fields.

Cowpe is an isolated village of eighteenth- and nineteenth-century houses, cottages in rows and scattered farms on the hill-sides above, all traditional—stone on stone, here white walls, there dark gritstone with white pointing a cheerful feature in local architecture. The wide panorama northwards is more green than grey, there are more hayfields than factories away to Hile, Cribden, Musbury Tor and Holcombe Moor. Kestrels wing over-head, where once hawks and falcons were caught to supply the royal mews. This is the landscape the workers survey during breaks, over the rims of their tea mugs, enjoying the fresh air. I watched them in the dye works, lifting hanks of wool dripping from tanks of yellow, green and orange.

Spinning is always associated with south-east Lancashire, but where impounded water was so plentiful as here, there bleaching, dyeing and finishing processes too, always in rural surroundings. The hay machine was loud in the meadows surrounding, sweet scents in the valley.

Industry was as pleasantly sited as in the valley rising from the chief village, Newchurch-in-Rossendale, to Whitewell Bottoms, Water, and branching off to Little Dean of the "singing larks".

Now old Newchurch has character. It was 'new' in the fifteenth century, when folk appealed to Henry VI for a place of worship of their own, journeys to Clitheroe being dangerous for "the old, the young, and women great with child". The church tower rises strong and proud, like the gritstone hills which gave their stone for walls, roofs, pavements and cobbled streets. Once narrow ways, hemmed in by old houses, ran down the hillside and strung out on the ancient highways up and down the valley. Inns were plentiful, these being common meeting places. 'The Boar's Head' keeps more of the village pub atmosphere. 'The Blue Bell', backing against the churchyard, has decided to go modern, so it is difficult to picture times when crowds in holiday mood milled around their walls, shouted and sang in the cobbled ways with sudden, secret corners—Mill Lane, Dark Lane, Church Lane.

The fairs used to attract the crowds and fill the 'Blue Bell', the 'Boars Head' and seven more inns and eight beershops, in the 1870s. Now it takes a home game of the Rossendale United football team to draw the crowds, especially when they are taking all before them as in the 1971–2 Cup season.

LANCASHIRE'S SOUTH-EAST CORNER, BACUP TO WHITWORTH

Open spaces are multiplying, environmental improvement seized upon, belts of landscaping, green lawns, rose beds, are extending along roads, riverside and railways. It is happening around Bacup, in and around Rochdale and Bury, but I think I would give the prize to Whitworth, transforming its rural urban district with energy and optimism.

Leaving Bacup the road passes through Britannia, a village famous for its 'Nutters' or coconut dancers, who, with blackened faces and a great click and clatter, make their way through local towns and villages, keeping alive, they say, ritual derived from the Moors, introduced to Cornwall and brought to Lancashire when tin miners came north for work in the mills.

Southwards small communities string along highways and railway, tight gripped between bare hills—Millgate, Shawforth and Leavengreave which almost joins Whitworth, an outgrown village and centre of local government. From their rocks half Lancashire was built, and floored and paved. York Stone is quarried here in Lancashire, and because of its fine texture, beauty of colour and superiority over all others, one walks on it in Trafalgar Square, Windsor Castle terraces and Canterbury Cathedral precincts.

From each village in the past two centuries stone hewers trudged up the rutted roads to Higher End and Lower End Moors to quarries, rock face and deep holes called Dule's Mouth (the devil was familiar hereabouts), Grime Hole, Matty's Face with similar evocative names.

The beauty of long-lost colour has recently been revealed. Sandblasting of smoke-darkened walls has been a Whitworth achievement; several terraced rows of early Victorian times have been cleaned, provided with wrought-iron railings and to complete the paved frontages, rows of flower containers; central heating has been installed—and tall roofline chimneys removed. Too often good stone-built streets have been demolished, and 'back-to-backs' also, but around Whitworth good sense has prevailed. The cleaning and conversions go on merrily. And completely new housing too where none has been before.

The Rochdale railway, a life-line for nineteenth-century industry, is no more. Long and narrow grass-turfed gardens at the road edge—pleasant places for mothers to sit and children to play— replace the railroad track. At Leavengreave there is great development: modern bungalows sit side by side on the railway, grass-laid embankment for front garden below and the rough moor slopes behind. "Three-bedroomed, £8.95 a week," I am told.

As though all this belongs to them by right, moorland sheep stray into gardens, public and private, whilst hill ponies feed with no hindrance in parks and by the highway. But, "We draw the line at our Civic Centre", Whitworth folk tell me. This is *some-thing*, shared with all its U.D. villages—not only splendid new all-the-year-round swimming baths, a *super* civic hall and council offices, but a new park area with trees, flower beds, rockeries, pools and a bowling green which is faultless. Three cheers for Whitworth and its attendant villages!

And long may Summerseat's Village Society flourish, long may Wardle keep its pleasant face, and Littleborough—by cherishing what it can of its old building—keep the past alive on the old road to Blackstone Edge.

How could the villages of south Lancashire survive, especially any on Manchester's perimeter, covering the "treasures of Lancashire, miles of coal measures about to render the county so renowned". From north Manchester to Worsley, west to Atherton and Wigan the coalfield extended. Here, as early nineteenth-century writers foresaw all was at hand and "well adapted to make use of natural advantages and with the manufacturing energies of the people bring about industrial prosperity with a rapidity unexampled anywhere else in the world".

Until the eighteenth century there had been villages by the score with homely names like Dumplington and Wickleswick, Barton and Booths, and manorial lords to control them—the nominees of Norman barons—were not averse to accepting land grants near Chat Moss, "black and frightful bog and waste 5 to 6 miles east to west, 7 to 8 miles north to south, being nothing but matted vegetable matter fit for nothing but to be cut into fuel for poor cottagers".

In the early days two of Lancashire's longest established families were here—Traffords south and Hultons farther north—neighbours of the Worsleys of Booths, lords of Workesley, and Wardleys, who led their tenants to fight in the Crusades; and Banastres of Makerfield and Langtons, Barons of Newton, Gerards of Ince and Bryn, Tyldesleys, Haydocks and Athertons, who adopted their village names for their own, and whose tombs are found in the churches of Winwick, Eccles and Leigh.

Because this is the region called 'black', who ever comes in search of villages here? Their fate was decided even before 1840, when Dodd was saddened by cheerless industrial landscape— "vapour like seething cauldrons, no sky only grey haze and masses of smoke lying over the rooftops like clouds of sublimated ink".

VILLAGES ON COAL

A century later modern travellers, appalled, talked of "lunar landscapes", and of south Lancashire as "featureless, filthy, cratered like a battle field" and as "a vast ocean of ugliness hopelessly, helplessly depressing, miles of dereliction".

One who anticipated the environmental improvers of the 1970s declared that the energy which made south Lancashire the mess it was could, given incentive, battle to restore it to something of its early state. Especially around the pit villages. It is noticeable that at pit heads here, as in South Wales and Durham, where winding gear and slag heaps dominate rural landscapes, that mining communities were villages and remained so. When their "se coles" were first dug near Worsley, Tyldesley, Astley, Atherton, Billinge and Winstanley, Aspull and Haigh, the coals were fuel for local forges making iron spades, tools and nails, long a major industry. Textiles later brought added prosperity, factories as well as forges providing local employment. There was still inexhaustible coal below; and cornfields above, open sky, larks and plovers, and cuckoos calling.

At first what travellers saw was very pleasant. They commented on the country lanes between Prescott and Wigan and Leigh, and very lovely oases like Winwick, "a truly sequestered spot in a manufacturing distict with ancient church on a little hill, loud cawing in the rookery and the spire a conspicuous landmark over the countryside"; 1820.

It can be seen near the M6, one of the finest churches by the motorway, "the richest rectory in the kingdom—fit for sons of the Earls of Derby, and the largest endowments for charity—one a year's remission of rent to six poor labouring families of exemplary conduct, industry and piety". Tradition claims that King Oswald had a fair palace here in Maserfeld, and nearby in 642 Penda the Mercian king and his pagans slaughtered Oswald, who thereafter became saint.

I like surprises. One day I was met by the president of the W.I. at Astley Green, a mining village on the rim of the old mossland, now sprawling wider though the fine Astley–Tyldesley coal pits are closed. I remember a long straight lane between flat fields, at the end of it a large farmhouse within a moat, ducks splashing thereon. Obviously the farm had seen better days, as a well-protected manor house, one of the many around Chat Moss. Tea was waiting. No sooner had we sat down when all the china began to tinkle, window glass vibrated; a few seconds later all was normal.

"Not to worry," my hostess remarked. "They're only firing a charge in the pit; it runs for miles under here." Runs for miles, and a mile deep—so interesting a mine that if it is never brought to life in working order it could become a typical coalpit 'museum'!

Take Blackley, on the grimmer outskirts of Manchester but with remaining shreds of countryside including Boggart Hole Clough, a wild spot now a public park, the landscape taking on the not-so-far away Pennine character; a village mentioned in Domesday Book.

Demolition is a constant threat. Considered 'ripe' for it—Crab Lane, "with pleasing village atmosphere and unique sense of community, its centuries-old buildings among the oldest and most picturesque around the city". "But demolished it shall not be," cried Blackley's Village Action Group. The Commons heard their cry, the Minister deliberated and threw the ball back to the city council. Should it be kept for general improvement, or scrapped? They must decide.

A modern 'revolution' by thinking people; it is going on all over Lancashire where folk are more and more conscious of their once-rural heritage, their once-village identity. Who would have cared twenty years ago? There is hope for Lancashire yet! Or, rather, let us hope that within the Greater Manchester Metropolitan County the many villages 'leaving south-east Lancashire' will retain their identity.

Index